GREAT ENDEAVORS

SENIOR AUTHORS
Virginia A. Arnold
Carl B. Smith

LITERATURE CONSULTANTS
Joan I. Glazer
Margaret H. Lippert

Macmillan Publishing Company
New York

Collier Macmillan Publishers
London

ACKNOWLEDGMENTS

The publisher gratefully acknowledges permission to reprint the following copyrighted material:

"American Heritage" by Elsie Walush is reprinted from INSTRUCTOR. Copyright © 1964 by The Instructor Publications, Inc. Used by permission.

"A Bird's Body" is an adaptation of pages 5-22 in A BIRD'S BODY by Joanna Cole. Copyright © 1982 by Joanna Cole. By permission of William Morrow & Company.

"The Birthday Treasure Hunt" by Mary Merrem Shaw appeared originally in *Cricket* Magazine. Copyright 1983 by Mary Elizabeth Merrem. Used by permission of the author.

"Buried Treasures" by Carolyn Jabs appeared originally in *3-2-1 Contact*. © 1982 Children's Television Workshop. Used by permission of Children's Television Workshop.

"Captain Kidd" is from A BOOK OF AMERICANS by Rosemary and Stephen Vincent Benét. Copyright 1933 by Rosemary and Stephen Vincent Benét. Copyright renewed © 1961 by Rosemary Carr Benét. Reprinted by permission of Brandt and Brandt Literary Agents Inc.

"Courage, Dana" is excerpted from the book COURAGE, DANA by Susan Beth Pfeffer, illustrated by Jenny Rutherford. Copyright © 1983 by Susan Beth Pfeffer. Reprinted by permission of Delacorte Press and Curtis Brown, Ltd.

"The Crew of Apollo 8" by Elaine V. Emans appeared originally in *The Christian Science Monitor*. Reprinted by permission of the author.

"The Daimyo's Daughter" by Kristen R. Morsy appeared originally in *Cricket* Magazine. Copyright 1981 by Kristen Morsy. Edited and used by permission of the author.

"Do You Have the Guts Not To Fight Back?" is adapted from pages 66 to 76 of BREAKTHROUGH TO THE BIG LEAGUE by Jackie Robinson and Alfred Duckett. Copyright © 1965 by Jackie Robinson and Alfred Duckett. By permission of Harper & Row, Publishers, Inc.

"A Dog Named Grizzly" is adapted from A FRIEND INDEED by D.J. Arneson. Copyright © 1981 by D.J. Arneson. Used by permission of Franklin Watts, Inc.

"Dreams" is reprinted from THE DREAM KEEPER AND OTHER POEMS by Langston Hughes. Copyright 1932 by Alfred A. Knopf, Inc., and renewed 1960 by Langston Hughes. By permission of Alfred A. Knopf, Inc.

"The Fallen Spaceman" is the abridged and adapted text from pages 1-10 in THE FALLEN SPACEMAN by Lee Harding. Text Copyright © 1973, 1980 by Lee Harding. By permission of Harper & Row, Publishers, Inc., the author, and the author's agent, Virginia Kidd.

"A Fiddler" by Walter de la Mare is reprinted by permission of The Literary Trustees of Walter de la Mare and The Society of Authors as their representative.

"The Fiddler Who Wouldn't Fiddle" is adapted from JIM BRIDGER'S ALARM CLOCK AND OTHER TALL TALES by Sid Fleischman. Text Copyright © 1978 by Sid Fleischman. Used by permission of Bill Berger Associates, Inc., for the author.

"Haiku" and photograph from HAIKU-VISION by Ann Atwood. Copyright © 1977 by Ann Atwood. Reprinted with the permission of Charles Scribner's Sons.

Macmillan Publishing Company
866 Third Avenue
New York, N.Y. 10022
Collier Macmillan Canada, Inc.

Printed in the United States of America

ISBN 0-02-160130-5

9 8 7 6 5 4 3 2 1

Contents

UNIT ONE LEVEL 12

MOMENTS OF COURAGE

PREPARING FOR READING

Learning Vocabulary

1. An <u>average</u> day became a very special one for Dana.
2. She <u>risked</u> her life to save a child who had run out into the street.
3. By the time the car came to a <u>halt</u>, she and the child were out of danger.
4. Dana <u>reluctantly</u> let go of the lamppost she had grabbed.
5. After her <u>experience</u>, Dana realized that she was a <u>heroine</u>.

average	risked	halt
reluctantly	experience	heroine

Developing Background and Skills
Sequence of Events

The order in which events take place is called a sequence. When writers describe events, they may not always tell about them in the order in which they happened. They may start by telling about the most important or exciting event first. They may want to gain their reader's attention or emphasize what is most important.

Read the story on the next page. Notice how the writer describes the **sequence of events**.

The ship *Eagle* finally left port at 5:00 P.M. yesterday. It did not leave at 3:00 P.M. as scheduled, because a message saying there was a bomb on board was received at 2:30. As the passengers were leaving the ship, the captain called the police. When the special investigators arrived, they searched but found nothing.

Order of Events in Story	Actual Order of Events
1. Ship left port.	1. Message was received.
2. Message was received.	2. Passengers left ship and captain called police.
3. Passengers left ship and captain called police.	3. Investigators arrived.
4. Investigators arrived.	4. Investigators searched ship.
5. Investigators searched ship.	5. Ship left port.

The first event described in the story was the last event to happen. Two events took place at the same time. The word *as* lets you know what they are.

The story "Courage, Dana" tells what happened to Dana before and after she became a heroine. As you read, notice how the writer tells about the sequence of events.

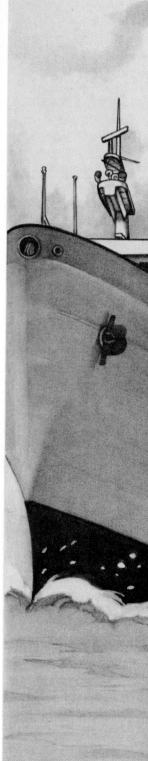

Courage, DANA

Susan Beth Pfeffer

It had been a pretty average day until I became a heroine.

We got back our spelling tests, and I'd gotten an 85, which was a relief. I was called on to do a problem in math, and I got it without too much trouble. We played soccer in gym, and I helped my team get a goal.

After school, I started walking toward home. The day was bright-blue sunny. "Where are you going?" Sharon asked. I hadn't noticed her running toward me.

"Home," I said. "Where else?"

"Oh, I don't know," she said, but I could tell from the look in her eyes she was thinking ice cream. Sharon and I have been best friends since kindergarten, and we knew each other's looks pretty well.

"Why not?" I said before she even had a chance to ask. It might be the last warm day until May, and a final farewell-to-summer ice cream cone sounded like a good idea. So we walked the few extra blocks to the Cream King and ordered soft vanilla cones.

Of course summer had officially ended the first day of school, but the end of our ice cream cones meant the end of it all permanently. I considered getting a second cone just to postpone the moment. It felt so good to be outside on such a beautiful day. Maybe things weren't perfect, but as long as the sun was shining and there were still flowers blooming, it was all right.

Like I said, it was a pretty average day.

Sharon headed for home and so did I. I got to the corner of Main and North streets just in time to miss the traffic light. I think they run that thing just for pedestrians to have to stand there. It's a busy corner, and you don't cross against the light.

I half noticed the people who were waiting for the light with me, the way you half notice things when you really aren't thinking about anything special, just waiting to cross the street. There was a woman carrying a shopping bag, and a man in a business suit who looked a little like my father, and a mother with a half-dozen packages in one hand, trying to control her little kid with the other. The kid was two or maybe three. I don't have that much experience with little kids, so it's hard for me to tell how old they are, or if they're boys or girls. This one was just a wriggling kid in overalls.

But then the kid managed to wriggle away from its mother. And before she even had a chance to notice, the kid had run smack into the middle of Main and North streets, with a big blue car coming right at it.

The funny thing is I didn't even think. If I'd taken one second to think, I never would have moved. I would

have stood there frozen and watched the car hit the kid. It couldn't possibly have stopped in time. I couldn't even be sure if the driver would see the kid, it was so little.

Not that any of that really registered. Instead, I ran into the street, right into the path of that big blue car, and pushed the kid out of the way. The momentum of pushing kept me going, and I stumbled along, half holding the hysterical kid and half holding my books.

I knew the car could hit us. It was roaring at us like a blue giant. But the funny thing was I felt like a giant too, an all-powerful one, like even if the car hit us, it wouldn't hurt us because I was made of steel, too. Like Superman. And as long as I was there, the kid was safe. I moved my giant steel legs and lifted the kid with my giant steel arms, and in what couldn't have been more than ten seconds, but felt more like ten years, I pushed both of us out of the path of the car.

By the time I'd gotten to the other side of the street with the kid, the blue car's brakes were screeching it to a halt. But over that noise, and the noise of the kid crying, I could hear its mother screaming from way across the street. It was amazing how far off she looked.

I really wanted to lean against the lamppost, but I wasn't going to let go of that kid. I'd already lost most of my books, since I wasn't about to go to the middle of the street and pick them up where I'd dropped them. So I stood there, holding on to the kid with my grip getting weaker and weaker as I started to realize just what I'd done, and just what the car could have done to the kid and me.

The man in the business suit stood in the middle of the street, holding his hand up to stop the cars, and picked up my books for me. The kid's mother, still screaming, crossed the street, walked over to where we were, and started weeping. She was shaking pretty hard,

too, but nowhere near as hard as I was. The kid ran to its mother, and the two of them hugged and sobbed. That left me free to grab onto the lamppost, which I did, with both arms.

"I couldn't see, I didn't see," the driver of the blue car cried at us. I guess she pulled her car over to the side of the street, because I watched her join us. She seemed like a nice lady, too, not the sort that drove blue giant monster cars and aimed them at kids. "I have two of my own. I never would have . . ."

"He just got away from me," the kid's mother said. "I was holding his hand, and then he just broke away."

"Here are your books," the businessman said, handing them to me. That meant I had to give up the lamppost, which I did reluctantly. That car could have killed me. I risked my life for some little kid—I didn't even know if it was a boy or a girl. I could have been killed trying to save some strange kid's life.

"I have to go home now," I said, trying to sound conversational. Nobody was paying any attention to me anyway. I grabbed my books, and took about a half dozen steps away from the corner of Main and North streets before my legs gave way, and I practically sank onto the sidewalk.

"I'll drive you home," the woman with the shopping bag said. "My car is right here."

I gratefully followed the woman into her car. She didn't say anything to me, except to ask where I lived. A couple of times, though, she patted me on the hand, as if to say things were going to be all right.

"Here," I said when we got to our house. What a beautiful house, too. I'd never noticed just how beautiful it was before.

"There's no car in the driveway," the woman said. "Are you sure your parents are home?"

"Oh, no, they aren't," I said. "They both work."

"I won't leave you here alone," she said.

"That's okay," I said. "My older sister should be in." I fumbled around, got the key from my pocket, and unlocked the front door. The woman followed me in, to make sure Jean really was there.

She was in the living room, sprawled on the sofa, watching TV, and eating an apple. I wanted to hug her.

"You see?" I said instead. "She's here."

"If you want, I'll stay until your parents come," the woman said.

"No, really," I said. "I'm okay."

"Dana?" Jean asked, turning around to face us. "What's the matter? What's going on?"

"You should be very proud of your younger sister," the woman said. "She saved a little boy's life. She's quite a heroine."

And that was the first time I realized that I really was one.

Questions

1. Where had Dana been just before she got to the corner of Main and North streets?
2. Why would the driver of the blue car probably not have seen the child who ran into the street?
3. What thoughts were going through Dana's mind as she pushed the child out of the path of the car?
4. If you had been with Dana, what would you have done?

Applying Reading Skills

The sentences below tell about some of the events in "Courage, Dana." Read the sentences, then write them in the correct sequence on your paper. Circle the two sentences that describe events that took place at the same time.

The child managed to wriggle away from its mother.
Dana pushed the child out of the car's path.
The blue car's brakes screeched as the car came to a halt.
The child ran into the middle of the street.
Dana missed the light at the corner of Main and North streets.
The child's mother screamed.
Dana saw a car heading for the child.
The child's mother crossed the street and the child ran to her.

You gain strength,
courage and confidence
by every experience
in which you really stop
to look fear in the face . . . .
You must do the thing
you cannot do.

Eleanor Roosevelt

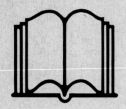

PREPARING FOR READING

Learning Vocabulary

1. Bill Welch's quick action prevented a <u>tragedy</u>.
2. A truck driver was <u>distracted</u> and did not see the train coming.
3. His truck burst into flames after it was hit by the train, and he was unable to escape from the <u>intense</u> heat by himself.
4. Karen Edwards rescued a drowning man and his son, who <u>revived</u> once she got them to safety.
5. Karen and Bill's medals are <u>enduring</u> reminders of their courage, which is an <u>inspiration</u> to us all.

tragedy	distracted	intense
revived	enduring	inspiration

Developing Background and Skills
Sequence of Events

Events take place in time. An event may take place before another event, after another event, or at the same time as another event. The order in which events take place is called the **sequence of events**.

Writers sometimes use words such as *first*, *then*, *next*, *finally*, and *afterwards* to help you understand the sequence of events.

Read the sentence below.

Bill called the police after he saw the accident.

The word *after* tells you the order of events: (1) Bill saw the accident; (2) Bill called the police.

What is the sequence of events in the sentence below?

The man called for help as he ran toward the overturned car.

The word *as* tells you that the two events took place at the same time.

Sometimes writers do not use words such as *after* and *as*. Then you have to read carefully to figure out the order of things. You can also use your common sense to figure out the sequence of events by asking "What order makes sense?"

The next selection is made up of three separate stories. Notice the order in which things happen in each story.

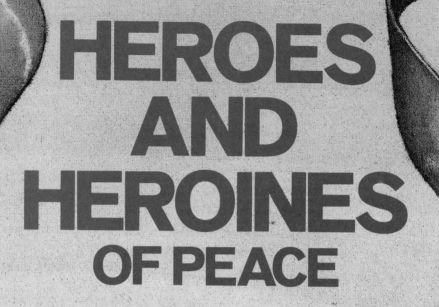

HEROES
AND
HEROINES
OF PEACE

L. B. TAYLOR

It was a spring afternoon on April 29, 1974, in Durham, North Carolina. It was pleasantly warm. Soft clouds drifted across the sky. A slight breeze was blowing as kids slowly made their way home from school. There was no hint of the tragedy that was about to take place.

To Phil Williamson, sixty years old, it was just another work day. Williamson drove an ice cream truck, and most of the kids smiled and waved at him as he passed them. But as he neared a railroad crossing, he became distracted for some reason. He didn't see the long train coming down the tracks. Suddenly, he turned and froze in horror as the speeding engine bore down on him. But it was too late. His truck was already on the tracks.

There was a terrible crash as the train ran into his truck, twisting its frame and knocking it down the tracks. The train's emergency brakes squealed. Then the great wave of sound caused by the crash and the sudden stopping of the train died out.

For a second or two there was a terrible silence.

Williamson was stunned and badly shaken by the awful blow. He was alive, but his body felt as if some giant hammer had just banged him all over. He ached from head to foot. But his pain suddenly gave way to pure fear. Flames leaped up out of the front end of the truck and were moving toward the cab. Williamson was afraid the flames would spread to the truck's gas tank, causing an explosion.

Frantically he tugged at the door handle, but it was badly bent and wouldn't open. He couldn't move. He was pinned in, trapped. The flames were getting nearer.

"Help!" he screamed. "Somebody help me." He didn't want to die in a blazing fire.

Several people stood across the tracks, almost in shock. They had heard the dreadful crash and seen Williamson's truck being hit. Then they saw the flames shoot up from the truck and heard his cries for help. Yet they still stood there, without moving.

29

One did not, though. Sixteen-year-old high school student William E. (Bill) Welch, Jr., ran toward the truck. Some of the kids shouted to him not to go, that the truck might explode. Bill either didn't hear them or didn't pay attention.

As he reached the truck, the flames from the front end jumped up. More fire broke out from beneath it. The heat was intense, but Bill Welch didn't stop. He pulled hard at the door, but it wouldn't open. Then he reached inside the open window on the driver's side. He threw his arms around Williamson and began to pull. At first he couldn't move the heavier driver. As the flames drew ever closer, Bill somehow found the strength to free Williamson. Then he pulled Williamson through the open window and dragged him away from the burning truck.

Stopping to rest a few yards away, Bill turned back. The entire cab was now on fire. A few seconds later the whole truck went up in flames.

Had Bill Welch not pulled him free, Phil Williamson would have died in his fiery truck cab. As it was, he soon recovered from his injuries.

Teen Hero Saves Man From Inferno

It was one of the first warm days of summer, June 17, 1972, in Duncansville, Pennsylvania. School was over, so the motel swimming pool was filled with swimmers.

Thirteen-year-old Karen Edwards was enjoying herself. She practiced her freestyle stroke for a while. Then she got out of the pool to dry off and rest.

Eugene Taylor, a thirty-seven-year-old truck driver, was resting by the pool. Suddenly he noticed his ten-year-old son in the deep end of the pool, struggling to stay above water. He couldn't swim. Taylor couldn't swim either, but he immediately jumped into the pool, trying to reach his son. Instead, he went under and did not surface.

Karen saw what was happening. While others stood by, she ran to the deep end and dived in. She reached the boy quickly and towed him to the side of the pool. Others lifted him out. Then she swam back to where Taylor had gone under.

13 Year Old Saves Two

Taylor outweighed her by nearly one hundred pounds. But Karen, drawing on strength she didn't know she had, somehow was able to bring him to the surface. Treading water as she caught her breath, Karen started toward the edge of the pool. Taylor began flailing his arms in the water, and Karen lost her hold on him.

Struggling for breath, Karen was nearly exhausted. But once again she grabbed Taylor under his arms and started for safety. Slowly, painfully, she worked toward the side. Finally, when she was close enough, someone held out a pool chair. She held on to it and was pulled to the side along with Taylor. Once out of the water, he quickly revived.

Had it not been for Karen's quick action, both Eugene Taylor and his son probably would have drowned.

Because they risked their lives to save others, Bill Welch and Karen Edwards were awarded medals by the Carnegie Hero Fund Commission.

Such medals, sometimes called the "Civilian Medal of Honor," are awarded each year to heroes and heroines from the United

From Drowning

33

States and Canada. There may be from fifty to one hundred-fifty or more awards given per year. Many of them are presented to young people.

Since the commission was founded, more than 6,000 awards have been made. More than $12 million has been given. The cash awards help students pay for their college educations.

Andrew Carnegie set up the commission in 1904. He had been thinking about the fund for years. Perhaps his inspiration came in 1886. In that year, a young boy named William Hunter lost his life while trying to save two other boys from drowning. The incident took place in a lake in Carnegie's native Scotland.

Carnegie gave money for a monument to Hunter bearing the following words: "The false heroes. . .are those who can only boast of the destruction of their fellows. The true heroes of civilization are those alone who save or greatly serve them. Young Hunter was one of those and [he] deserves an enduring monument."

Andrew Carnegie

Eighteen years later, Carnegie learned about the heroic deaths of two rescuers in a coal mine tragedy in Pennsylvania. He gave $5 million to set up the commission. He had long felt that while soldiers had always been given medals and honored for their actions in war, there was no award for those whom he called the "heroes of peace."

The medal is a little larger than a silver dollar. The front has a likeness of Carnegie. On the other side is the quote "Greater love hath no man than this, that a man lay down his life for his friends."

Questions

1. What do Bill Welch and Karen Edwards have in common?
2. What incidents inspired Andrew Carnegie to establish the Carnegie Hero Fund Commission?
3. Why do you think the people who heard Phil Williamson call for help did not try to help him?
4. Do you know of anyone who deserves a Civilian Medal of Honor? What did the person do?

Applying Reading Skills

Each sentence below makes a statement about sequence of events in "Heroes and Heroines of Peace." Number your paper from 1 to 6. Write **T** after the number if the statement is true. Write **F** if it is false.

1. Karen Edwards got Eugene Taylor out of the pool before she got to his son.
2. Carnegie set up his Hero Fund Commission after the death of William Hunter but before the death of the Pennsylvania coal miners.
3. Bill Welch saved Phil Williamson after Karen Edwards saved Eugene Taylor.
4. Taylor jumped into the pool after his son before Karen Edwards did.
5. Bill Welch reached Williamson's truck at the same time that flames jumped up from the front end.
6. Williamson's whole truck went up in flames before Bill Welch could drag him away.

WRITING ACTIVITY

WRITE A FEATURE STORY

Prewrite

What makes a person a hero or heroine? Dana became a heroine in "Courage, Dana." Karen Edwards and Bill Welch risked their lives for others in "Heroes and Heroines of Peace."

Imagine you are a feature story writer for your local newspaper. A feature story is a story about a subject of interest to many people. Unlike a news story, it tells more than just the facts about an event. A feature includes more details and often presents the writer's feelings about the subject.

As a feature writer, whom will you choose as the subject of a story about heroes and heroines? It can be one of the people in the first two stories in this book. You may want to write a feature about someone you know who has done something for others. People do not have to risk their lives to be heroes and heroines.

Before you write, do some reading about your subject. If you choose to write about someone you know, plan to interview that person for your story.

These questions can help organize your writing. Write the answers as sentence notes.

1. Who is the subject of your feature story?
2. What experience did he or she have? When? Where?
3. Why is the person or what they did of interest to people?
4. How do you feel about what the person did?

Write

1. Read your questions and answers.
2. Plan how you will organize your story. The first part may tell what the subject did. This part of your feature story is like a news story. The facts are told in sequence. Use words like *first*, *then*, *next*, and *finally* to help your readers follow the sequence of events.
3. The second part of the feature story may tell about the person's feelings, your feelings, and why the subject is of interest to people.
4. Think of an interesting headline for your feature story. A headline should give a hint about the story and attract the attention of the readers.
5. Use your Glossary or dictionary for spelling help.

Revise

Read your feature story. Did you give the facts about what the person did in a clear sequence? Did you tell about the person's feelings as well as your own feelings? Will your readers feel as if they know the subject when they have read your feature story? If not, rewrite now.

1. Did you use correct end punctuation for each sentence?
2. Did you capitalize all proper names?
3. Did you use complete sentences?

PREPARING FOR READING

Learning Vocabulary

1. A man told his sons, "I will give a diamond to which-ever one of you <u>accomplishes</u> the noblest <u>deed</u>."
2. One son's deed was <u>generous</u> but not truly <u>noble</u>.
3. Another son rescued a child caught in the current of a <u>swift</u> river.
4. The third son, however, did something very <u>rare</u>.

accomplishes   deed   generous
noble   swift   rare

Developing Background and Skills
Draw Conclusions

Maria always arrived at school after her friend Jane. Maria's hook on the hall coat rack was number 17, Jane's was number 16. One day when Maria went to hang up her coat, there was no coat on hook number 16. Maria decided that Jane had not come to school that day. She was very surprised to see Jane sitting at her desk when she walked into the classroom. Jane had not worn a coat that day!

When Maria decided that Jane had not come to school, she was **drawing a conclusion.** A conclusion is a decision based on information and experience.

Drawing conclusions is an important reading skill. As you read, you are presented with information that the writer gives you. You use this information along with your own experiences to draw conclusions.

Read the paragraph below. What conclusions can you draw?

An old man was dying. He wanted to leave his only wealth, a diamond, to one of his sons. But he could not decide which son to leave it to.

You might reach two conclusions about the old man. One might be that he was not wealthy. Although the writer does not directly say this, you can conclude it because you know that a diamond is his only wealth.

You might also conclude that the old man did not have a favorite son. He could not decide which son to leave the diamond to. If he did have a favorite son, that son would certainly be given the diamond.

As you read the next selection, think about the information the writer gives you. Use the information and what you know from your own experiences to draw conclusions about each of the characters.

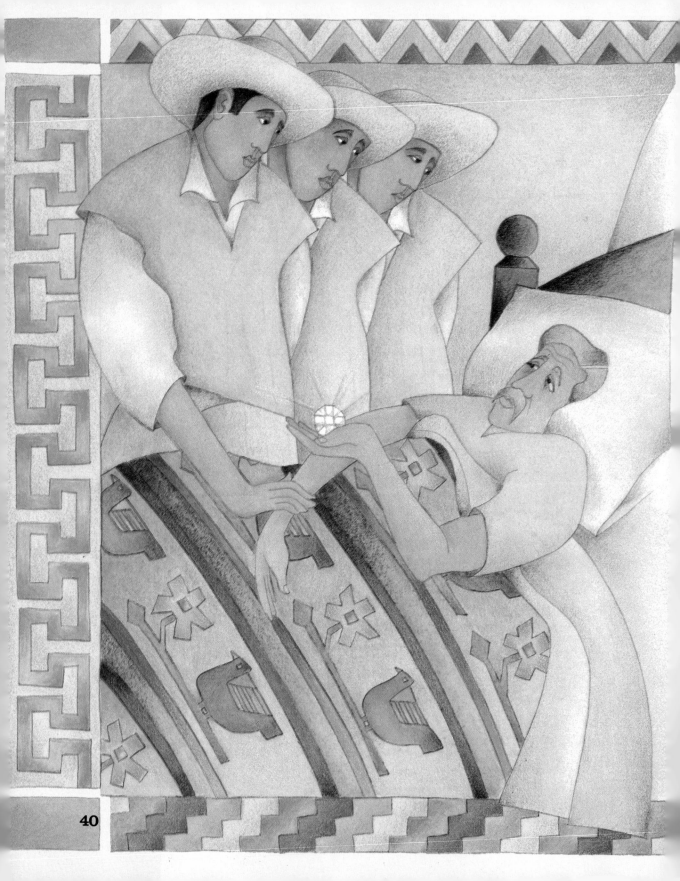

THE NOBLEST DEED

GRANT LYONS

Once there was a very old man in Guadalajara (gwäd′ əl ə här′ ə) who was about to die. He wanted to leave a diamond, the only wealth he had, to one of his three sons. But he could not decide which one. He called the three sons into his room, and this is what he told them.

"My sons, I am not a rich man. The only thing I have that is worth much is this diamond. It has been in our family for generations, and I would not want it sold. Because it cannot be sold or divided, I can give it to only one of you. The diamond will go to whichever of you accomplishes the noblest deed in a week's time. Go now. Return in a week to tell me what you have done."

A week passed, and the sons returned. They found their father even weaker than before and unable to leave his bed. He asked each in turn to tell his story.

"My father," said the first son, "I thought and thought of a deed that would be worthy. Finally, this is what I did. I gathered together all of my property, divided it in half, and gave one half to the poor people of the city."

The old man shook his head. "Ah, that is a good deed," he said, "but not truly noble. After all, it is our duty to be as generous as we can to the poor."

"When I was returning home from work one day," said the second son, "I saw a little girl caught in the swift current of the river. Though I can hardly swim myself, I jumped into the river and pulled her out. The current was so swift, I almost drowned."

"That, too, is a good deed, and yet not noble," said the father. "All should be willing to risk their lives for the sake of a child."

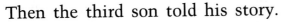

Then the third son told his story.

"Father, a wonderful thing happened to me. I was walking high up in the mountains very early one morning. There I saw a man, wrapped tight in a blanket, sleeping at the very edge of a cliff! I could hardly believe my eyes. For if he turned this way or that, if he moved at all in his sleep, the man would be certain to fall over the cliff—thousands of feet to the valley below! I crept closer, as quietly as I could, for I didn't want to startle him. And guess who the man was? Sancho, my bitterest enemy! Many times he had threatened to kill me if he got the chance.

"I moved as close to this man as I could. Gently I put my arms around him. Suddenly his eyes opened and looked into mine. I saw he was afraid. 'Do not fear,' I said. With that I pulled him toward me and rolled with him, away from the cliff.

"We both stood up, and he said, 'I came this way last night. It was so dark that I could not see my own feet! I was too tired to go on, so I stepped off the path to sleep. I had no idea where I was! I see now that if I had walked a little farther, or turned in my sleep, I would have become food for the vultures in the valley. You have saved my life, amigo—I, who have threatened to kill you!'

"We threw ourselves into each other's arms and swore to be friends forever. We wept for joy. Each of us found a friend, where before there had been an enemy!"

"Ah, my son!" exclaimed the old man. "That is a beautiful story, and a truly noble deed. It is a rare person who will risk his life for the sake of his enemy. A *noble* person. The diamond is yours!"

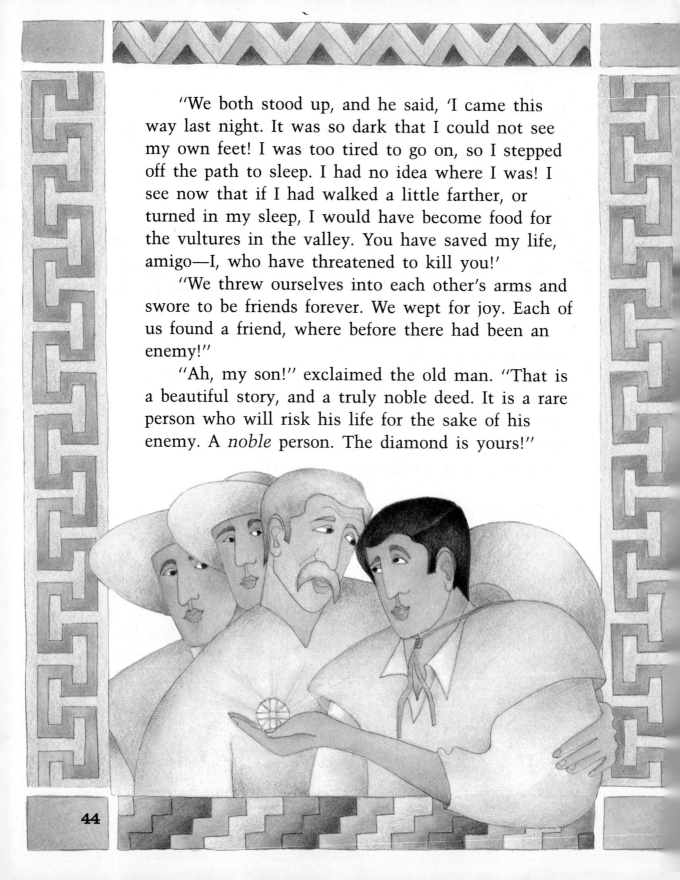

Questions

1. What did the dying man ask his sons to do? How long did they have to do it?
2. Did the second son plan what he was going to do as a good deed?
3. Do you agree that the third son's deed was the noblest? Why or why not?
4. Do you think the father should have sold the diamond and divided the money among all three of his sons? Explain your answer.

Applying Reading Skills

The numbered sentences below are conclusions that could be drawn about the characters in "The Noblest Deed." The lettered sentences each support one of these conclusions. Number your paper from 1 to 5. Write each conclusion and the sentence that supports it.

1. One son was fairly well off.
2. One son was brave.
3. One son was forgiving as well as brave.
4. The father believed that being noble was important.
5. Each son wanted to have the diamond.

a. Although not a good swimmer, he jumped into the river to save a girl.
b. He risked his life for the sake of an enemy.
c. He would leave all his wealth to his noblest son.
d. He told his father about a deed he hoped was the most noble.
e. He had property he could divide and give to the poor.

PREPARING FOR READING

Learning Vocabulary

1. Jackie Robinson believed in the <u>sincerity</u> of the offer from the Brooklyn National League club.
2. It was an <u>opportunity</u> to address an issue that had long been avoided in professional sports.
3. Although the country was <u>democratic</u>, in 1945 black players and white players did not compete in the same baseball leagues.
4. Robinson was warned that it would take <u>discipline</u> to control his feelings about the <u>injustice</u> he would have to face.

sincerity   opportunity   democratic
discipline   injustice

Developing Background and Skills
Draw Conclusions

You know that a **conclusion** is a decision or judgment based on information. As you read, you can draw conclusions about the information a writer presents. All the information should support the conclusion.

You also know that what you have seen, read, done, or heard about can help you draw conclusions. Using what you know from your own experiences is important. A writer may not always state information directly. What you know can help you to figure out what the writer means.

Read the following paragraph. What conclusions can you draw?

Clyde Sukeforth was a scout for the Brooklyn Dodgers. He knew who the best players were on every team in every league. He told Branch Rickey, the Dodgers' manager, about Jackie Robinson. Rickey decided to see Robinson. He asked Sukeforth to set up a meeting.

The writer does not say why Branch Rickey wanted to see Robinson. You probably concluded, however, that Rickey was interested in getting Robinson to play for his ball club.

You also may have concluded that Clyde Sukeforth had seen Robinson play. That's what scouts do. The writer did say that Sukeforth knew who the best players were. Sukeforth probably told Rickey that Robinson was a good player. His recommendation led to the meeting between Robinson and the Dodgers' manager.

The next selection is part of Jackie Robinson's autobiography. An autobiography is the story of a person's life written by the person himself or herself. As you read, think about the information Robinson presents and the conclusions you can draw about it.

JACKIE RO

Jackie Robinson played his first game as a Montreal Royal on April 18, 1946.

DO YOU HAVE THE GUTS NOT TO FIGHT BACK?
Jackie Robinson

Jackie Robinson always wanted to be a professional athlete. But in 1945, black men and white men couldn't play professional baseball together. So Jackie joined the Kansas City Monarchs, a baseball team in the Negro American League. Later that year, Clyde Sukeforth, a scout for the Brooklyn Dodgers, came to talk to Robinson. Clyde invited him to come to Brooklyn to talk to Branch Rickey, the Dodgers' manager. Robinson didn't know why the manager of a major league ball club would want to meet with him, but he was going to find out soon.

On the morning of August 28, 1945, Clyde Sukeforth and I walked into Mr. Rickey's office. He fixed his eyes on me as if he could see how I felt and knew what I was thinking.

"Are you under contract to the Monarchs?" he asked.

I answered that I was not, that I had a month-to-month, payday-to-payday agreement.

The Dodger boss leaned forward in his chair.

"Do you have any idea why I want to talk to you?" he demanded. "Do you really understand why you are here?"

"Well, Mr. Sukeforth said you wanted to talk to me about your new Brown Dodgers Club."

"That's what Mr. Sukeforth was supposed to tell you," Mr. Rickey said. "The truth is you are

Robinson played himself in a movie about his life called *The Jackie Robinson Story*.

not here as a candidate for the Brooklyn Brown Dodgers. I've sent for you because I'm interested in you as a candidate for the Brooklyn National League Club. I think you can play in the major leagues. How do you feel about it?"

There it was! The realization of a dream I'd been pushing out of my mind because I simply couldn't believe it would ever come true.

How did I feel? It was hard to say. I didn't know how to put it into words. I was dazzled, shocked, delighted, scared to death. I don't know whether I even answered the question. I know I answered the next question because it was specific—as specific as the pinch that wakes you out of a dream.

"You think you can play for Montreal?"

"Yes," I said.

Robinson signs his contract with the Dodgers for the 1950 season in Branch Rickey's office.

Montreal! The Brooklyn Dodgers' top farm club! This was the training school, the trial division to which Dodger hopefuls were taken.

Mr. Rickey considered my answer. Then he turned to Sukeforth.

"Think he can make the grade?" he asked the scout.

"He's good," Sukeforth answered. "He can run. He can field. He can hit."

Suddenly Mr. Rickey wheeled his swivel chair to face me. He pointed a finger challengingly.

"I know you are a good ballplayer," the Brooklyn boss said. "What I don't know is whether you have the guts."

"Guts," I repeated to myself wonderingly. I'd had a lot of things said about me, but no one had ever accused me of being a coward or running away from an issue—or even a fight.

What did Mr. Rickey mean? His voice was deep and rumbling as he told me.

"I'm going to tell you the truth, Jackie. I've investigated you thoroughly. They said at UCLA that in basketball you had trouble with coaches, players, and officials. I just want to tell you that my investigation convinced me that the criticisms are unjustified, that if you'd been white it would have been nothing. So I'm dismissing these rumors as not amounting to a hill of beans."

His rich voice deepened.

"The thing I want to convince you of is that we can't fight our way through this, Jackie. We've got no army. There's nobody on our side. No owners, no umpires, very few newspaper reporters.

Robinson first put on the Dodgers' uniform in 1947.

During his ten seasons with the Brooklyn Dodgers, Robinson helped the team win six National League pennants and one World Series title.

We'll be in a tough position, Jackie. We can win only if we can convince the world that I'm doing this because you're a great ballplayer and a fine gentleman."

Mr. Rickey continued and it was almost as if he were talking to himself as well as to me.

"So there's more than just playing," he said. "I wish it meant only hits, runs, and errors—only the things they put in the box score. Because you know—yes, you would know, Jackie—that a baseball box score is a democratic thing. It doesn't tell how big you are, what church you attend, what color you are, or how your father voted in the last election. It just tells what kind of baseball player you were on that particular day."

"It's the box score that really counts—that and that alone—isn't it?" I asked.

"It's all that *ought* to count! But it isn't! Maybe one of these days it *will* be all that counts. That's one of the reasons I've got you here, Jackie. If you're a good enough man, we can make this a start in the right direction. But let me tell you, it's going to take an awful lot of courage. Have you got the guts to play the game no matter what happens?"

He had left his desk and was leaning over in front of me, his face close to mine, his eyes measuring me.

"I think I can play the game, Mr. Rickey," I said. My nervousness was leaving me. I was filled with an excitement about what this man wanted to accomplish. It wasn't just making me the first in the majors. It wasn't just the buildup of one new

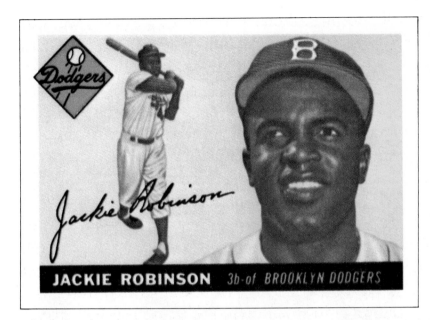

JACKIE ROBINSON   3b-of BROOKLYN DODGERS

The Dodgers' bench rises to congratulate Robinson after his home run in the playoff games of 1951.

The Sluggers: Duke Snider (center field), Gil Hodges (first baseman), Jackie Robinson (second base), PeeWee Reese (shortstop), and Roy Campanella (catcher).

star. We were standing at a closed door where many had knocked and none had been admitted. We were going to take hold of the knob, turn it, and walk in. But we had to walk carefully or it wouldn't work.

Mr. Rickey began to predict the kind of problems I would face: having bean balls thrown at me, being called names. He told me I'd have to permit all these things to happen to me and not lose my temper. I must never lose sight of our goal.

In those few minutes, experiences from most of my twenty-six years came to mind. I had always prided myself that I didn't start things but that I stood my ground when someone else did.

What was this man asking of me now? Was he calling upon me to sell my manhood for some fame and money which might come to me?

"Mr. Rickey," I demanded suspiciously, "are you looking for a Negro who is afraid to fight back?"

"I'm looking for a ballplayer, Jackie," he rumbled, "with guts enough *not* to fight back."

My interview with Branch Rickey lasted three hours. Once he had convinced me of the sincerity of his purpose I was completely in tune with him. He proceeded to dramatize for me some of the problems I would have to face. He did it so well that several times I had to make an effort to keep from getting angry, to make myself realize that he was acting a part and didn't mean some of the things he said.

"You're fielding a ground ball. A white player charges into you. He sneers at you, 'Next time get out of my way, you dirty ___,'" Mr. Rickey said. "Can you walk away from him?"

"They'll taunt you, goad you. Anything to make you fight. Anything to bring about a race riot in the ball park. If they succeed, they'll be able to prove that having a Negro in baseball doesn't work. They'll be able to frighten people so they'll be afraid to come out to games."

Branch Rickey did more than talk. He acted. He became an umpire, not only calling unfair decisions but adding racial sneers to his injustice. He became a restaurant owner, telling me I couldn't eat with the rest of the team but that he would prepare sandwiches for me to take out.

Jackie Robinson was elected to the Baseball Hall of Fame in 1962.

Rae Robinson stands in front of a picture of the stamp issued to honor her husband's achievements.

I didn't know, sitting there in his office, how I would be able to discipline myself, to control my rebellion at injustice. But I knew I would do it because I must. I had to learn to conquer and control myself because I sensed that the opportunity being offered me meant more than success for one Jackie Robinson. I had to do it because success would mean so much to the kids who would be coming up behind me. I wanted them to be able to feel that the color of their skins wouldn't hamper their dreams of making it in the majors. I had to do it because of my mother and the rest of my family and because of Rae, the girl I wanted to marry. Finally—to be perfectly honest—I had to do it for myself.

Questions

1. What team was Jackie Robinson playing for when he went to see Branch Rickey in August, 1945?
2. What sport had Robinson played at UCLA?
3. Why had Robinson stopped dreaming about the idea of playing for a major league team?
4. Do you think Robinson's decision to join the Dodgers was a courageous one? Do you think it took courage for Rickey to make the offer? Explain your answers.

Applying Reading Skills

Number your paper from 1 to 2. Choose the best answer for each question by drawing conclusions. Write each conclusion on your paper.

1. Why did Branch Rickey want Jackie Robinson to think their meeting was about the Brooklyn Brown Dodgers?
   a. He thought Robinson wouldn't want to play for the Brooklyn National League Club.
   b. He didn't want anyone to find out about his real plans.
   c. He wanted to surprise Robinson.

2. Why did Robinson know that he would be able to control his rebellion at injustice?
   a. He had not been upset when Rickey dramatized the problems he would have to face.
   b. He wanted to do it for his family, his wife-to-be, himself, and for those who later would get a chance because he succeeded.
   c. He had never been in trouble in sports before.

PREPARING FOR READING

Learning Vocabulary

1. Mrs. Sherman read an article about joint <u>ventures</u> in which elderly people bought their own house to live in.
2. At first, she thought the idea was <u>impractical</u>.
3. Mr. Pepper thought it was a <u>logical</u> <u>alternative</u> for some, but not the <u>majority</u>.
4. The judge said, "The court <u>commends</u> the spirit of those who try to build lives for themselves."

ventures	impractical	logical
alternative	majority	commends

Developing Background and Skills
Character's Motives or Feelings

Can you figure out if your friend is in a good mood or in a bad mood? You probably can. What your friend says or does usually reveals his or her feelings. Writers reveal the **feelings** of the characters in their stories in the same way. They describe what the characters say or do. They offer other clues, too. They may describe how a character talks or acts. They may also describe the character's appearance, or what the character looks like.

Read the following paragraph and notice how the writer describes Mrs. Anderson's feelings.

Mr. Wells is a lawyer, so he knows all about joint ventures. He commends the elderly people who want to buy a house in his neighborhood. But the majority of his neighbors disagree. Mrs. Anderson came storming into his house. Her face was red as she said loudly, "We don't want a boarding house next door!"

How does Mrs. Anderson feel about the elderly people's plan? There are several clues that let you know.

1. what she says—   "We don't want a boarding house next door."

2. how she says it—   loudly
3. what she does—   storms into Mr. Wells' house

4. her appearance—   red in the face

It's not difficult to figure out that Mrs. Anderson does not support the plan, and that she is angry about it.

As you read the next selection, try to figure out the feelings of the characters.

The Rocking Chair Rebellion

Eth Clifford

The Rocking Chair Rebellion! The way Mom used the phrase, you could almost see people meeting in out-of-the-way places, wearing trench coats and giving passwords out of the corners of their mouths, just like in the old-time movies.

Let me tell you what really started the Rebellion. It began when Mrs. Sherman saw this article in the *Indianapolis News*. You wouldn't think such a small item, buried way in the back of the paper someplace, would even be noticed, much less saved. It was just a few lines about how some elderly people had rented a big old house for senior citizens to live in. That was in Chicago, or maybe Los Angeles. I can't remember. Anyway, the whole point is, Mrs. Sherman began to talk about it. I heard about it first when I was at the Maple Ridge Home for the Aged. I'm one of the volunteers who help out there.

"How I admire them, Opie," Mrs. Sherman said, giving me the clipping to read. "Think of these ten people taking their courage in their hands and starting out fresh."

"What are you talking about, Serena?" said a voice from the doorway. Mr. Pepper was standing there, looking interested.

"Read this article, Simon, and tell me what you think about it."

He skimmed over it quickly.

"It would be lovely, Simon, wouldn't it? To have a place of one's own again? But of course it's impractical."

Mr. Pepper didn't think it was impractical. He took the whole idea seriously.

"What we would need would be three or four others to come in on something like this with us," he told her, kind of thinking out loud. "Someone like Smithers. You know how he's always puttering around here, fixing things. And easy to get along with. That's very important. And Georgeby. That man can grow. Why, we could have home-grown vegetables all summer long."

That was true. Mr. Georgeby had started a vegetable garden out in the backyard at Maple Ridge. I thought Mr. Pepper's idea of including Mr. Georgeby was terrific.

"If there were enough of us, we could pool our income," Mrs. Sherman said thoughtfully. "But what about the down payment on a house?" She sighed. "It's not as easy as this clipping makes you believe."

"Mrs. Longwood," I blurted out. "She's got lots of money."

"I'm not exactly poor myself," Mr. Pepper said. "We wouldn't need any money from Madeline."

"I'll go get Mrs. Longwood," I offered and ran out of Mrs. Sherman's room before either one could say anything. I really wanted them to try this idea. It wasn't the kind of idea that would work for most people at Maple Ridge, not the really old people, or the sick ones. But for Mrs. Sherman and some of the others, the ones who were in good shape physically . . .

"What's the child talking about?" Mrs. Longwood asked

when I brought her to Mrs. Sherman's room.

"Here," said Mr. Pepper. "Don't say another word until you've read this article."

Mrs. Longwood read it once, then she read it again. Then she turned the article over and looked at the back of it, as if it could give her some additional information. "You mean to tell me that people our age have actually done this? They are living the way they want to live?"

"The way Simon and I would like to live when we get married. But we can't do it alone," said Mrs. Sherman.

"It would take several people to take care of the house," I said. I was so eager about it you'd have thought it was my idea in the first place.

"Who were you thinking of?" Mrs. Longwood asked, looking at Mr. Pepper.

"Georgeby, to take care of the grounds. Smithers, to do the handiwork around the house. And me. I'm a mighty handy man with tools myself. Serena to do some of the cooking."

"I could take care of some of the housekeeping. Wouldn't it be grand to have a house to fuss over again?" Mrs. Longwood's face was all lit up.

"But what would Mr. Ver Lees say?" Mrs. Sherman asked suddenly. "If we moved out, he might take it as a reflection on himself and how he runs Maple Ridge."

They all fell silent. They liked Mr. Ver Lees.

"Well," Mr. Pepper said after a while. "It was nice dreaming about it anyway."

I got so upset. It seems like people give up so easily. I guess I'm like my dad; when I want something I kind of dig in my heels and fight for it. I shouldn't be so quick to judge, though. Then it came to me that there was one very logical thing to do.

"Why don't you just go into Mr. Ver Lees' office and ask him? The worst thing that can happen is that he'll say he doesn't think much of the idea."

"Opie's right," Mr. Pepper said. "It's about time we stood up to be counted." He turned to Mrs.

Sherman. "There's no time like the present. Come on, Serena."

I tagged along. I don't think they even noticed that I was there, they were so busy gathering up their courage to talk to Mr. Ver Lees.

Mr. Ver Lees was just on his way out, but when Mr. Pepper insisted, they all went into his office. Me, too. He read the article. And he listened to them speak, interrupting each other because they were so anxious to get him to understand how important this was to them.

When they stopped talking, there was this long silence.

"You're against the whole idea, aren't you?" Mrs. Longwood snapped. "I might have known."

"Now, Madeline," Mr. Ver Lees said mildly. "As a matter of fact, I've known about these joint ventures for some time now. I think it's the wave of the future.

Not for everybody. We'll always have some people living in institutions of one kind or another. But we recognize the very real need for this particular type of housing for some of our active senior citizens."

"Then you wouldn't be against our trying to find a place of our own?" Mrs. Sherman asked.

"You would have my whole-hearted support. Some of you are here because you have had no alternative. Now that you have found an alternative, I'll do whatever I can to help you."

I don't think I ever admired anybody more than I did Mr. Ver Lees just then. Except for maybe my dad.

I wasn't around when they got their group together—Mrs. Sherman, Mr. Pepper, Mr. Smithers, Mr. Georgeby, Mrs. Longwood, and Mrs. Gibson, who's one of the practical nurses at Maple Ridge. I know Mr. Pepper talked to a lot of real-estate agents about finding a house in the right area.

Boy, was I surprised when Mr. Pepper found a house right in my neighborhood! Mr. Crystal put his house up for sale, and he and Mr. Pepper got together and made a deal.

Three of our neighbors came to our house to discuss the Crystal house soon after.

"I think we can excuse Opie," Mr. Hartman said, glaring at me, waiting for me to leave the room.

Can you imagine? Wanting to throw me out of our own living room?

"She does live here," my mom said frostily. She didn't like the way Mr. Hartman spoke to me. She can talk to me any way she wants to, and she does, you better believe me. But let somebody else try it, and zing! she's a tiger defending her young.

Mrs. Anderson tried to smooth matters over. "You know we had a meeting of all the neighbors, Chet."

"We're sorry you couldn't be there. You would have found it very enlightening to know how everyone on the street feels about this," Mrs. Boight added.

"It was my sister's birthday," my dad said.

"You could have called the meeting for another evening," my mom said, sounding a little resentful.

Mrs. Anderson's voice got very tight. "The neighbors took a vote and decided to go to court to stop the sale of the house."

My dad didn't look pleased. He was the one who had told Mr. Pepper and the others that they would have to get what he called a "variance" on the zoning regulations in our area.

Mrs. Boight and her group went before the zoning board and argued that the old people wanted to set up a rooming house.

They lost, but they weren't giving up, because here they were, asking my dad and mom to support their case in court.

Mrs. Boight said, "After all, we

66

don't want those people coming in here and setting up a rooming house right on our street."

My mom got mad. She snapped, "What do you mean by 'those people' Ida May? You've know Simon Pepper for years."

Mrs. Anderson glared at my mother. "Are you going to sit there, Elizabeth, and tell us that a rooming house right on our block wouldn't disturb you?" Mrs. Anderson stood up, she became so agitated.

"Do we take this to mean that you are not on our side in this matter?" Mrs. Boight asked, her lips pulled together in such a tight line it was a wonder her voice could get through.

"I hadn't planned on taking sides," my dad explained.

My mom interrupted. "You can take it to mean that if Simon Pepper wants that house, Chester and I will do whatever we can to help him."

My mom looked beautiful to me then, she honestly did, all fire and flame, defending Mr. Pepper's rights.

"Never mind, Ida May," Mr. Hartman said. "I'm positive the court will overrule the zoning board's decision."

"You're not going to go through with this, are you, John?" My mother couldn't believe that he was so worked up about the whole thing.

"Am I ever," he said frostily. "I will take them to court and I will fight them tooth and nail. I will not have that sort of place next door to me, I promise you that!"

"If that's the mean way you're going to act," I shouted, "then okay, we'll see you in court."

"Do be quiet," Mrs. Boight told me sharply.

Dad walked over to me and put his arm around my shoulders.

"I think Opie has said it for us," he told her, giving my shoulder a little squeeze. "If that's the way you want it, well then, yes. We'll see you in court."

I had never been in the City-County Building. We went up to the fifth floor—that's where the circuit courts are. Mr. Ver Lees showed up, which surprised me. I don't know how he found the time.

We practically filled all the seats in the courtroom, which isn't hard. The courtroom isn't all that big. We sat in these really comfortable chairs that are behind a railing, separated from the real action. Straight ahead, on a raised platform, is the judge's desk, which is called a bench.

Over on the right, on another raised platform that was lower than the judge's bench, were twelve orange seats. They were for the jury, only *Hartman* vs. *Pepper* wasn't a jury case. It was going to be heard by Judge Ephraim Hydecker.

After about twenty minutes, the judge came out through a little door in back of the court.

I was kind of disappointed. I expected to see the judge in a black flowing robe. He was wearing an ordinary business suit with a tie that looked homemade. He had a no-nonsense,

let's-get-on-with-it look on his face that worried me.

He ruffled some papers on his desk and then he looked over his glasses and asked, "Is counsel for the plaintiff here?" Schuyler Withers nodded. "Is counsel for the defendant here?" My dad nodded.

After both lawyers agreed they were present, Judge Hydecker made a little speech to the spectators, explaining that this was not a jury hearing but a trial by court (which was himself). He would listen carefully to all the facts in the matter and from those facts make a judgment.

Mr. Withers got up to address the court. "Your Honor," his opening statement began, "my client objects to the establishment of a rooming house next to his property on a street zoned for one-family residences. We expect to prove that the house, presently known as the Crystal residence at four-fifty Horizon Drive, is going to function as a boarding house."

When it was my dad's turn, he got up and said, "Your Honor, far from being a rooming house, as learned counsel contends, the Crystal residence is and will remain a one-family residence, as we expect to prove."

The first witness called was Mr. Hartman. First Mr. Withers asked a few ordinary questions, like who Mr. Hartman was and where did he live, and was his house next door to the residence known as the Crystal house. Then Mr. Hartman was asked, "Are you alone in wanting your street maintained as a strictly residential area of one-family homes?" Mr. Hartman told him that more than half the people on the block agreed with him.

"We called a meeting of all the neighbors on the block. We all agreed, since this is a democracy and the majority is supposed to rule," he said, with a fierce look at Dad, "that we would take the matter to court and abide by the decision of the judge."

"All the neighbors at that meeting were in agreement?"

"Not at first, no. But as I said, they finally said they would accept a court ruling."

I'm not going to go through the whole hearing because it just went on and on. First there were all the witnesses that Mr. Withers called. Then there were the witnesses that Dad called, like Mr. Ver Lees, who of course said he was in favor of what Mr. Pepper wanted to do.

When Mr. Withers cross-examined Mr. Ver Lees, he said, "As an expert, what do you think the chances are for this group of elderly," he put a lot of emphasis on elderly, "people making a go of this venture?"

Mr. Ver Lees shrugged. "Who's to say? It might work out very well. It might fail."

Mr. Withers pounced. "It might fail?"

"Your Honor," my dad protested. "That's hardly the issue here. . . ."

But Mr. Ver Lees was still talking. "However, that's not the point. The point is that they should have the same right to try something and succeed, or fail, just like anyone else."

When it was Mr. Pepper's turn on the stand, Dad asked him, "Mr. Pepper, won't your house, in effect, be a boarding house?"

Mr. Pepper shook his head. With an absolutely straight face, he said, "Boarders? Certainly not. The home would belong to me and to my future wife, Mrs. Sherman. As for Mrs. Longwood, Mr. Georgeby, Mr. Smithers, and Mrs. Gibson—why, we would be taking them on as helpers. Mrs. Gibson is a fine nurse and cook. She is willing to help us. And Mr. Smithers will, too. He is an excellent handyman. And Mr. Georgeby already has made plans for the garden."

Nothing could shake Mr. Pepper, not even the sharp questions Mr. Withers got up to ask him.

Then both lawyers made their closing statements, which I don't remember word for word, because my mind was wandering. What I was thinking was lawyers start off by telling you what they're going to say, then they say it, and then they wind up the whole thing by telling you what they just told you.

Judge Hydecker was scribbling away all the time.

After a while, he looked up and said, "It is the opinion of this court that the Crystal residence, if purchased by the defendant Simon Pepper, would not become either a boarding house or a home for the aged.

"This court commends the spirit of these six *individuals*," he emphasized the word, "who in the best American tradition are attempting to build lives for themselves by their own efforts and labor. The court finds in favor of the defendant Simon Pepper."

The judge got up and left the courtroom quickly. I guess he didn't want to have to stop us all from cheering.

Questions

1. Who were the six individuals in the group that wanted to buy a house of their own?
2. Why were they concerned about what Mr. Ver Lees might say about their plan?
3. Who is the plaintiff in a court case? Who is the defendant?
4. If you had been the lawyer for the defense, what would you have said in your closing statement?

Applying Reading Skills

The sentences below are from "The Rocking Chair Rebellion." Number your paper from 1 to 4. Write a word or phrase to describe the feelings of the character whose name is under-lined. Then write one or more of the phrases below to tell what helped you to know.

the character's words   the character's actions
how the character spoke   the character's appearance

1. "I'll go get Mrs. Longwood," I offered and ran out of the room before either one could say anything. (Opie)
2. "I could take care of some of the housekeeping. Wouldn't it be grand to have a house to fuss over again?" Mrs. Leonard's face was all lit up.
3. "Well," Mr. Pepper said after a while. "It was nice dreaming about it anyway."
4. Mrs. Anderson glared at my mother. "Are you going to sit there, Elizabeth, and tell us that a rooming house right on our block wouldn't disturb you?" Mrs. Anderson stood up, she became so agitated.

AMERICAN HERITAGE

The Declaration of Independence,
The Constitution with its Bill of Rights:
These are the bulwarks of our heritage,
These are our nation's guiding lights.

Freedom of speech, freedom of press,
Freedom to worship as we please,
The right to assemble, the right to petition,
Are some of the freedoms we recite with ease.

The right to life, the right to liberty,
The right to the pursuit of happiness,
The right to equality, the right to security,
The right to live without undue stress.

But what of the many other rights,
Not written in our laws:
The right to labor, the right to suffer,
The right to fight for freedom's cause?

For these are rights our forefathers chose,
When they laid our country's foundation,
And these are the rights we must assume
To preserve our precious nation.

Elsie Walush

WRITING ACTIVITY

WRITE A BUSINESS LETTER

Prewrite

Mr. Pepper, Mrs. Sherman, and their friends wanted to buy a house in "The Rocking Chair Rebellion." Imagine you know the people in the story. You have decided to write a letter to the editor of the local newspaper explaining why you think Mr. Pepper and his friends should be allowed to buy the house on Horizon Drive.

Your letter to the newspaper editor will be a business letter. A business letter is short and to the point. Your letter should explain who you are and the purpose you have for writing the letter. Then the letter should state your opinion and give reasons that explain or support it.

Reread the story. Write sentence notes that explain exactly what Mr. Pepper and his friends want to do and why. Be sure to write notes that explain how the people on Horizon Drive feel also.

Then write notes that explain your opinion. Remember, opinions are statements about what a person believes or feels. If you want people to support your opinion, you must give good reasons to explain why you believe or feel as you do. Your opinion will be respected if you present a good case for it.

Write

1. Read your notes.
2. Address your letter to:
   Ms. Myra McDonald, Editor
   The Daily Eagle
   227 West Main Street
   Indianapolis, Indiana 46204
3. Use the correct form for a business letter.
4. Your first paragraph should introduce yourself and state the purpose of your letter.
5. The next paragraph should explain Mr. Pepper's plans and how people on Horizon Drive feel about those plans.
6. The last paragraph should give your opinion and the reasons that support or explain it.
7. Use your Glossary or dictionary for spelling help.

Revise

Read your business letter. Did you introduce yourself and clearly state the purpose of your letter? Did you make very clear what Mr. Pepper wants to do? Did you give reasons that explain why you have your opinion? If you need to rewrite any part of your letter, do so now.

1. Did you capitalize names correctly?
2. Did you use the correct punctuation in your letter?
3. Did you use the correct form for a business letter?

PREPARING FOR READING

Learning Vocabulary

1. From far away, the boy's home looked so small that a crow could <u>pluck</u> it from the ground.
2. The boy found an injured bird and took it to the old man's <u>dwelling</u>.
3. The old man's trailer was filled with broken arrows of <u>warriors</u> and other things used by his <u>ancestors</u>.
4. He had a collection of stuffed birds, their eyes <u>replaced</u> by pieces of glass.
5. The boy <u>clutched</u> the injured bird and ran.

pluck	dwelling	warriors
ancestors	replaced	clutched

Developing Background and Skills
Character's Motives or Feelings

You know that writers reveal a **character's feelings** in several ways. They tell what a character does and says. They describe how a character talks, acts, or looks.

Writers also present information about a **character's motives,** or reasons for saying or doing something.

Read the sentences below. See if you can find the motive of each character whose name is underlined.

Sarah worked after school to earn money for a new bicycle.

"I want to win the race," said David, "so I am going to practice every day."

Because she wanted her son to know she was serious, Mrs. Wolcott had a stern look on her face.

You probably found it easy to find each character's motive. Sarah's motive was to earn money for a new bicycle. David's motive was to win the race. Mrs. Wolcott's motive was to let her son know she was serious. What did each person's motive lead him or her to do or say?

As you read "The Scared One," look for the motives behind what the Scared One does and says. It is helpful when looking for motives to ask "Why?" or "What was the reason or purpose?" Often in a story, there will be a single motive behind many things that a character does or says.

79

THE SCARED ONE

Dennis Haseley

They call me the Scared One
because I run from things,
because I am afraid
of the night
and the big dogs
even when those in our village
who are smaller than me
are not afraid.
And anyone can call me
the Scared One.
Anyone can say
what they like about me
and I will stay and smile
for the others know
I am most afraid
of being alone.

And in the school they told us
that my tribe was once proud
although today
only a few old people
know the language.
And they said that once
a young man of this tribe
would go to a wild place
by himself,
would go without his food,
without his sleep,
until an animal
came to him
in a dream
to be his guide
for all his life . . .

and in the classroom
I closed my eyes and tried to see
the animal that would
come for me—
a bear
or a deer—
and the boys laughed
when they saw me
and told the teacher
I was dreaming
of a little mouse.

And that night at the table
my mother looked at me
for a long time
and then she asked
if I would like to talk.
I shook my head.
"I understand," she said.
"You are almost a man."
I nodded, then I
walked from the room
quickly so she would not see
and put my face down
on my cot
and my tears flowed
from my little mouse heart.
I slept then,
but it was during the night
that our goat
chewed through his rope,
and in my dream
of running from my village
I heard his bell
grow softer
and softer.

And in the morning
my mother gave me
a piece of jerky
and a rope
and sent me off
through the fields
all alone
running to keep up
with my heart.

My house grew so small
a crow could pluck it.
My house!

And when I was so far away
and alone
I lay by a rock . . .

After a time
the sun grew warm
on my back and I woke
and saw the goat
nuzzling the grass.
I reached and grabbed his rope . . .
and then I saw the bird!

He stood near me
with his wings stretched
the length of my arms
and they were bright, like flames,
and his eyes stared into mine.

I sat up slowly
but he did not move.
"Go," I said. "Fly." And he
tilted his head.
Then I saw the crook
in his wing
like a twig
broken by a storm.
"You can't fly," I said,
and his eyes seemed
to know my words.
I took my shirt—
my heart was beating
like a caught bird—
and I put it over his folded wings,
and then I lifted him gently.
He was light.

And then the goat
and the bird
and I went through the fields
toward my village.

When we returned
it was night
and I tied the goat
and went into my house.
My mother was cooking
and I lifted the shirt
and she turned and looked at me
a long time.
"You cannot keep him,"
she said. "He will die here."
I looked down.
His eyes were closed,
and I felt afraid.
"If you want to help him," she said,
and her voice was soft
like it had not been for a long time,
"then you must take him
to Old Wolf. He
knows of such things."

That night I did not sleep.
In the dark of the room,
the bird and I looked at each other.

And at the first light
I wrapped him in my shirt
and walked through the village
while the families were eating,
and the boys came to their windows
and called out to me:
"Hey, Scared One, mouse,
where are you going?"
And I nodded and smiled,
though I did not want to,
and walked up the road,
alone,
to the dwelling of the man
who would help my bird fly.
He was a member of the tribe
though now he lived by the highway
and sold things to the visitors
who came to see the village.

When I got to the door
of his trailer
it seemed like he was
waiting for me.

I spoke fast like a rabbit.
"I have a bird that is sick.
I was told you could heal him."
He looked at me and did not smile.
Then he said for me
to show him the bird.
When I lifted the shirt
his eyes opened wide.
"This bird is very sick," he said.
"I will do what I can.
You go home, now."

I gave him my bird,
but when I turned to go
my heart felt sick
though I did not know why.
Then I heard a
flapping of wings,
and I turned and saw
Old Wolf holding on to my bird
while the bird beat his wings.
But when the bird
saw me
he stopped
and tilted his head.
And it was as if
everything slowed down.

I looked around
the walls of the trailer . . .
and saw the broken arrows,
the chipped flints
of warriors,
the rusted knives
beneath the glass.
And along the walls
on perches
I saw the birds,
frozen there,
with their wings spread,
who would stay and never fly,
and I saw how my own bird might look,
frozen, never moving,
his eyes replaced with glass,
his legs on a metal stand,
a tag on his neck,
and oh, I wished to see him fly!

Then I grew very still
while something in my chest
began to beat,
strong and steady,
trying to get out,
and I said, "No,"
sharply, and I took my bird
and I turned
and ran from his trailer,
and I could hear Old Wolf
shouting
in the language of my ancestors.

And when I reached the road
I saw
the boys from my village
waiting for me
and they were not smiling.
"Give us what you have," they said.
"Give us what is in the shirt."

I looked at them as
they walked toward me,
and I felt the beating
in my chest,
and I took my bird
from my shirt
and he leapt
onto my arm,
my bare arm,
and he clutched there
with his claws,
and the boys stood back,
and then, oh,
I raised him
and the words came from inside.

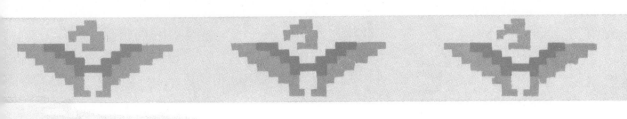

"*WaNyaka Michante!*
Behold my heart!
WaNyaka Mi wowaske!
Behold my strength!"
And how the sun was rising,
and he stretched out his wings
his flashing wings,
his wings of flame
and I said, "You must fly now,"
and he clutched my arm
and like my own fire
my blood ran!
"*Kinan Po!* Fly now!" I cried.
"*Ake Akisne!*
You must grow strong
while you fly!"

And I thrust my arm
into the air . . .
He tilted his head
at me. He looked
into my eyes . . .
and he turned
and rose
and, oh, I could feel his wings
beating in my chest
and I cried
"I will never fear!
I will never die!"
And he rose
into the flame of the sky
into the blood of my life!

Questions

1. Why was the boy called the Scared One?
2. How did the Scared One discover the injured bird?
3. Why did the Scared One's mother think that if he kept the injured bird it would die?
4. Do you think the Scared One will change because of his experience with the bird? Why or why not?

Applying Reading Skills

Choose the ending for each sentence below that best describes the motive for what the Scared One did. Number your paper from 1 to 3. Write the completed sentences.

1. The Scared One walked away from the dinner table because _____.
   a. he wanted to go to sleep
   b. he did not want his mother to see him cry
   c. he was afraid his mother might make him talk about his sadness

2. The Scared One took the injured bird to Old Wolf because _____.
   a. he wanted Old Wolf to heal the bird
   b. he wanted Old Wolf to add the bird to his collection
   c. he wanted Old Wolf to sell the bird to someone who could take care of it

3. The Scared One stood up to the boys of the village because _____.
   a. he knew he could frighten them with the bird
   b. he wanted to show them that he was not afraid
   c. he wanted to protect the bird from them

PREPARING FOR READING

Learning Vocabulary

1. The sound of a bear cub rummaging for food was not <u>familiar</u> to the dog, Grizzly.
2. He <u>boldly</u> leapt at the <u>massive</u> mother bear who came to find her cub.
3. The bear's <u>wrath</u> was directed toward the brave <u>rescue</u> dog.

familiar   boldly   massive
wrath   rescue

Developing Background and Skills
Sequence of Events

You know that a writer has several ways of letting you know the order in which things happen, or the **sequence of events**. Words such as *first*, *last*, *next*, *then*, and *finally* help you to know whether one event took place before or after another event.

What is the sequence of the events described in the paragraph below?

At first Mrs. Gratias ignored the noise, but later she left the cabin to investigate. Before she went outside, she untied the dog.

If you read carefully you know the correct sequence.

1. Mrs. Gratias ignored the noise.
2. She untied the dog.
3. She left the cabin.

Sometimes a writer does not use clue words but tells the events in the order in which they happened. The sentences in the paragraph below describe the events in the order in which they happened.

Mrs. Gratias ran for the door. She turned the corner of the house and came face to face with a bear. The bear reared up on its hind legs. Mrs. Gratias leaped sideways to avoid it, but slipped on the ice and fell.

Writers do not always use signal words or write about events in the order in which they happened. Then you must use your experience and your common sense to figure out the right sequence.

As you read the next selection, think about the order in which things happen. What clues does the writer give you? What must you figure out for yourself?

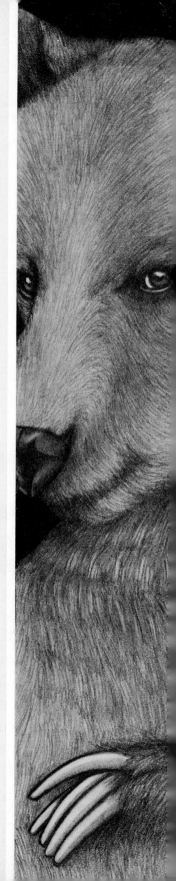

A DOG NAMED GRIZZLY

D.J. ARNESON

Mrs. David Gratias was preparing the noon meal for her husband and their little daughter, Theresa. Mr. Gratias was tending to the many chores that were constantly in need of doing around the place. He would come for lunch when he was called—if he wasn't too far off to hear.

Theresa, just two years old, was sound asleep in the front room near the door of the family cabin.

As she worked alone in the kitchen, Mrs. Gratias thought she heard a noise coming from somewhere in the clearing behind the cabin. "Oh, it's probably just the wind," she said. She glanced across the kitchen to where the family dog lay sleeping in a lazy, furry heap. The dog didn't stir, and so Mrs. Gratias forgot about the noise and went on with her work.

But the dog wasn't exactly sleeping. He had heard the noise too and was listening. His sharp senses quickened. Though he was still young, years of fine breeding caused him to be alert. St. Bernards are not only excellent rescue dogs, they are fine watchdogs as well. Though not yet full-grown, the Gratias's dog was large. Because of his size and weight, he was called Grizzly Bear.

Grizzly Bear didn't look or act like a real bear. He was nothing at all like a real grizzly, one of the largest and fiercest of all wild creatures. Instead, he was a friendly, easygoing, and gentle family pet. But he had come from a long line of heroic mountain dogs that had been bred to rescue lost travelers in the Swiss Alps. Alaska was a fitting place for a St. Bernard called Grizzly Bear.

Grizzly focused his sleepy eyes on the kitchen door and listened. He was familiar with the sounds of the surrounding forest, but the sound he heard was not familiar. He sniffed the air.

Mrs. Gratias again paused and this time turned her ear toward the window. "I *do* hear a noise," she exclaimed aloud. "There's something in the yard."

Grizzly's ears were perked. He no longer lay in slumber. He sat up in a crouch, watching his owner.

"It's probably nothing more than some birds fighting over scraps," Mrs. Gratias said, again out loud. "But I better take a look, just to be sure." She started walking toward the front door, the only entrance to the cabin, when she noticed that Grizzly was sitting up. The dog, leashed to a heavy table, was looking at her eagerly. "Oh, all right," Mrs. Gratias said, and she turned back and untied the leash. "You might as well get some exercise too. At the rate you're growing, you're going to be too big to get back inside the cabin before long." She laughed and went to the door.

As Mrs. Gratias stepped outside into the sunlight, she glanced back at Theresa, who continued to sleep soundly near the door. She smiled warmly at her tiny daughter. Instead of closing the door, she left it open just a crack.

The air was brisk and refreshing. Mrs. Gratias hugged herself to keep warm as she walked to the rear of the cabin. As she neared the backyard, she paused to listen. Clearly, something was in the yard behind the house. She stepped boldly around the corner to see what it could be.

"*Oh, my goodness!*" Mrs. Gratias's arms came up in surprise. She stopped dead in her tracks. Rummaging near the back wall of the cabin, scraggly and very hungry-looking, was a grizzly bear cub. The cub was just as startled as she.

"Arrunnk," the cub grunted.

The sound was enough to shock Mrs. Gratias to
the awful truth of what she had stumbled upon. She
knew enough about the wilds of Alaska to know
that grizzly bear cubs are seldom very far from their
mothers. She also knew that a mother bear separated
from her cub was one of the most dangerous creatures
in the world.

"Theresa!" Mrs. Gratias screamed, suddenly
remembering that she had left the front door open.
She whirled on the snow-covered ground and raced
toward the front of the house. She had to get to the
door and make sure that Theresa was safe. Nothing
else mattered.

The instant she rounded the corner of the house,
her worst fears came alive. The mother grizzly, looking for her own wandering offspring, stood face to
face with the terrified woman.

The bear reared up onto her hind legs. She was
so huge that she blocked out the sun.

Panic gripped Mrs. Gratias. The bear blocked the
way between her and Theresa. There was only one
thought on Mrs. Gratias's mind. She had to protect
her daughter.

Mrs. Gratias leaped sideways but slipped on the
icy ground beneath her feet and fell solidly to the
frozen earth, striking her head sharply. Her vision
blurred. She was totally helpless now.

The bear dropped to all fours. Then the giant bear opened her huge mouth.

Mrs. Gratias struggled, but she was already wounded and much too weak to fight. The giant

head came toward her. The razor-sharp teeth were only inches away.

Then, without warning, there was a flash of brown-and-white fur in the air. The huge bear grunted aloud as Grizzly crashed headlong into her chest. The sudden blow knocked the beast away from Mrs. Gratias. The bear staggered backwards, stunned by the powerful flying leap of the attacking dog.

The bear's attention was no longer on the fallen woman, who weakly struggled to regain her feet. Instead, the wild creature's wrath was directed toward the dog. The bear roared. Her huge lips curled. Fangs sharp as knives sparkled white against the red flesh of her mouth.

Grizzly jumped and darted back and forth between the bear and the woman. The bear couldn't get close to her. Each time she tried to move forward, Grizzly barked and leaped, driving the bear back. Grizzly snapped at the bear's massive paws and repeatedly struck her in the head and chest with solid blows from his thick paws. He refused to let the bear advance a step closer to the woman lying dazed on the ground.

Mrs. Gratias watched in horror the terrible battle between the real grizzly bear and her own beloved Grizzly. Mrs. Gratias grew weaker. She slipped into unconsciousness as the battle went on.

A few moments later, Mrs. Gratias blinked her eyes opened. There was silence. The bright yellow sun was shining down on her. She could feel its pleasant warmth on her back. She felt the cold snow beneath her and knew she was alive. As she pain-

fully raised her head, she felt something warm and wet on her cheek. Mrs. Gratias blinked her eyes open again. Grizzly, his fur torn, put his big, sad face next to that of his mistress and licked her wounds.

"Grizzly," Mrs. Gratias murmured. Then she remembered!

"Theresa!" she screamed as she struggled to her feet. What if the bear wasn't really gone? She staggered to the front of the cabin. The door was open.

Grizzly bounded past Mrs. Gratias and leaped through the open door, his big furry tail wagging rapidly to and fro.

"She's all right," Mrs. Gratias gasped in relief, holding onto the open door for support. "Theresa is all right." She peered into the friendly warmth of her cozy cabin home. Theresa lay sound asleep, exactly where her mother had left her. And curled up alongside the little girl, wounded and frightfully dirty but with his tail wagging happily, was Grizzly.

Mrs. Gratias threw her arms around the big, bold dog. Tears of thankfulness filled her eyes. "You saved both our lives, Grizzly," she said, hugging him tightly, "Theresa's and mine."

Questions

1. Why did Mrs. Gratias leave the cabin?
2. In what ways was Grizzly like a grizzly bear? In what ways was he different?
3. Why was Mrs. Gratias worried about Theresa even though the child was inside the cabin?
4. Did Grizzly show true courage in his defense of Mrs. Gratias, or was he just following his instincts? Explain your answer.

Applying Reading Skills

The sentences below tell about some of the events in "A Dog Named Grizzly." Write the sentences in the correct sequence on your paper.

Mrs. Gratias slipped into unconsciousness.

Mrs. Gratias saw the bear cub rummaging near the cabin wall.

Mrs. Gratias fell, striking her head sharply.

Mrs. Gratias raced to the front of the cabin, where she saw the mother grizzly.

Mrs. Gratias heard an unfamiliar noise coming from the clearing behind the cabin.

Mrs. Gratias felt something warm and wet on her cheek.

Mrs. Gratias threw her arms around Grizzly with thankfulness.

Grizzly directed the bear's attention away from Mrs. Gratias.

PREPARING FOR READING

Learning Vocabulary
1. Minako had an <u>abundance</u> of <u>desire</u> to learn.
2. She also had the <u>dedication</u> needed to become a <u>scholar</u>.
3. Her self-defense skills helped her to become a <u>victor</u>

abundance   desire   dedication
scholar   victor

Developing Background and Skills
Character's Motives or Feelings
Understanding the **motives and feelings of characters** in stories can make your reading more enjoyable and interesting. Some characters may have feelings that you have. They may have motives, or reasons for doing things, that you share. As you read about these characters you may say, "I've felt that way before" or "I know why she did that."

Writers help you to understand their characters' motives or feelings in several ways. They may explain them directly. They may also give you information that you can use to figure out what the feelings and motives are. Writers tell about a character's actions and appearance. They also explain what a character says.

Read the following paragraph. Notice how the writer reveals the character's motives and feelings.

Yoko was as curious as she was beautiful. She had an incredible desire to learn and always found reasons to visit her brothers' school. She would deliver messages to her brothers or bring food and flowers to the teachers. One day, a teacher invited her to study with his class. Yoko's face glowed, and her voice shook as she quickly accepted.

What are Yoko's motives for visiting the school? How does Yoko feel when she is invited to study?

By reading carefully, you know that Yoko was curious and that she had an incredible desire to learn. Curiosity and a desire to learn are Yoko's motives for her visits to the school. They are also clues to Yoko's feelings about the offer to study. You can probably guess that she is delighted. The writer says that Yoko's face glowed, and that her voice shook as she quickly accepted the offer.

As you read the next selection, try to determine the characters' feelings and motives. Use information that is plainly stated, and pay attention to appearance, action, and speech. Focus particular attention on Minako, the main character.

THE DAIMYO'S DAUGHTER

Kristen R. Morsy

Dusk is a dreaming time for storytellers. My imagination wanders to a far away time when a great warlord, a daimyo (dī′ myō), governed this valley.

The daimyo Imazu lived with his three sons and one daughter, but he spent little time enjoying his children. Much of his time was spent directing his samurai warriors against bandits.

One bandit in particular haunted his dreams. The farmers called this bandit the Rice-Fox. No one had ever seen the face of Rice-Fox. He always wore the battle mask of a samurai on his raids. Legend told that the Rice-Fox had once been a great samurai warrior whose lord had been killed in battle. Rather than obey the victor, Rice-Fox had chosen to become a bandit.

The daimyo Imazu's chasing of the bandit distracted him from his children and their education. Although the best teachers were hired, the daimyo's sons wanted to hunt and ride. They rarely visited the classrooms. His daughter, Minako, however, was even more curious than she was beautiful. Her hands were busy arranging flowers, but her mind was roving like a butterfly.

Every day Minako brought gifts of rice and flowers to the school. One afternoon she carried branches of camellia piled so high that she could not see the path before her, and she stumbled over a monk in the courtyard. Camellias fell out of her arms into his lap.

"Forgive me, Honorable Master," she said, regaining her balance. "I did not expect to meet anyone at this hour."

"I spend many hours in thought," the monk said, "since so few are required for teaching."

"Master," Minako blurted, "how I wish you could teach me! My brothers are foolish to waste their opportunities. They should be forced to study with you."

"Can the gardener force the bush to bloom?" the master said, fingering the pink petals of camellia. "The teacher cannot force the pupil to learn. The teacher is only a guide to self-discovery. The path to self-discovery is not an easy one. First, you must have desire."

"I have desire in abundance," Minako said.

"You need discipline as well," he told her. "You must focus on the teacher and copy every movement."

"Yes, Master," Minako agreed. "I will discipline my mind and body to follow your teaching."

"But there is more, Minako," the master cautioned. "You must show dedication. No learning of any value is gotten overnight. You must spend long hours in study."

"I will have the dedication," Minako said.

"Then you will be the perfect pupil," he said. He rose, brushing flowers from his lap, and they bowed to each other.

The next morning, Minako arrived at the school dressed in her youngest brother's old clothes. She kept her promises to the monk and was welcomed by the other teachers. She excelled as a scholar, an artist, and an athlete. Her intelligence and modesty soon became known to all but her father.

The daimyo Imazu, meanwhile, continued to chase the Rice-Fox. The bandit never harmed the farmers or villagers, as did some common robbers. He only raided the warehouses of the rice the daimyo took for taxes. The daimyo vowed to punish the Rice-Fox. He prepared to lead his samurai on an attack of the robber's mountain hideaway.

Before he left, he called his sons to him. "I have had you trained for this day of your man-hood," he told them. "You must take on your duties as rulers now and free me to capture the Rice-Fox."

The daimyo Imazu then told his sons to demonstrate their skills. To his amazement, they could neither read nor calculate nor defend themselves in combat. "Sad day!" Imazu cried. "You are utterly useless. When I die, this valley will be a plum for any enemy to pluck. Your lives will be worth less than a puff of smoke. Send the teachers at once! I will punish them as a warning to all against laziness in my service."

The teachers lined up silently before the daimyo, but Minako ran forward and threw herself at his feet. "Honorable Father," she said, "the

teachers should not be punished for my brothers' laziness. The teachers have worked long and well."

"Show me proof," Imazu said.

Minako bowed, then took up a scroll and brush. She wrote a letter to the Emperor as skillfully as any scribe. She read aloud from a treaty Imazu had signed that year with a neighboring daimyo.

Minako then selected a handful of tax receipts. She added the sales of rice, subtracted the taxes, and wrote the correct amount in the accounting scroll.

Without warning, a bodyguard rushed at Minako with a shout. She turned out of the man's hold and glided away from him. He charged again. This time she caught his wrist and threw him down on the mat.

Minako bowed to her father. "Honorable Father," she said. "I would like to play a song for you I wrote, so you might know I have not neglected a lady's education."

She settled her skirts around her and tuned the samisen. As she sang, her father rose to his feet. "Minako," he said, "you are my best and only hope. Your fingers run as swiftly and surely across the abacus as across the strings of the samisen. You step as lightly through the patterns of self-defense as through a dance. I will leave you in charge of my estates while I am gone."

"Thank you, Father," Minako said. "I am honored to use my skills in your service."

"Then, when the Rice-Fox is caught," the daimyo said, "I will marry you to an ally. I shall be sorry to lose you."

"Do not lose me then!" Minako cried. "If I prove myself an able ruler, why must I marry an ally?"

"Soldiers will not obey a woman," the daimyo Imazu said. He gave her his most commanding gaze. "You will obey me, of course."

"Yes, Father," Minako said. Sadness lowered her voice to a whisper as she bowed and left the room.

Minako went outside to think. Her thoughts were so troubled that she almost missed a small rustle of movement in the dark courtyard. The sound alerted her to danger.

"Eeeeeee-yites!"

Before her attacker could touch her, Minako had stepped aside, and he fell into the reflecting pool. Minako looked around to see that she was surrounded by bandits.

"Very good," said a voice from the shadows. "I have heard that you are quick as well as clever, Lady Minako."

"Who are you?" Minako demanded.

"I am called the Rice-Fox," the voice said, "and I have come to steal you away. Your ransom will save us the trouble of raiding the daimyo's warehouses. I doubt your father is searching for me so close to his own fort."

"Then your legend is correct," Minako said. "You are a very great samurai to outwit the daimyo. But I must ask you one favor that, as a samurai, you can grant me. Do not set your men on me like dogs on a bone. If you intend to capture me, let me defend myself against each of you, one at a time."

"Your request is a fair one," the Rice-Fox answered. "But I have eight men with me. Can you resist so many?"

"I can try," said Minako.

The Rice-Fox laughed with delight. "I like your spirit, Minako. Defend yourself against me alone, and I will free you." He stepped out of the shadows. Minako stared in amazement at the tall and terrible figure. He grabbed her kimono but she twisted and stepped aside. The silk slipped out of his hands. Back and forth they moved, the advantage changing moment by moment. He was stronger; Minako quicker. It seemed that neither could win.

Finally, the two faced off. "Have I won my freedom?" Minako said, gasping. "You have earned yours."

"I have never been your captive," said the Rice-Fox.

"You are a slave to the life of the bandit," Minako said. "I can free you from that. And you are the only obstacle between me and the power of daimyo. My father believes that no soldier will obey a woman. But if I am the woman who presents the Rice-Fox alive to him in his own court, I will earn the respect of his samurai. Then they will obey me."

"How will you catch me when you cannot escape me?" the Rice-Fox asked.

"You have proven yourself a worthy samurai," Minako said. "You would hold your rightful place in our land today if it were not for the one battle in which your lord was killed. I will restore the title of samurai to you."

She smiled at the eyes behind the battle mask. "You can make me daimyo," she said, "and I can make you samurai. Together we can bring peace to this land."

Rice-Fox stood still beside the reflecting pool. Suddenly he lifted his battle mask, and Minako saw his face for the first time. She marvelled at his beauty and dignity. He smiled and dropped to his knees before her. "My lady," he said.

Minako proved herself as wise with the people of the valley as she had with Rice-Fox. He was as able and loyal a leader as she had hoped. The entire land prospered in peace. The story of Minako lives to this day in the imaginations of storytellers.

Questions

1. Who was the Rice-Fox and why did Imazu spend time chasing him?
2. Why did Minako wear her brother's clothes when she went to school?
3. Do you think Imazu was right when he said that soldiers would not obey a woman? Explain your answer.
4. What qualities do you think leaders need to earn the respect of their followers?

Applying Reading Skills

Number your paper from 1 to 4. Finish each incomplete sentence below by choosing the best word or phrase. Write the complete sentences on your paper. Then write **F** if the sentence describes a feeling or **M** if it describes a motive.

1. Imazu's sons neglected their studies because _____.
   a. they wanted to ride and hunt
   b. of their dislike of the teachers
   c. they wanted to become bandits

2. When the master accepted Minako as a pupil, she was _____.
   a. worried   b. happy   c. confused

3. The Rice-Fox's raids made Imazu _____.
   a. jealous   b. happy   c. angry

4. The Rice-Fox tried to take Minako captive because he thought he would _____.
   a. get a large ransom for her return
   b. be able to force her to marry him
   c. make the daimyo jealous

A weightless balloon
slips from the hand of a child
the wandering moon

Two things the moon steals:
a light from the trunks of the trees,
a day from my life.

Ann Atwood

UNIT TWO   LEVEL 12

TRUNKFULS
OF
TREASURE

PREPARING FOR READING

Learning Vocabulary

1. Aunt Mim told Cindy that they were going in a cab and that Gwen's Rock Shop was their <u>destination</u>.
2. Cindy found it difficult to be <u>patient</u> while they were traveling.
3. In the back of the shop were piles of <u>sorted</u> rocks.
4. Gwen lifted the cover of a machine to <u>reveal</u> a saw blade.
5. She explained that <u>erosion</u> is a process of wearing away.
6. Gwen told Cindy that <u>minerals</u> can form bands of color in rocks.

destination   patient   sorted
reveal   erosion   minerals

Developing Background and Skills
Make Generalizations
Read the story below.

Jim's hobby is rock collecting. He belongs to a rock club that meets every Saturday. Sometimes the group spends the whole day on field trips searching for new and different kinds of rocks. After school Jim often works on identifying, mounting, and labeling all the specimens he has collected.

Suppose you were asked to make a single statement about Jim and his rock collection. You might say *Jim spends a lot of time on his rock collection.* A statement of this kind is called a **generalization.** A generalization is a broad, or general, statement that is based on facts or information. The particular facts or information should support the generalization.

Now reread the story carefully to find the facts that support the generalization that *Jim spends a lot of time on his rock collection.* You should be able to see that the facts below support and lead to the generalization.

1. Jim belongs to a rock club that meets every Saturday.
2. The group sometimes spends the whole day on field trips.
3. Jim often works on his collection after school.

As you read the next selection, think about what generalizations you can make about what the writer tells you. Keep track of the facts or information that support your generalizations.

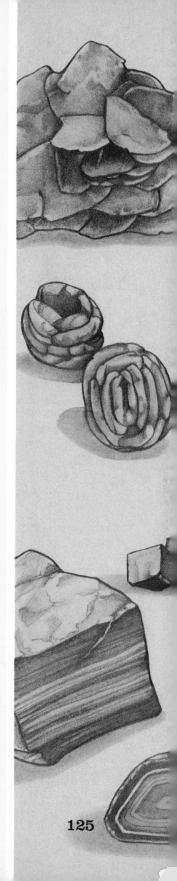

THE BIRTHDAY TREASURE HUNT

Mary Elizabeth Merrum

"Aunt Mim! Aunt Mim!" cried Cindy excitedly. "You got here!"

"Sure I got here. You know I wouldn't miss my favorite niece's birthday," Aunt Mim said, smiling as she paid the cab driver. Both of them enjoyed the private joke that had started when Cindy was just a baby— Cindy had to be Aunt Mim's favorite niece because she was her only niece.

Cindy didn't see her aunt that often because she was always traveling. Aunt Mim was a geologist and worked for an international oil company, but she never forgot to come home for Cindy's birthday or to bring her an unusual gift from another country. Once she had given her a set of little wooden boxes from the Orient, each smaller than the last and each containing a tiny carved animal. The following year she had brought her a beautifully carved and painted bird from Russia. Cindy had set aside an entire shelf in her bookcase for the gifts Aunt Mim gave her.

Now Aunt Mim took a brown package from her large tote bag and handed it to Cindy. "Here's your present," she said. "You can hold it, but you can't open it yet. Be careful with it. I've been carrying this thing around ever since I left Mexico a month ago!"

Cindy was surprised at how heavy the package was. "Thank you, Aunt Mim," she said. "But when can I open it?"

"Well, you can't see it here. I asked the cab driver to return in thirty minutes," Aunt Mim said. "We have a mysterious destination," she added in a whisper. "We're going on a treasure hunt of sorts!"

"Oh, where?" pleaded Cindy.

"You'll see soon enough," answered Aunt Mim. "Let's get my bags in the house first and leave your mother a note—you can write it. Just tell her we're on an errand and we'll be back by four."

Cindy had just finished the note when she heard the cab honking outside. As she hurried out, she almost dropped the heavy box. What could it be, she wondered. She couldn't hear any rattling noises from inside.

"It's well packed," said Aunt Mim, seeming to read her mind. "Thirty West Thorpe Street," she told the driver.

In the cab Cindy sighed and asked, "Just a little hint, Aunt Mim?"

"Hmmm," said Aunt Mim, thinking. "All right, let's see. It's something I've seen and yet I really haven't. In fact, no one has. It may contain something we'll like," she smiled, "and it may not."

"No one has seen it?" asked Cindy in disbelief. "How could no one have seen it?"

"You'll find out. Be patient a little longer," said Aunt Mim. "We're almost there!"

The cab pulled into a shopping center and stopped in front of a store. The sign read, GWEN'S ROCK SHOP.

Inside, a plump, gray-haired woman approached them. She stared at Aunt Mim for a moment, a puzzled look on her face. "Miriam . . . Miriam Carlson, is that you?" she asked.

"It is indeed, Gwen," said Aunt Mim. "My goodness, it's been so long—it's a wonder you recognized me! Gwen, this is my niece Cindy. Today is her birthday, and that's why we're here. This is Mrs. Cole, Cindy. I think she knows every rock in the state! She led most of the geology field trips when I was at the university."

"Happy birthday, Cindy," said Gwen. "What can I do for you?"

"Why don't you open your package?" said Aunt Mim before Cindy could answer.

Cindy lifted the box lid, but when she saw the contents, her mouth opened in surprise and disappointment. Two large, ugly rocks lay in shredded newspaper. One was hourglass shaped, and the other looked like a rough cannonball.

Aunt Mim patted her shoulder and said, "Don't be upset, Cindy. With luck Gwen may help us find our hidden treasure after all!"

"Treasure in these?" Cindy asked, trying to hide the doubt she felt.

"These are geodes (jē' ōdz), Cindy," said Gwen, "and I'll bet I know what your aunt wants me to do."

They followed Gwen to the back of the store where piles of different-colored rocks of all sizes lay sorted in wooden bins. A large machine sat nearby. Gwen lifted its metal cover to reveal a large, round saw blade.

"Where did you find these, Miriam?" asked Gwen, taking the round rock from the box and studying it.

"In Mexico," Aunt Mim answered. "I picked them up where some blasting was being done. These two looked fairly promising. Actually I was sorry I couldn't bring back more."

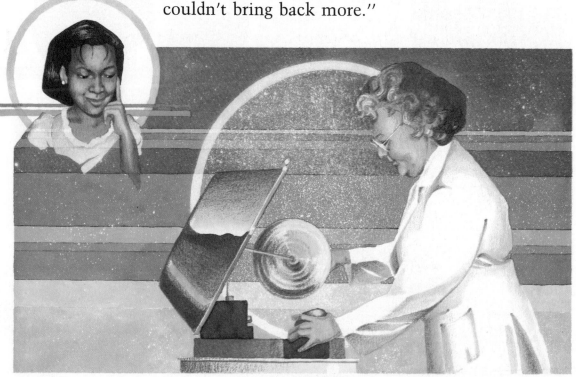

"They feel light for their size. That's a hopeful sign," said Gwen as she placed the round stone in the viselike grip of the machine. After placing the protective cover over the saw, she pushed the "on" button, adding, "We'll soon see, Cindy. Your aunt could have brought you something very beautiful or something completely ordinary."

Whatever it is, it must be inside these ugly rocks, thought Cindy. That's why Aunt Mim said no one had ever seen my present.

A whining, grinding noise began. Through a clear window in the cover Cindy could see the saw start working its way through the center of the round rock. A liquid suddenly splashed on the rock and window.

"What's that brown stuff?" asked Cindy.

"That's called coolant," answered Gwen. "It keeps the saw from getting too hot while it cuts the rock. It's a mixture of oil and other things with a low flash point. In other words, it won't catch fire in case the metal saw strikes sparks from the rock."

"How can the saw cut through such hard rocks?" Cindy asked.

"Well," answered Gwen, "that saw blade is tipped with industrial diamonds to make it hard enough to do the job."

"Real diamonds?" asked Cindy in amazement.

"Yes, but they're not the kind of diamonds a person wears," replied Gwen. "Your aunt can tell you they're also used in the oil fields on drilling bits that cut through rock."

Aunt Mim nodded, still watching intently.

"But I still don't know what these rocks are or what you're looking for," said Cindy.

"A geode," explained Gwen. "It starts as a hole inside a soft type of rock such as limestone. Water seeps through the rock for thousands of years and picks up minerals such as quartz (kwôrtz), leaving them inside the hole. The layers of minerals become beautiful bands of color. Sooner or later, after still more thousands of years, the soft rock wears away, leaving the harder substance that was deposited in the hole. If this erosion takes place before the hole is entirely filled with mineral deposits and a hollow area still remains, it's a geode. Now we're about to see if we have trash or treasure here!"

All three watched as the sharp blade made its way to the final edge of the geode. Suddenly it was through!

Gwen stopped the machine and picked up the halves of the rock. "Beautiful!" she exclaimed. "Miriam, you haven't lost your touch."

"Oh, Aunt Mim," sighed Cindy as she took one of the rocks. Bands of soft gray-blue and white circled a hollow center filled with sparkling crystals. "It's just like a big piece of jewelry!"

"Yes, indeed," sighed Aunt Mim, relieved. "Now let's do the other one, Gwen."

"By the way, Cindy, geodes don't just come from Mexico," said Gwen as she anchored the second geode and started the machine. "They're also found in our own country, particularly in the Midwest, and they come in all colors."

"Let's hope this one is as good as the first!" said Aunt Mim.

Cindy found it difficult to be patient this time as she watched the saw cut through the rock.

Finally the geode came apart, and Gwen stopped the saw and picked up the halves. "We're lucky again! How lovely—a double geode!" she said.

Cindy took the hourglass-shaped rock and gasped with pleasure. A pinkish, speckled stone surrounded two hollow areas, one in each half of the hourglass shape. The hollows were filled with thousands of crystals, dark and sparkling. Cindy hugged her aunt and whispered, "Thank you, Aunt Mim. It *is* hidden treasure, just like you said. You're great!"

"And lucky," sighed Aunt Mim gratefully, looking at the stone halves. Then she hugged Cindy back and added, "In more ways than one!"

Questions

1. What did Aunt Mim do for a living?
2. Why was Cindy surprised and disappointed when she saw the two rocks in the box?
3. Do you think Cindy should have hidden her disappointment over her present from Aunt Mim?
4. Has anyone ever given you a present that opened up a new field of interest for you? Explain you answer.

Applying Reading Skills

Read the paragraphs in the story referred to after each number below. Then choose the generalization that can be made from the facts found in each paragraph. Number your paper from 1 to 3. Write the generalization after the numbers.

1. Third paragraph on page 126 (continues on page 127)
   a. Aunt Mim likes to travel.
   b. Aunt Mim always thinks carefully about the presents she gives Cindy.
   c. Boxes from the Orient always come in sets.

2. First paragraph on page 129
   a. Gwen knows a lot about rocks.
   b. Gwen always recognizes her old friends.
   c. Mim always takes Cindy to the rock shop for her birthday.

3. Sixth paragraph on page 132
   a. Most geodes are found in Mexico.
   b. Most geodes are found in the Midwest.
   c. Geodes are not extremely rare.

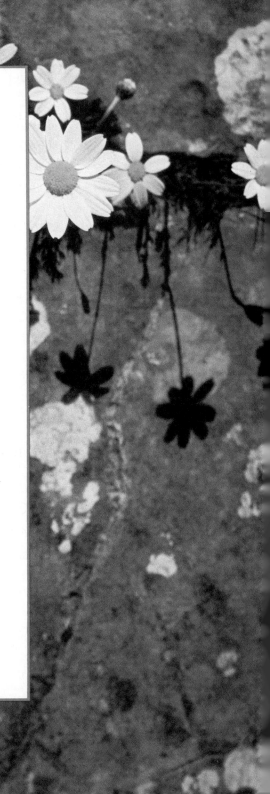

STONE

Go inside a stone.
That would be my way.
Let somebody else become a dove
Or gnash with a tiger's tooth.
I am happy to be a stone.

From the outside the stone is a riddle:
No one knows how to answer it.
Yet within, it must be cool and quiet
Even though a cow steps on it full weight,
Even though a child throws it in a river;
The stone sinks, slow, unperturbed
To the river bottom
Where the fishes come to knock on it
And listen.

I have seen sparks fly out
When two stones are rubbed,
So perhaps it is not dark inside after all;
Perhaps there is a moon shining
From somewhere, as though behind a hill—
Just enough light to make out
The strange writings, the star-charts
On the inner walls.

Charles Simic

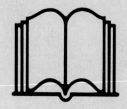

PREPARING FOR READING

Learning Vocabulary

1. Although many minerals are rare, others, such as quartz, are <u>common</u>.
2. Some rocks are made up of tiny <u>particles</u> of different minerals.
3. Under <u>ideal</u> conditions, each mineral would be a well-formed crystal.
4. Sometimes you can <u>identify</u> rocks by their <u>patterns</u>.

common   particles   ideal
identify   patterns

Developing Background and Skills
Make Generalizations
Read the paragraph below.

Agate is a red, brown, or orange variety of quartz found in many places in our country. Especially nice agates come from the beaches of Lake Superior. Clear, glittering crystals of quartz found in New York are called "Herkimer Diamonds." A variety of quartz known as amethyst is a purple color. People look for amethysts in South Carolina. In Ohio and many western states, a kind of quartz called flint was once used by the American Indians to make arrowheads.

Suppose you were asked to make a general statement based on the information in the paragraph. You might say *Quartz is common in the United States*. A statement of this kind is called a generalization. A **generalization** should be supported by particular facts or by other information.

Every sentence in the paragraph you read stated a fact that supports the generalization *Quartz is a common mineral in the United States*. The paragraph mentioned several different kinds of quartz found in several parts of the United States.

You should remember that a generalization is a broad statement that is true most of the time or for almost all examples. Reread the generalization above. Are *all* kinds of quartz common in the United States? Is quartz common in *all* parts of the United States? To know for certain, you would have to find more facts, but your common sense tells you that the answer to both of the questions is "no."

Think about what generalizations you can make as you read the next selection. Identify the facts that support your generalizations.

CAROLYN JABS

BURIED TREASURES

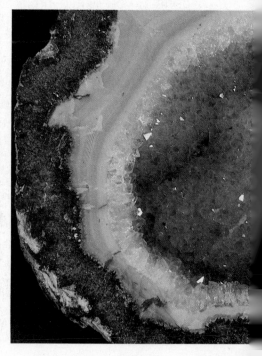

Winnifred Parker went out looking for rocks one day in Murfreesboro, Arkansas. She was a rock collector, or *rockhound*. What made this rockhunting trip special was what she found. Lying on the ground was a small, shiny stone. She picked up the rock and took it home. It turned out to be a big diamond! Mrs. Parker's find became known as the "Star of Arkansas."

Thousands of other rockhounds like Mrs. Parker make a hobby of collecting rocks. Have you ever walked along a beach and noticed a colorful rock lying in the sand? If you picked it up and put it in your pocket, you may be a rockhound, too.

Most rockhounds don't expect to find a diamond. They think more common rocks can be very interesting, too. Look closely at a few stones, and you'll see

BURIED TREASURES

Left to right:
Amethyst, the most valuable form of quartz, may get its purple color from small amounts of iron.

Amethyst can sometimes be found inside volcanic rocks called Thunder Eggs.

Quartz can be found in many different colors. The colors result from impurities in the crystals. Clear quartz is the purest form of quartz.

why. You will notice that they often have streaks of color or tiny specks. These tiny particles that make up rocks are called *minerals*. Granite is a common rock. It is made up of the minerals mica (mī′kə), feldspar (feld′ spär′), quartz, and hornblende.

Minerals come in different colors. There are more than 2,000 different kinds of minerals. These include rare ones, like gold and silver, and common ones, like iron and quartz.

Every mineral forms crystals in its own special shape. Under ideal conditions, each mineral would make a large, well-formed crystal. Rockhounds are always looking for these crystals, but they're hard to find. In most rocks, several minerals are jammed together so that none of the crystals is perfect.

BURIED TREASURES

mica   feldspar

quartz   hornblende

BEAUTIFUL ROCKS

A rock doesn't have to be as rare as a diamond to be beautiful. Quartz, for example, is a common mineral in the United States. Because it comes in many different lovely colors and shapes, rockhounds enjoy looking for it. What quartz looks like depends on where you are looking.

Agates (ag′ its) are a kind of red, brown, or orange quartz. If you hold an agate up to the sun, the light shines through. Agates are found in many places. The ones on the beaches of Lake Superior in Wisconsin are especially nice.

In New York, rockhounds hunt for a kind of quartz so clear that it glitters like diamonds. These rocks are called "Herkimer Diamonds." In South

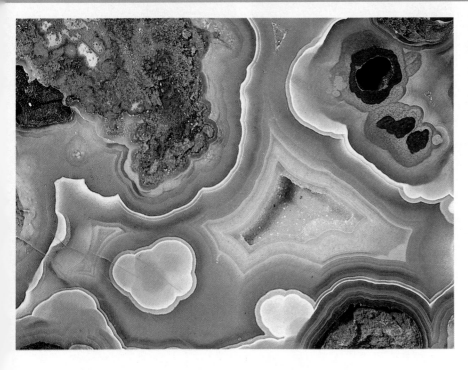

Left to right:
Mica, feldspar, quartz, and hornblende are minerals found in granite.

Agate is another form of quartz. The sample shown comes from Mexico.

Carolina, rockhounds are very excited when they find the deep purple quartz called *amethyst* (am′ ə thist). In Ohio, they search for a kind of quartz called flint. It was used by the American Indians to make arrowheads. In Montana, quartz shows up as moss agate. This clear stone has wavy green marks in it.

In Oregon, quartz shows up again. This time it's in Thunder Eggs. These rocks were formed long ago inside volcanoes. They are lumps about the size of a tennis ball. A lump of rock doesn't sound very exciting. But there's a surprise inside. Break open a Thunder Egg and you'll find a beautiful piece of quartz.

BURIED TREASURES

Left to right:
This glittering "Herkimer Diamond" looks very much like the real diamond below it. It is really very clear quartz crystal.

The Thunder Egg shown here has smoky quartz crystals inside.

You don't have to go far to hunt for rocks. Even your own backyard may have many treasures waiting to be discovered.

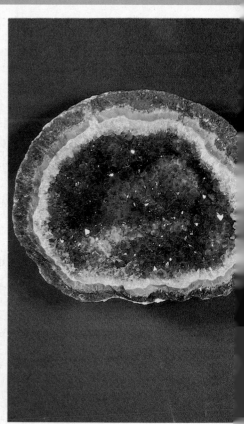

BECOME A ROCKHOUND

Looking for rocks can be a real adventure. No matter where you live, some kind of rock is just waiting to be collected. You don't need much equipment to be a rockhound. Just find the following things:

1. A strong bag or knapsack to hold your rocks
2. Newspaper to wrap the rocks you pick up so that they don't get chipped or scratched
3. A brush for cleaning off rocks you find
4. A magnifying glass for a closer look at your rocks
5. A spray bottle of water, since many rocks look prettier when they are wet

BURIED TREASURES

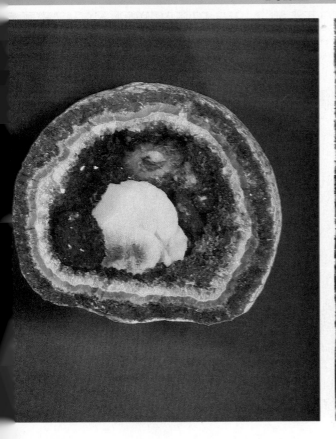

WHERE TO LOOK

The great thing about rockhunting is that you can do it almost anywhere. You can look for fancy stones while you're traveling with your family. Or you can start in your own backyard or in the park down the street.

Streams and beaches are also good places to look. The water makes the rocks shine so they are easier to spot. Places where people are digging to build a new house or a road are often full of rocks. But you should get permission before looking in those spots.

BUILDING YOUR COLLECTION

Finding rocks is just the first step for a rockhound. When you get your rocks home, you will want to figure out just what you have. A book on rock

BURIED TREASURES

A rocky shore is a wonderful place to hunt for rocks. The water brings out the beauty of the rocks.

When you bring your rocks home, you can label them.

The Mohs Scale can help you to identify the minerals in the rocks.

collecting with loads of pictures will help you decide what rocks you've found.

Look carefully at the markings of the rocks you find. Some rocks have stripes on them. Others have flecks or specks of a different color. Still others have lines or marks that seem to make a picture. Many rockhounds collect rocks just so they can look at the designs on them. Looking carefully at the patterns will also help you identify the rock.

Another way to identify a rock is by its hardness. That may sound silly. But not all minerals are hard. A scientist named Friedrich Mohs (frēd′ rik mōs) figured out a hardness scale from 1 to 10. Minerals which get a 1 for hardness are as soft as the talc which is used to make baby powder. Minerals which get a 10 are as hard as a diamond. This mineral is so hard that chips of it are used on saws to cut other rocks.

BURIED TREASURES

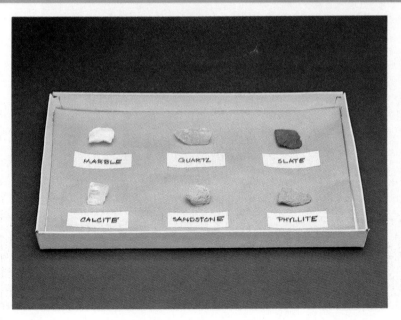

MOHS HARDNESS SCALE

Mineral	Hardness	Common Test
Talc	1	Can be scratched
Gypsum	2	by fingernail
Calcite	3	Can be scratched by copper coin
Fluorite	4	Can be scratched
Apatite	5	by knife or glass
Feldspar	6	Will scratch a knife
Quartz	7	or glass
Topaz	8	
Corundum	9	
Diamond	10	Will scratch all common materials

To figure out the hardness of the minerals in your rock, try these tests. Can you scratch the mineral with your fingernail? If so, its hardness is around 2. If your fingernail doesn't work, can you scratch it with a penny? Then the hardness is around 3. Next try using the mineral to scratch a piece of glass. If the mineral scratches the glass, its hardness is about 6.

Your book may suggest other tests that will help you identify your rocks. When you think you know the kind of rock you have, write the name on a card with the place where you found the rock. Then you can display your collection on a shelf. Some rockhounds like to store their rocks in a glass jar so they can see them next to each other. If you fill the jar with water, it will make the colors in the rocks look brighter.

BURIED TREASURES

Questions

1. What is a rockhound? Tell what things rockhounds do.
2. Why do you think rock collecting is such a popular hobby?
3. In what places do you think it is all right to pick up rocks without permission? In what places should you ask for permission to collect rock specimens?
4. Describe how you might label and display a rock collection.

Applying Reading Skills

Number your paper from 1 to 8. Read the generalizations below. If the generalization can be supported by a fact found in "Buried Treasures," write the fact next to the number.

1. A diamond is a very rare mineral.
2. Quartz is found in all parts of the United States.
3. The rarer a mineral is, the more interesting it is.
4. Most Indian tribes used rocks to make tools.
5. Collecting rocks is an expensive hobby.
6. Most minerals are below 5 on the Mohs Scale.
7. You can find rocks anywhere.
8. Rockhounds spend a lot of time outdoors.

PREPARING FOR READING

Learning Vocabulary

1. The king was looking for an heir who showed honesty, patience, and <u>perseverance</u>.
2. His minister posted a <u>proclamation</u> announcing a needle-hunting contest.
3. To <u>ensure</u> honesty, the king had the needle inscribed with secret words by a goldsmith who knew his <u>craft</u> very well.
4. The king's minister figured out a <u>plot</u> to make his son the king's heir.

perseverance   proclamation   ensure
craft   plot

Developing Background and Skills
Plot, Setting, Mood, Theme

Have you ever told a friend about a book you read and liked? If you have, you probably described what the characters did and what happened to them. You were telling the story's plot. Whatever characters do and whatever happens to them is part of the **plot**. The plot is the series of events that takes place in a story.

Plot is only one of four basic parts of a story. The other three are **setting, mood,** and **theme.** Let's take a look at each of them.

The setting of a story is when and where the story takes place. The time may be the present, the past, or the future. The place may be real or imaginary.

Mood is the feeling that the story creates for a reader. A story may make readers laugh or cry. It may keep them in suspense, or it may scare them.

Finally, every story has a theme. The theme is the idea on which the story is based. The theme of a story is not usually directly stated in the story. It is sometimes the most difficult story part to identify. The theme may be a message, a lesson, or a moral. In Aesop's fables, the theme is a moral or proverb. The theme of the fable *The Tortoise and the Hare* is "slow but steady wins the race."

As you read "The Needle in the Haystack," think about the plot. See if you can identify the setting, mood, and theme.

THE NEEDLE IN THE HAYSTACK JOHN HAMMA

Once in another time, there lived a King and Queen who had no children. The King worried about who would take his place when he grew too old to rule, so he asked his chief counselor what to do.

"Why not adopt a son, Your Majesty, and teach him the laws of the land?" his counselor suggested.

"But how will I find the right boy?" the King asked.

"Look for one who shows honesty, patience, and perseverance," the counselor told him. "It will be like looking for a needle in a haystack, but if you search wisely and well, you will find someone who is worthy."

"That's it!" the King exclaimed. "A needle in a haystack! Who would be more patient and persevering than a young man who could find a needle in a haystack? I will order my goldsmith to make a golden needle. Then I will hide it in one of the royal haystacks. The man who finds it will become Crown Prince. And to ensure honesty, I shall have the needle inscribed with words only I know. That way no dishonest man will bring me a false needle."

Pleased with his decision, the King went to the goldsmith's shop that very afternoon. Franz, the son of

the goldsmith, was the only one there. He explained that his father was sick with a fever.

"But perhaps I can help you, Your Majesty," Franz said. "My father has taught me all the secrets of his craft."

"Could you make a needle of gold?" the King asked.

"Yes," answered Franz.

"And could you write words on the needle?"

"Why I could write a whole song on the head of a pin," Franz said.

"And," asked the King sternly, "could you keep the secret of what is written on the needle?"

"Yes," Franz said simply.

"Very well," said the King, and told Franz how he wanted the needle made. As he turned to leave, the King warned, "Remember, *only* you and I are to know the words on the needle."

Two days later, Franz brought the needle to the castle. The King examined it closely with a magnifying glass and praised the young man. "You have done all you said you could, Franz. Your father must be proud of you. Here is your payment—and remember, not a word to anyone!" Franz bowed and accepted the bag holding twenty gold pieces.

That night the King set out secretly to hide the needle. The next afternoon he ordered Joseph, his first minister, to appear before him. After Joseph had bowed, the King said, "Last night I placed a golden needle in one of the royal haystacks. Today you will post a proclamation. All young men between the ages of eighteen and twenty-five have three days to search for this needle. The one who finds and brings the needle to me will become heir to the throne."

"Right away, Your Majesty," Joseph said, and after several more bows, he left the room. He rubbed his hands as he walked into the courtyard. What a good thing I saw young Franz hand the golden needle to the King yesterday, he thought. It has given me the chance I've been waiting for. I shall see to it that my son, Joseph II, presents a golden needle to the King and is pronounced heir. Through him I shall rule the kingdom.

First Joseph had to find out which haystack the King had visited. He asked the farmers who worked the fields surrounding the castle. Finally he found an old man who said he had seen a man put something in one of his haystacks and leave. Joseph noted that the haystack stood near a blue and white windmill. Then he went to visit the royal goldsmith's shop.

He found Franz making a silver bird and complimented his work. Franz thanked him and asked, "How may I help you, Your Excellency?"

"I am here on the King's business," Joseph said. "You are the one who made the golden needle for His Majesty, are you not?"

Franz said nothing. He was going to keep his promise to the King.

Joseph read his silence correctly. "I know that the King has sworn you to secrecy, so you need not answer. Just listen. The King has lost the needle. He was drinking from a well of fresh mountain water, and the needle fell in. He now asks that you make an exact copy."

Franz nodded, and Joseph placed twenty gold pieces on the counter. "Can you have it ready for me by tomorrow afternoon?"

Again, Franz nodded.

"I see I need not warn you about keeping my visit a secret. If word got out that the King had lost the needle, the kingdom would be in an uproar."

The next day, the first minister picked up the new needle from Franz. He hurried home to give it to his son, along with instructions about what he must do for his part of the plot.

The following morning, Joseph II joined the other young men from all over the country who were searching through the royal haystacks. At first, he deliberately looked in the wrong haystack. Then as evening neared, he rode to the haystack near the blue and white windmill. Some of the young men were standing near the field, with hay all over their clothing and in their hair. They shouted to Joseph II that he was wasting his time, for they had already flattened the haystack without finding the needle.

He just smiled and started searching through the scattered mounds of hay. Suddenly he shouted in triumph and stood up, holding the golden needle in his hand.

Later that evening, Joseph II kneeled before the royal throne and proudly presented the needle to the King. The King took it from him, reached into the pocket of his royal robe, and brought out his magnifying glass. As he read the inscription, his face grew dark with anger. "Where did you get this needle?" he demanded.

"Why, in the h-h-haystack, Your Majesty," Joseph II stammered.

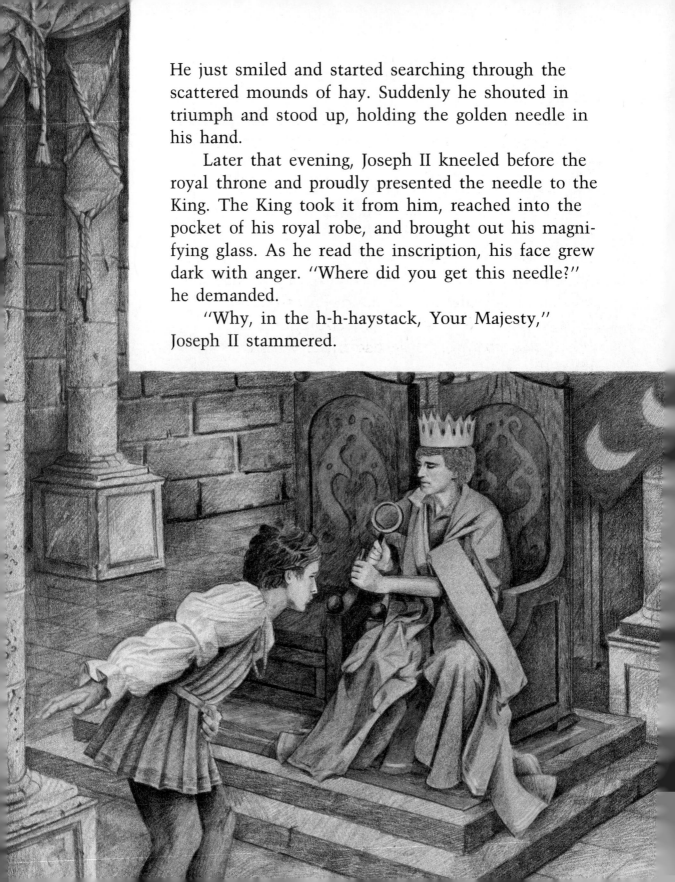

The King turned to his first minister. "Perhaps *you* have an explanation?"

"For what, Your Majesty?" the older Joseph said.

"Come here," the King commanded, "and read this."

The first minister read the writing on the needle: *Exact copy of first needle: Patience, Perseverance, Honesty.* Color left his face.

The next day, Franz heard that the first minister and his family had been banished from the kingdom and that the needle search had been called off. His heart sank. Surely this had something to do with the second needle he had made without asking the King!

He was ready for the worst when he heard a knock on the door and saw the King standing outside with his royal guard. But to his surprise, the King gave him a very friendly smile as he entered the shop.

"No doubt you have heard that I have called off the contest," the King said to Franz, "and that I have banished the first minister for trying to trick me with the second needle?"

"Yes, Your Majesty," Franz answered in a low voice.

"I have called off the contest for three reasons," the King continued. "The first reason is that everybody knows by now which haystack the needle is in. Secondly, the contest was not a good idea; the hay is ruined—thrown all over the field, and I will have to have my royal harvesters gather more. And finally, I have found my heir."

"You have?" Franz asked.

"Yes," said the King. "You."

"Me?" Franz looked at the King as if he had gone mad.

"Yes, you," repeated the King firmly. "It took patience and perseverance to craft the needle and honesty not to betray a confidence. And more importantly, you are intelligent. You knew that if I had truly lost the needle, the words 'exact copy' would not matter, and if I had not lost it, the words would reveal a trickster to me. I am proud to make you my royal heir and son."

So Franz, the goldsmith's son, came to be the King's heir. In time he ruled the kingdom with patience, perseverance, honesty—and intelligence.

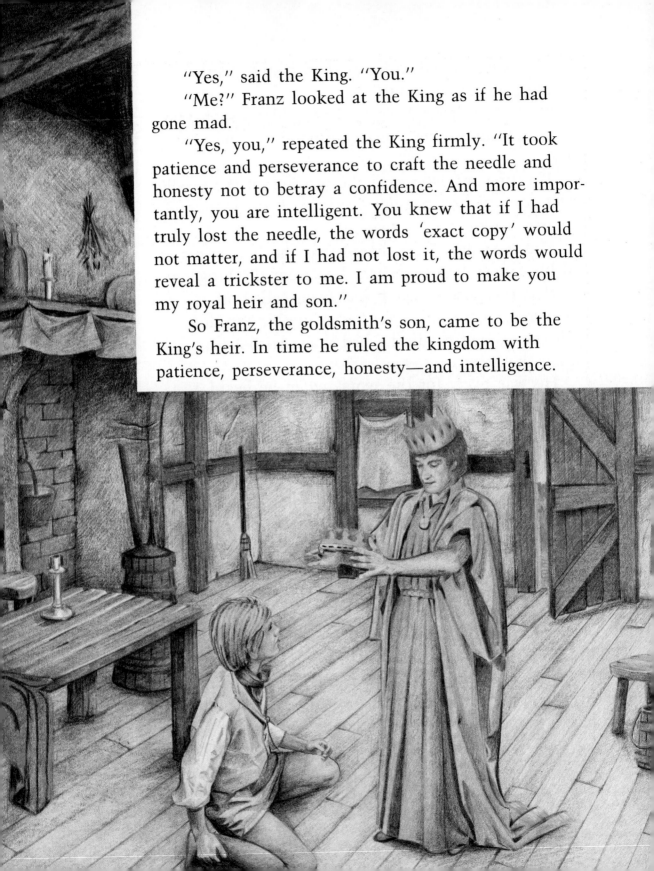

Questions

1. Why was the King looking for an heir? What qualities did the King want the heir to have?
2. How would words inscribed on the needle ensure the honesty of the person who brought it to the King?
3. Do you think the needle hunt was a good way to find an heir with the qualities the King demanded? Explain your answer.
4. Think of another fairy tale or legend in which a contest is held to find a worthy person. Describe the contest and the reason for it.

Applying Reading Skills

Number your paper from 1 to 4. Then answer the following questions about "The Needle in the Haystack" by using complete sentences.

1. When does the story take place? Where does it take place?
2. What are the main events in the plot of the story?
3. Describe the mood of the story.
4. Do you think the following is a fair statement of the story's theme: *Virtue is rewarded, evil is punished*? Explain your answer.

PREPARING FOR READING

Learning Vocabulary

1. As soon as the professor began to <u>operate</u> his machine, all the television screens went blank.
2. He would not <u>reverse</u> the process until the towns-people met his <u>requirements</u>.
3. The mayor appointed a <u>committee</u> to find a way to <u>avoid</u> the professor's demands.

operate   reverse   requirements
committee   avoid

Developing Background and Skills
Plot, Setting, Mood, Theme

You know that a story has four parts: **plot, setting, mood,** and **theme.** Plot is the series of events that takes place in the story; setting is the time and place in which the story takes place; mood is the feeling the story creates; and theme is the idea on which the story is based.

It shouldn't surprise you that a play has the same four parts that a story does. Many plays are just stories written as dialogue, or conversation. Most plays are written for performance on the stage or on television.

Read the dialogue from a play that appears on the next page.

PROFESSOR: (hears knock at the door) Who's there? (goes to door and opens it) Oh, it's just you, Rupert. (pulls him into the room)

RUPERT: Professor, I've just brought you this important message from the Mayor. (He reaches into jacket pocket, but finds nothing.) Oh, no! I've lost it! (He crosses to table, sits down, and buries his head in his hands.)

When you read a play, you learn about the plot through the characters' lines, through descriptions of what the characters do, and through directions to actors who play the characters.

The descriptions and directions are usually enclosed by parentheses. It is important to pay close attention to the words in parentheses when you read a play. If you don't, you will probably miss some of the action that takes place.

It is easy to determine the setting of a play. Playwrights usually tell you the setting at the beginning of each scene.

As you read the play "A Treasure Without Measure," try to identify the plot, setting, mood, and theme. Think about the special ways the playwright develops the plot and lets you know the setting.

A TREASURE WITHOUT MEASURE

SHEILA L. MARSHALL

CHARACTERS

PROFESSOR GIBBS, scientist
RUPERT, his assistant
MAYOR GREEN
MR. BUCKS, the banker
MR. BRITE, the jeweler
MISS LEWIS, the town librarian
MR. LONG

MRS. LONG
KAREN
JULIE
SALLY   children of
MIKE   Mr. and Mrs. Long
JOE

SCENE ONE

SETTING: The laboratory of Professor Gibbs, in a cave in Black Mountain. Moss and cobwebs hang from the ceiling. There is a large table, center, with an enormous machine. It has knobs, levers, dials, lights, wires, and tubes. On the rear wall is a large clock, reading twelve. An entrance is at left.

AT RISE: PROFESSOR GIBBS, in a white lab coat, with white hair and beard, stands at a table, adjusting equipment. Hammering is heard from offstage. Then RUPERT enters.

RUPERT: Everything is all set, Professor Gibbs. I've just connected the last cable.

PROFESSOR: Excellent, Rupert. Now I only have to throw this last switch and the deed will be done.

RUPERT: *(going to PROFESSOR)* What exactly is going to happen, Professor?

PROFESSOR: As soon as this machine begins to operate, every television set in the town of Oakville will go on the blink. All the TV screens will be blank. Not one of them will work. No game shows, no soap operas, no evening news—not even a test pattern!

RUPERT: Will anyone be able to fix them?

PROFESSOR: Impossible! My machine is unbreakable. Once the process has begun, only I can reverse it. There will be no more television in Oakville.

RUPERT: The people of Oakville depend on their TV sets. Without television, I don't know what will happen. Why do you want to do this to the quiet, sleepy little town of Oakville?

PROFESSOR: Very simple, my boy. I've been planning this for a long, long time. You see, many years ago, when I was a young man, I lived in Oakville. I wanted to make some friends, so I invited a few people over for dinner.

RUPERT: What happened?

PROFESSOR: It was a disaster! I gave a dinner party on a Monday night. When the guests arrived, they looked everywhere for my television set to watch Monday night football. When they learned I didn't have a TV set, they ate as fast as they could so they could get home by half-time. They wouldn't even stay for dessert!

RUPERT: How awful! Then what happened?

PROFESSOR: It happened again and again. I kept trying to make friends, but the results were always the same. It was love me—love my TV set in Oakville. Finally I couldn't stand it anymore, so I moved here to this cave on Black Mountain. I worked for years to invent this machine. *(points to machine)* At last it is ready. Unless the people of Oakville meet my conditions, I will turn off their TV sets forever.

RUPERT: But, Professor Gibbs, when the screens go blank, won't the people think it's a power failure?

PROFESSOR: No, no! I shall broadcast my conditions to them on their TV sets. Come, now, I think everything is ready. And just in time. *(pointing to clock)* It's exactly twelve noon. Let's go! *(They begin to push buttons and pull a large switch on the table. Lights begin to flash on and off.)*

RUPERT: We've done it, Professor! It's working!

PROFESSOR: *(into microphone)* People of Oakville! This is your former neighbor, Professor Gibbs, speaking. Do not try to adjust your television sets. There is nothing wrong with them. I am in complete control of them, and I will keep your television sets in darkness for twenty-four hours. Listen carefully! I will return your television sets to normal operation, if you will bring me a treasure—a treasure without measure—at my cave on Black Mountain. You have twenty-four hours. Remember, a treasure without measure in twenty-four hours, or no more television in Oakville! *(putting down microphone)* Now, Rupert, all we have to do is wait!

CURTAIN

SCENE TWO

TIME: *Morning of the following day.*

SETTING: *Same as Scene 1. Clock points to eleven.*

AT RISE: PROFESSOR GIBBS *paces the floor.* RUPERT *is asleep on the floor, leaning against the table.*

PROFESSOR: *(striding over and waking* RUPERT*)* Wake up, Rupert! Wake up!

RUPERT: *(rubbing his eyes)* What's happening?

PROFESSOR: Nothing! Nothing is happening. What's keeping them? There's very little time left and we haven't heard a word from them.

RUPERT: Wait! I hear someone outside. *(*MAYOR GREEN *enters.)*

MAYOR: Professor Gibbs? I'm the Mayor of Oakville. My name is Green.

PROFESSOR: How do you do, Mayor Green? How is your peaceful little town?

MAYOR: You ought to know. It's total confusion down there!

PROFESSOR: Are you ready to meet my demands?

MAYOR: I don't know yet, you see. But we're working on it.

PROFESSOR: What do you mean?

MAYOR: I've set the wheels in motion. I have appointed a committee to look into the problem. They'll begin their investigation into your demands as soon as they've elected a chairperson.

PROFESSOR: How long will that take?

MAYOR: I don't know exactly. But I'm sure we'll have an answer for you in a month or so. You can't expect us to take action sooner than that.

PROFESSOR: I see through your clever plan. No committees, Mayor Green. No stalling for time. If my conditions aren't met in one hour, your TV screens will be dark forever!

MAYOR: No! No! Not that! Don't do anything hasty! I'm sure we can work things out somehow. I just happen to have brought along some treasure. *(goes to entrance and calls)* Oh, Sam! Sam Bucks! Will you come in here? We need you. *(MR. BUCKS, the banker, enters, carrying a brief-case.)* Professor, this is Sam Bucks, the banker.

MR. BUCKS: Professor—you win! We had hoped to avoid having to give in to your conditions. But we're desperate to get our televisions back. *(opening briefcase)* So here you are. Treasure! *(He shows rows of dollar bills. He takes some out and holds them.)* All this beautiful money!

PROFESSOR: I don't want your money.

MAYOR and MR. BUCKS: *(together)* You don't want it?

MR. BUCKS: Why? Isn't it enough?

MAYOR: There's enough

money here to keep you happy for the rest of your life.

PROFESSOR: I asked for a treasure without measure. But I didn't mean money!

MR. BUCKS: Money is a treasure.

PROFESSOR: To you, maybe, but not to me! That wasn't the kind of treasure I had in mind.

MR. BUCKS: What kind of treasure could be better? *(to* MAYOR*)* Your Honor, I wash my hands of this whole deal! Refusing my money—the very idea! *(He closes briefcase and leaves in a huff.)*

PROFESSOR: Time is running out, Your Honor.

MAYOR: *(anxiously)* Wait! Wait! Our time isn't up yet! There is someone else outside with a treasure. I'm sure it is just what you have in mind.

PROFESSOR: O.K. Bring him in, but remember, no treasure, and—poof! No television.

MAYOR: *(goes hastily to entrance and calls)* Mr. Brite! *(*MR. BRITE *enters, carrying a small chest.)* Professor, this is Mr. Brite, the jeweler.

MR. BRITE: Professor, I have something here which I'm sure

will interest you. *(He places chest on the table and opens it dramatically, pulling out jewelry and letting it slide through his fingers.)* Look—gold, pearls, diamonds, rubies! Treasures—a whole chestful. Their value cannot be measured! They are priceless.

PROFESSOR: *(picking up several and examining them)* They certainly are beautiful!

MR. BRITE: This must meet your requirements. It surely is a treasure without measure. Won't you please turn our TV sets back on now?

PROFESSOR: *(returning jewelry to box)* I asked for a treasure without measure. Jewelry isn't what I had in mind.

MR. BRITE: How can you say that? Why, these gems can be sold for millions! Or, you can just sit and enjoy looking at them—the way I do.

PROFESSOR: They might be a treasure to you, but not the kind of treasure I want.

MR. BRITE: What could possibly be better? There's no one who doesn't like diamonds! I'll take them back to the store. *(Shaking his head in disgust, he packs chest and leaves.)*

PROFESSOR: I'm afraid you'll have to give up, Mayor Green. *(PROFESSOR starts toward table again when there are loud noises at the cave entrance and MISS LEWIS enters, followed by MR. and MRS. LONG and KAREN, JULIE, MIKE, SALLY, and JOE. MISS LEWIS carries two shopping bags.)*

MISS LEWIS: Wait! Wait!

MAYOR: Miss Lewis! The Long family! What are you doing here?

MISS LEWIS: We came to help.

PROFESSOR: You can't. It's too late. Besides, I know you won't have the treasure without measure. Nobody does.

MISS LEWIS: Oh, but I'm sure we do, Professor. Look! *(unpacking books from shopping bags)*

169

PROFESSOR: Books!

MISS LEWIS: Yes, books!

MAYOR: Miss Lewis, these are just ordinary books. They aren't a treasure. They aren't valuable at all.

MISS LEWIS: I'm surprised at you, Mayor Green. Books are indeed a treasure! And one without measure, at that. *(turning to* PROFESSOR*)* Professor, would you like to go to Spain?

PROFESSOR: I suppose so, but I don't have time for a long trip.

MISS LEWIS: You don't need much time—just this book. *(holds up the book)* It will take you there in one evening. *(holds up another book)* Are you sad? Here's a joke book to cheer you up. *(She holds up another volume.)* Do you want adventure? Has your life been a little dull lately? Try this mystery. *(*SALLY, MIKE, *and* JOE *begin to take books out of bags.)*

MIKE: Wow! Here's one about horses—*Black Beauty*. It looks great. *(begins to read)*

SALLY: And one about baseball—*The Life of Babe Ruth*. He was the greatest. Just look at this. *(She holds up a book, then sits to read it.)*

JOE: I have one that looks exciting. Have you read *The Phantom Tollbooth*? *(He opens book.)*

MAYOR: *(reaching into the bags and taking out several volumes)* Hmm! Here's one for me— *How To Direct Committee Meetings*. Just what I need! And here's one about making decisions. That should be a big help! *(starts to read)*

MRS. LONG: Professor, when you turned off our TV, we didn't know what to do without it. We'd been sitting in front of our television set for so long that we forgot about the other wonderful things there are to do—like reading.

MR. LONG: Then Miss Lewis suggested we read some of the new books at the public library.

MRS. LONG: We found books to interest all of us. I took out some how-to-do-it manuals.

MR. LONG: And I'm reading a new spy novel.

KAREN: I found some wildlife adventure books.

JULIE: And there are so many books I like that I hardly know where to begin.

SALLY: If you turn on our TV sets, we'll never go back to watching them all the time, the way we used to.

MIKE: We promise to watch only the very special shows.

JOE: We're going to need all the free time we can get for these terrific books.

MR. LONG: Why, there are new books all the time, and each one is better than the last.

MISS LEWIS: You see, Professor, books are really a treasure without measure. They've begun to change the lives of our townspeople already.

PROFESSOR: *(picking up several books in an interested way)* They do seem to be a valuable treasure. But—it's just that. . . .

MISS LEWIS: Yes? What's wrong? Tell me.

PROFESSOR: All this started because I wanted to make new friends. It will be fun to read these books, and I'm delighted that everyone will cut down on watching television. I'm still going to be all alone in the evenings, though. No book will ever change that!

MISS LEWIS: Wait a minute! I have just the thing for you! *(She reaches into the bottom of the bag and pulls out several books.)* Here is a book called *How to Win Friends and Influence People*. Here's another one on how to be popular. *(holding them up)* And this is one of my favorites: *How to Give Great Dinner Parties*. Professor, if you read these, and do what they suggest, you'll have lots of friends. They'll be begging for invitations to visit you. I'd love to come myself!

PROFESSOR: You would? Really? Let me see those books! They sound marvelous! About that dinner party book—would you like to come next Thursday and help me try it?

MISS LEWIS: I'd be delighted!

PROFESSOR: You wouldn't rather watch TV, would you?

MISS LEWIS: Not at all!

PROFESSOR: I can see we're going to be good friends. Mayor Green! (MAYOR, *reading his book, does not hear him.* PROFESSOR *goes to* MAYOR *and shakes his arm.)* Mayor Green, I'm disconnecting my machine. You may tell the people of Oakville that they may watch television again. I have found my treasure without measure now, so I'm keeping my promise!

MAYOR: What? Oh, thank you, Professor—but I have some even better news for Oakville! Wait until I tell the rest of our citizens about all the wonderful books in the public library. They've all been so busy watching television that they didn't bother to read them, but they're going to hear all about them now—from me!

JULIE: We'll help, Your Honor, by telling all our friends about our discovery.

OTHER CHILDREN: *(looking up from books)* Hooray for books!

PROFESSOR: A treasure forever!

THE END

CURTAIN

Questions

1. What demands did Professor Gibbs make for returning the television sets to normal operation?
2. Why did the professor turn off the TV sets? Do you think he had something in mind as treasure?
3. Do you think the professor should have accepted the money or the jewelry as the treasure he demanded? Explain your answer.
4. What would you do if you were unable to watch TV?

Applying Reading Skills

Number your paper from 1 to 5. Choose the best answer choice to complete the following sentences about "A Treasure Without Measure." Write the completed sentences on your paper.

1. The plot of the play revolves around a professor who ____.
   a. turns off TV sets and demands a ransom
   b. performs TV experiments in a remote laboratory
   c. tries to make friends

2. The play takes place in ____.
   a. Oakville   b. a cave in Black Mountain
   c. an imaginary city

3. The time of the play is probably the ____.
   a. past   b. present   c. future

4. The mood of the play is ____.
   a. serious   b. suspenseful   c. humorous

5. The theme of the play is the pleasure of ____.
   a. reading   b. watching TV   c. having friends

There is No Frigate Like a Book

There is no frigate like a book
To take us lands away,
Nor any coursers like a page
Of prancing poetry.

This traverse may the poorest take
Without oppress of toll;
How frugal is the chariot
That bears a human soul!

Emily Dickinson

175

WRITING ACTIVITY

WRITE A COMMERCIAL

Prewrite

In the play "A Treasure Without Measure," Miss Lewis and the Long family convince Professor Gibbs, or make him believe, that books are a treasure without measure. Could you convince your friends that books are a treasure?

One way people try to convince others is through advertising. You see advertisements in magazines and newspapers. Television and radio advertisements are commercials. A commercial presents a product in such a way that people will want to buy it. Commercials often make use of slogans such as "Buy Your Cars at Weird William's and Get a Monster of a Deal."

Choose your favorite book. You are going to write a commercial for that book. If you do a television commercial, you may need pictures and costumes. Such things are called props. If you choose to write a commercial for the radio, you may want to use music or other sound effects.

To get ready to write, think of a few facts about your book. Write a slogan that will "grab" the attention of your audience.

1. Name of the book
2. Author of the book
3. Publisher and date of publication
4. One or two exciting characters and events in the plot

Write

1. Read your facts and slogan.
2. Think about how you will start your commercial. You might start with your slogan.
3. Give the facts about the book. Remember, you want to sell a product. You want people to remember its name, so make sure you use the title of the book more than once in your commercial.
4. Commercials have short snappy sentences. Writers of commercials choose clever verbs, adverbs, and adjectives to interest their audience.
5. Plan how your pictures, costumes, or music will fit into your commercial.
6. Use your Glossary or dictionary for spelling help.

Revise

Read your commercial. Would you want to buy the book? Did you use short, snappy sentences? Is your slogan going to "grab" your audience? Now is the time to rewrite any parts of your commercial you think could be more interesting.

1. Did you choose clever verbs, adverbs, and adjectives?
2. Did you use commas correctly?
3. Did you capitalize proper nouns?

PREPARING FOR READING

Learning Vocabulary

1. In the 17th century, ships loaded with <u>cargo</u> were no match for storms at sea.
2. Sunken ships left few <u>traces</u>, so treasure hunters are always excited by any new <u>lead</u>.
3. Treasure <u>items</u> can sometimes pay the high cost of <u>modern</u> <u>salvage</u> operations.

cargo   traces   lead
items   modern   salvage

Developing Background and Skills
Maps

Suppose that you wanted to know in what direction Cape Canaveral is from Tallahassee, or how far it is from Jacksonville to Miami. How could you find out? The easiest way to find out is to look at a **map.** You probably know that the places mentioned are all in Florida, so you would find a map of Florida.

Look at the map of Florida on the next page. The arrow shows you which way north is. Use the north arrow to see what direction Cape Canaveral is from Tallahassee.

Find the scale on the map and use it to find the distance between Jacksonville and Miami in miles and kilometers.

Notice that on the main map of Florida there is also another map. This map is set into the main map, so it is called an inset map. What large area does the inset map show? What part of the inset map is highlighted?

The inset map is useful in helping you see where Florida is in relation to the rest of the United States.

As you read the next selection, use the maps to find the sites of the sunken treasure ships. Think about how maps can sometimes help you better understand what you read.

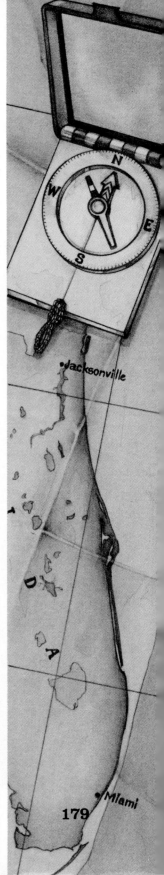

GOLD

This is the moment he has been waiting for. As he swims along the ocean bottom, Mel Fisher spots something shiny. Could it be what he hopes? Yes, it's gold!

"Once you've seen the ocean carpeted with gold coins, you'll never forget it," Mel says. He should know. For 17 years, he has searched the warm clear waters of Florida for shipwrecks. Mel is an underwater treasure hunter.

There are plenty of shipwrecks near the Florida coast to keep Mel busy. In the 17th century, many Spanish ships sailed in the area. They carried gold, silver, copper, dyes, and tobacco. But when loaded with cargo, the ships were no match for bad storms at sea. Many of them sank. Treasure hunters like Mel Fisher have been trying to find those ships and bring up their wealth.

THE LONG SEARCH

Mel Fisher became interested in two shipwrecks. The *Atocha* and the *Santa Margarita* sank within sight of each other during a hurricane in 1622. Both carried great riches. Over the years, there had been many different rumors about where the sunken ships were. Mel chose one spot and searched there for five years. But he found nothing. Then a fresh clue was found.

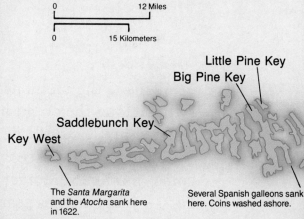

WHERE LOST SHIPS LIE IN THE FLORIDA KEYS

ATLANTIC OCEAN

Florida

GULF OF MEXICO

FLORIDA BAY

Florida Keys

N

0 ——— 190 Miles
0 ——— 244 Kilometers

0 ——— 12 Miles
0 ——— 15 Kilometers

Little Pine Key
Big Pine Key

Saddlebunch Key
Key West

The *Santa Margarita* and the *Atocha* sank here in 1622.

Several Spanish galleons sank here. Coins washed ashore.

"One of our researchers discovered an old paper that told about where the ships sank," Mel says. The paper was found among other ancient papers in Spain. Excited by this new lead, Mel and his team immediately moved their entire operation 100 miles (161 km) to the west.

For nearly a year, Mel and a team of divers searched an area called "The Quicksands" near Key West. Still no treasure. The two ships had left almost no traces.

Then one summer day, diver-photographer Don Kincaid went down to photograph an old anchor. Suddenly, he saw links of a gold chain poking out of the sand. "The first chain I found was eight and a half feet (2.5 m) long," he says. He came up with the links draped across his arm and shoulder. Mel knew that at last they had found what they were looking for. It was the wreck of the *Atocha!*

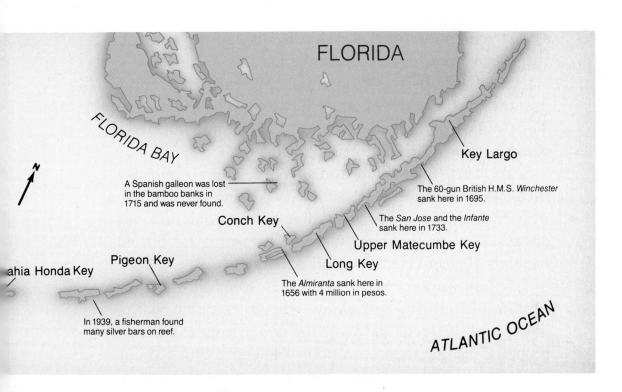

FLORIDA

FLORIDA BAY

N

Key Largo

A Spanish galleon was lost in the bamboo banks in 1715 and was never found.

The 60-gun British H.M.S. *Winchester* sank here in 1695.

Conch Key

The *San Jose* and the *Infante* sank here in 1733.

Upper Matecumbe Key

ahia Honda Key

Pigeon Key

Long Key

The *Almiranta* sank here in 1656 with 4 million in pesos.

In 1939, a fisherman found many silver bars on reef.

ATLANTIC OCEAN

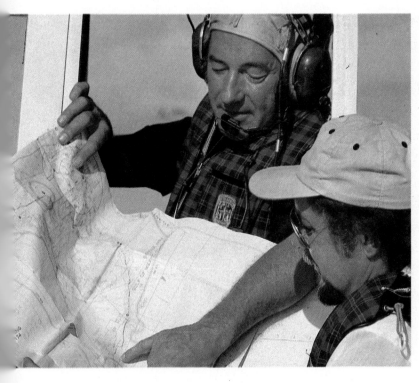

Mel Fisher and a crew member study a map of the Florida Keys. Originally, historians thought the *Atocha* and *Santa Margarita* sank near Upper Matecumbe Key. After his researcher's discovery, Mel and his crew were able to locate the wreck near Key West.

Divers found other jewelry. Beads and rings lay on the ocean floor, covered with sand.

They found silver coins, too. "We call silver coins 'biscuits' because that's what they look like," says Mel. The coins had melted together. One clump of silver coins weighed 105 pounds (47.6 kg).

To hurry the search along, Mel's divers often use metal detectors. The detectors beep when they come near metal. But even when divers find gold, it's not always easy to uncover it. Some treasures lie buried beneath 20 feet (6 m) of sand and mud.

To dig into the sand, Mel uses something he invented himself. It is an elbow-shaped tube that slants downward. It forces the whirling water from the boat's propeller against the ocean floor. Sand gets whisked out of the way. Divers watch the sand for signs of gold.

Opposite page, left: A crew member uses a metal detector to search for hidden treasures.
Opposite page, right: A diver displays gold chains from the *Atocha*.
Left: The elbow-shaped tubes mounted on the ship will be submerged to direct the whirling water that will clear away the sand that may cover treasure.
Above: A crew member digs up a clump of silver coins, or "biscuits." After being in saltwater for many years, the coins have become black.

HISTORY COMES TO LIGHT

Mel is also interested in what his finds can tell modern people about life long ago. He knows that plates, silverware, and other everyday items can tell a lot about the life of the people on board ship. For example, a gold whistle about the size of a pencil stub may have been used by the ship's first mate.

"There were a lot of people on board who were forced to work. They came from different countries, and a lot of them didn't speak Spanish," explains Don Kincaid. "In order to give commands, the mate used a whistle. They had 24 different signals, many of them

still used at sea today. The whistle had another advantage over the human voice. You could hear it despite high winds."

Mel works with scientists who are called *marine archaeologists*. They study the wrecks of old ships and everything that is brought up from them. If they find parts of the original ship, they take pictures. The scientists make a map that shows where each item of treasure was found. These records help people figure out how the ship sank. They also show how ships were built in the 17th century.

Far left: Marine archaeologists try to identify some of the jewelry found in the *Atocha* by looking at old paintings.
Top left: This whistle was probably used to give commands to a crew.
Bottom left: Gold chains were the first treasures to be uncovered by the crew. So far, they have found treasures worth more than 60 million dollars.

GREAT ADVENTURE

Mel is one of only a few underwater treasure hunters at work today. "It began as a hobby," he says. "Now it's a challenge."

Although finding treasure is a great adventure, it can also be dangerous. Modern pirates who hear about Mel's plans may try to get there first or steal what he's already found. To protect himself, Mel files a claim to a wreck in court. When the claim is granted, he gets the rights to all treasure he finds at that spot. If other people approach his claim, Mel can call the Coast Guard for protection.

Treasure hunting can also be expensive. Once he has permission to salvage a wreck, Mel hires divers and gets special equipment. With a fleet of seven ships and a crew of 70, he can spend as much as $7,000 a day to operate a salvage project. But it may take weeks—or years—before the first sign of gold shows up. After finding the *Atocha*, it took Mel nine more years to find the *Santa Margarita*.

The treasure taken from the *Atocha* and the *Margarita* so far is worth more than 60 million dollars. Mel Fisher continues to search for more underwater riches. Many silver and gold bars from the *Atocha* still lie off the coast of Key West. Mel hopes to find them!

Questions

1. Give two reasons for Mel Fisher's interest in sunken treasure ships.
2. Explain how you think the old paper might have shown or told where the Atocha and the Santa Margarita sank.
3. Do you think that treasure from sunken ships should belong to the person who finds it? Who else might have a claim?
4. Would you like to search for sunken treasure? If so, what would your motives be?

Applying Reading Skills

Number your paper from 1 to 4. Use the maps on pages 182 and 183 to answer the questions below. Write your answers in complete sentences.

1. What is the name of the area in Florida where the sunken ships lie?
2. Does the main map of the Florida Keys or the inset map show the area in greater detail?
3. What does the boxed area on the inset map on page 182 show you?
4. In what direction would you sail from Pensacola to the area of the lost ships?

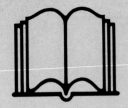

PREPARING FOR READING

Learning Vocabulary

1. The boys dug a <u>pit</u> in hopes of finding buried treasure.
2. First, <u>barriers</u> blocked the way, then the area flooded.
3. To <u>drain</u> the flooded area, a new <u>shaft</u> was dug.
4. After a dam built to keep back the ocean water <u>collapsed</u>, <u>engineers</u> began to study the problem.

pit	barriers	drain
shaft	collapsed	engineers

Developing Background and Skills
Maps

Most people find a map useful at one time or another. A **map** can show you where places are. It can help you figure out the best way to get there. Sometimes a map helps you follow written directions more easily. And if you lose your way, a map may help you find it again.

You know that an inset map is sometimes included with a main map. The inset map may show a large area of which the main map is just a part. It may also show a small area of the main map in greater detail.

Look at the map and inset map on the next page.

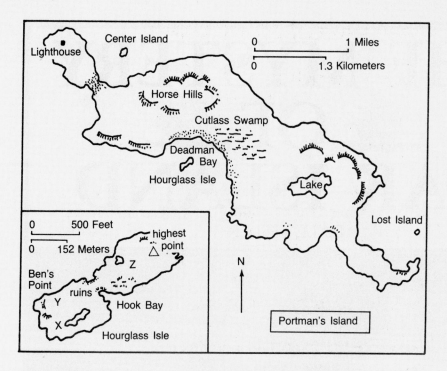

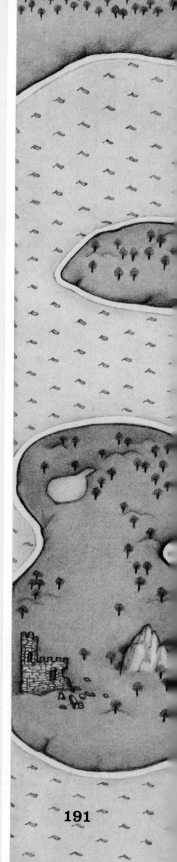

Suppose you found these directions to a buried treasure:

The treasure is on the small island shaped like a peanut lying in the wide bay on the south side of Portman's Island. It is buried at the place where a line between the castle ruins and the island's highest point crosses a line drawn directly east of the island's northernmost lake.

Which map, the main map, or the inset map will help you find the buried treasure? At which place, X, Y, or Z, would you start digging?

Refer to the main map and the inset map on page 192 as you read "The Mystery of Oak Island." Think about how the maps help you as you read, and add to your enjoyment and understanding of the story.

THE MYSTERY OF OAK ISLAND

DALE TITLER

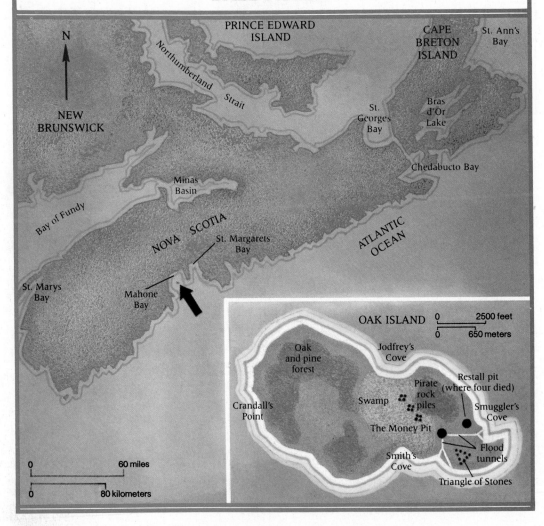

PRINCE EDWARD ISLAND

N

Northumberland Strait

NEW BRUNSWICK

CAPE BRETON ISLAND

St. Ann's Bay

St. Georges Bay

Bras d'Or Lake

Chedabucto Bay

Minas Basin

Bay of Fundy

NOVA SCOTIA

St. Margarets Bay

ATLANTIC OCEAN

St. Marys Bay

Mahone Bay

0   60 miles

0   80 kilometers

OAK ISLAND

0   2500 feet

0   650 meters

Oak and pine forest

Jodfrey's Cove

Restall pit (where four died)

Pirate rock piles

Swamp

Smuggler's Cove

Crandall's Point

The Money Pit

Flood tunnels

Smith's Cove

Triangle of Stones

Every buried treasure has a strange history. Maybe none is more mysterious than the Oak Island treasure. One of the 364 islands of Mahone Bay, tiny Oak Island lies just beyond Nova Scotia's coast. Its secret has cost four lives and wasted more than two million dollars. Every recovery expedition for the past 188 years has failed. Even today no one knows just what is buried there. Experts agree that it is the world's most perfectly buried treasure.

The treasure site was first discovered in 1795 by three teenage boys. On a hill near the shore they found a giant oak tree with a sawed-off limb sticking straight out from its trunk. The limb was long dead, but it still showed signs of deep cuts—perhaps from a heavy rope. Under the sawed limb they discovered a round sunken place in the ground. It looked like the dirt had settled after something was buried there. These clues could mean only one thing: something heavy had been lowered into the ground with a rope wrapped around the limb. A pirate chest?

The next day the boys returned to the island with shovels and picks. Ten feet (3 m) down they hit something hard. It was a platform of rough oak boards, six inches (15 cm) thick. Did it protect the treasure? They removed the boards and dug on, day after day. At twenty feet (6 m) and at thirty feet (9 m) wooden barriers stopped their work again.

An early winter sent the boys back home to Nova Scotia. When they asked about Oak Island, old-timers told them that fifty years ago strange ships had anchored there. One night two fishermen from the town went ashore to find out what was happening. They were never seen again.

The boys were excited by this news, but they could find no one to help them. Years later, one of them interested a local doctor, John Lynds, in the venture. They raised money and hired a small crew. In 1804, they began digging.

Every ten feet (3 m), oak boards delayed the digging. The crew also found layers of coconut matting, charcoal, and ship's putty. At ninety feet (27 m) they uncovered a new puzzle: a flat stone with strange markings. No one at that time could break the code. (A hundred and twenty-five years later, a professor of languages finally did translate the inscription. It read: *"Beneath this stone, two million pounds are buried."*)

After removing the stone, the crew continued to dig furiously. At ninety-seven feet (29.1 m) below the surface, a worker pushed a metal rod into the wet ground. He struck wood. Lynds believed that this was the last barrier to the treasure. He ordered the work stopped until the next morning. But when the men returned to work, they found that water had filled the shaft! They bailed and pumped for weeks, but the underground stream kept filling up the pit. Winter came and all work stopped.

The next summer, Lynds' crew dug a new shaft to drain the flooded treasure pit. At 110 feet (33 m) into

10 feet — Oak log platform

20 feet

30 feet — Level of high tide

Charcoal

40 feet — Ship's putty

50 feet — Coconut fiber

60 feet — Stone inscribed with hieroglyphics

70 feet

80 feet — Chest or barrels filled with loose metal

90 feet

98 feet

104 feet

Heart-shaped stone

Underground tunnel from Smith's Cove

Underground tunnel from Smuggler's Cove

Unusually heavy oak platform at 122 feet

Parchment and old bosun's whistle

Oak box in cement chamber at 154 to 158 feet

the second shaft, three workmen began to tunnel sideways toward the treasure. As their shovels broke through the last few feet of dirt, tons of water burst suddenly into the new shaft. The men escaped, but the water rose to sixty feet (18 m). Lynds' crew had to give up the search.

Forty years later, in 1845, still haunted by his near-success, Lynds tried again. His crew used a drill and hit a wooden container at 100 feet (30 m). When they raised the drill, they found three links of gold chain on it. A shout went up. They had hit the treasure!

There were wood shavings with the links. This made them think that the treasure was in oak chests or barrels. Because the flood water was salty, the crew believed that the two pits were connected to the ocean. A search of Smuggler's Cove, about 500 feet (150 m) away, revealed a hidden drain with five tunnels that sucked the Atlantic Ocean into the pit. Now they were certain a marvelous treasure must lie there. Why else would anyone go to so much trouble to protect it?

They built a dam to hold the ocean back, but the strong tide collapsed it. Then they dug a shaft more than 100 feet (30 m) deep on the pit's south side to keep the water out. But they couldn't work fast enough. Water in the tunnel burst through and collapsed the third shaft. The bottom of the treasure pit fell in, and Lynds and his men gave up again.

A few years later, in 1850, a third company tried to block the tunnels that flooded the pits. It also failed.

In the next ten years, two more companies lost more than $70,000 trying to get the treasure.

In 1894, the Oak Island Treasure Company was formed by Frederick Blair. Blair's men reopened the first shaft and widened it. Engineers studied the samples the drill brought up. They discovered that the material was an early type of hand-mixed cement.

They continued to drill and discovered a tiny ball of parchment, with *w* and *i* written in black ink. They also found a tiny bone whistle, shaped like a violin.

In 1955, Charles Green began excavation operations on Oak Island.
As others before him, he was not successful in discovering any treasure.

But the drainage tunnel from Smuggler's Cove still kept them from the big treasure. Like Lynds' crew, they tried to cut off the water. The shafts filled anyway. To find out where the water was coming from, Blair's men forced red dye into the pits. When no dye appeared at the cove, they were confused. But—at the *south* side of the island, at Smith's Cove, the beach was stained red. There was not *one* tunnel guarding the treasure—there were *two*!

The work went on four more years. When his company folded in 1898, Blair was still convinced that he could recover the treasure. He raised more money and kept digging—all for nothing. Finally, in 1903, he gave up.

In 1909, young Franklin Roosevelt, who was to become President of the United States, became interested. With three friends he raised $5,000 to dig on Oak Island. They believed the pit held the Crown Jewels of France. But when winter came, they went home, defeated.

Twenty-seven years later, in 1936, Gilbert Heddon, a rich manufacturer from New Jersey, decided to recover the treasure. He bought land on the island and hired a mining and drilling company. His crew used electric high-speed pumps. They cleared out the original pit to a depth of 155 feet (46.5 m), but after five years they had to give up.

World War II put a stop to treasure hunts. When it was over, new groups came to Oak Island every summer. Since the first pit was dug, more than two million dollars have been spent. More than forty water-filled shafts have been dug. More than twenty expeditions have failed.

Who thought of this grand puzzle? No one really knows. The people who buried the treasure are still the only ones who understand the secret.

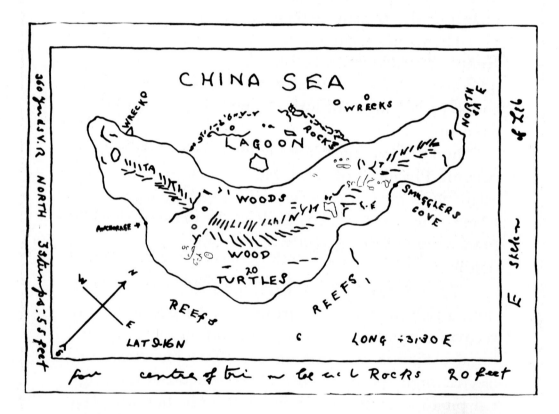

Captain Kidd's Treasure Map
This map shows an island that looks like Oak Island. It was found in Captain Kidd's chest.

Questions

1. What clues have led people to believe that there is buried treasure on Oak Island?
2. Explain how red dye appearing at Smith's Cove led to the conclusion that a second tunnel guarded the treasure.
3. Do you think the loss of lives and the money spent justifies the continued search for the treasure? Explain your answer.
4. Do you think there really is treasure on Oak Island? Why or why not?

Applying Reading Skills

Number your paper from 1 to 4. Write the answers to the following questions. Use complete sentences.

1. What does the main map on page 192 show? What does the inset map show?
2. In what part of Oak Island is the pit located?
3. Which flood tunnel is longer, that from the pit to Smuggler's Cove or that from the pit to Smith's Cove?
4. What is the greatest length of Oak Island? What is its width between Jodfrey's Cove and Smith's Cove?

WRITING ACTIVITY

WRITE A MYSTERY

Prewrite

"The Mystery of Oak Island" is a real-life mystery story. Is there a treasure? If there is, who buried it?

You can write a mystery story about buried treasure. A mystery story like other stories has characters and a setting. There is a problem to be solved in the plot of a mystery. In your mystery, the problem may be finding a buried treasure.

Begin your mystery by introducing the characters and the setting. Then describe the events in the plot that lead to the climax, the turning point or most exciting part of the story. The discovery of the treasure could be the climax of your story. The end of the story should describe what happens to the characters after the climax.

Organize the information for your mystery story by writing sentences to complete this chart.

1. Characters	
2. Setting	
3. Problem	
4. Plot Events	
5. Climax	
6. Ending	

Write

1. Read your chart before you begin to write.
2. Start your mystery story with an interesting paragraph that introduces your characters and setting.
3. Use dialogue, or conversations between your characters. Try to make your characters say things real people might say.
4. Remember, you are trying to build suspense or excitement. Short sentences with interesting adjectives and adverbs can help.
5. People who read mystery stories often try to solve the mystery as they read. Give them clear clues, but don't give away the mystery until the climax of your story.
6. Use your Glossary or dictionary for spelling help.

Revise

Read your mystery. Could you solve the mystery with the clues you gave? Did the events in your plot lead to an exciting climax? Now is the time to rewrite and change any parts of your mystery that are not clear.

1. Did you use adjectives and adverbs that really describe what is happening in your story?
2. Did you use correct punctuation for dialogue?
3. Did you use correct end punctuation for each sentence?

PREPARING FOR READING

Learning Vocabulary

1. The pirate captain <u>strutted</u> up and down the deck.
2. The unseen children played tricks on the pirates, <u>panicking</u> them.
3. Even though the captain was a <u>villain</u>, the children didn't want to see him dropped overboard.
4. The captain ordered the crew to <u>stalk</u> the ship to catch the "ghosts."
5. Mark felt <u>peculiar</u> when he was turned into a turtle.

strutted   panicking   villain
stalk   peculiar

Developing Background and Skills
Plot, Setting, Mood, and Theme

You know that **plot, setting, mood,** and **theme** are the basic parts of a story. Let's review what each part is.

plot   the series of events that takes place in the story

setting   the place and time in which the story takes place

mood   the feeling that the story creates

theme   the idea on which the story is based

Read the paragraph below. It is the beginning of a story.

Jane had not really believed that a genie would appear when she rubbed the lamp, but there it was. The lamp was magic after all! The genie bowed to Jane, saying, "Your wish is my command. It is in my power to grant you three wishes." What fun this would be, thought Jane. She had always wanted to solve a mystery with Sherlock Holmes. The first thing she would ask for would be a Sherlock Holmes adventure.

Think about the setting of this story. It may take place in London, or it may take place where Jane is. But in what time will it take place? Will Jane go back in time to the past in which Holmes lived? Will Holmes come into the present in which Jane lives? Or will the story switch back and forth in time between the past and the present?

The story you are about to read, "Magic by the Lake," will take you back and forth in time. To enjoy the story, you will have to believe in the magic on which the story is based. As you read, think about the plot, setting, mood, and theme in the story.

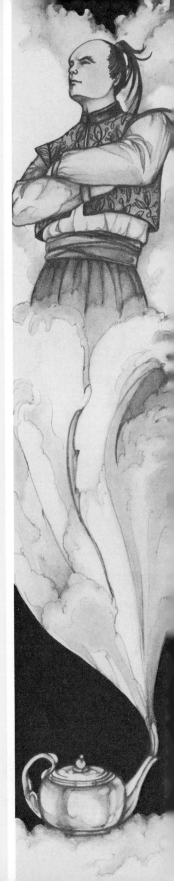

MAGIC BY THE LAKE

Edward Eager

You may have heard of a magic lamp, a magic coin, or a magic carpet. But have you ever heard of a magic turtle? Martha, Katharine, Jane, and Mark discover just such a turtle while they are enjoying a summer vacation at a lake. The turtle grants all their wishes—even when they ask for an adventure with pirates!

The ship was dark and its sails were black. A skull and crossbones was its flag. Among the figures on the deck walked a tall man in high boots. From the way he strutted up and down you could tell even at a distance that he thought it was quite a glorious thing to be a pirate king.

The ship was so near now that the four children could hear the pirate's voice plainly as he gave orders to drop the anchor and man the longboat.

A few seconds later the long-boat began to descend.

"Let's hide," said Martha suddenly, and all agreed that the suggestion was excellent.

The island had little shelter except palm trees, but the four children were soon behind two of these.

The bow of the longboat ground against sand, and the pirate chief leaped ashore. The children could see that he was handsome, with beautifully curling black whiskers.

"Up with the treasure and after me," he said to his men. "Bring the spades, picks, and shovels."

Some of the men heaved a great chest up out of the boat. Others followed with tools for digging. The black-whiskered one strode to a sandy spot just in front of the two palm trees. He pointed with his fine, gentlemanly hand.

"Dig," he said.

And the men dug long and deep in the sand.

"This treasure," he muttered, "will rest safely here, but only until I am ready to retire and take my place in the world as a gentleman."

Katharine chose this moment to sneeze.

The pirates jumped. So did the four children.

"Hark!" said Chauncey Cutlass. "What was that? Probably a sea gull."

"Can't they see us?" hissed Jane, from behind her tree.

"I guess not," Mark hissed back. "Katharine wished grownups wouldn't notice and

I guess they're grownups, the same as any."

"How the wind whispers in the trees," said Chauncey Cutlass, just to prove it.

"Hurry up with that digging," said Chauncey Cutlass to his men, "and back to the ship. I like not this shore. The very trees seem to be staring at me, and the air seems full of voices. Now. In with the box."

The digging men stopped digging and heaved the treasure chest down and into the hole. Then they started to shovel the earth in on top of it.

"Heel it down firmly," said Chauncey Cutlass, and they did, with a flat stone on top to mark the spot. Then the pirate king knelt down and carved his initials on the stone with a diamond from one of his rings.

The four children meanwhile had boarded the longboat. The others were soothing Martha, who wanted to steal the boat now while all backs were turned and row away with it. And she wasn't interested in staying to play tricks on the pirates, either.

"It wouldn't be right," she said. "What did they ever do to us?"

"Honestly!" said Jane. "Imagine bringing up a thing like that at a time like this! They're *pirates*! They *ought* to be preyed on!"

"Yes, I suppose that's true," said Martha. She wrestled with her fears for a minute, then set her jaw grimly. "All right," she said. "It's war to the teeth."

"Good," said Jane.

When Chauncey Cutlass had finished his carving and strode

to the shore, his men clambered after him.

"Careful," said Mark to Katharine. "Don't do anything till we get on the ship. Once we're aboard, the world is ours."

As they scrambled out of the longboat onto the deck, Mark called the others around him in a whispering huddle. They made a few quick plans and then separated. Mark hurried forward to the captain's cabin while the three others ran to the mainmast. Katharine untied all the knots she could see. Jane cut a few ropes here and there. The sails were soon sagging and flopping like wet sheets that you try to hang on the line on a windy washday.

"Sink me!" cried one of the pirates, looking up. "What wind is this, fouling our rigging while the sea be all calm as glass and nary a breeze is stirring?"

"Sure the ship be haunted!" cried another.

Katharine found the line for the skull-and-crossbones flag and started to let it down. A moan went up from the deck.

"We be all doomed! See the flag standing at half-mast for the whole crew of us!" cried all the pirates.

As for Martha, she knew no bounds. "Pinch them!" she cried. Then running among the pirates, she suited the action to the words. The pirates began howling with fear and swatting at the air. One or two even climbed the rail, ready to plunge overboard and escape the ghostly pinches.

"Belay!" cried Simon Sparhatch, taking command of the

panicking men. "The doom need be for only one of us! And who but that great captain who landed us on that island and caught us this swarm of spirits in the first place? Over the side with him and rid us of these pinching pests!" He started for the captain's cabin. All the pirates ran after him, and Jane and Katharine and Martha ran with the others.

Meanwhile, Mark had entered the captain's cabin and looked around. The captain was standing before a mirror curling his black whiskers. Mark stole up behind him, removed the pistols from his belt, gave them a good dousing with the captain's own perfume, and replaced them. The captain didn't seem to notice, exactly, but an uneasy expression crossed his face.

"Am I alone?" he said into the air. "I thought I was alone."

Mark closed the door behind him. "Now we can have a really good talk," he said.

The captain didn't seem to hear the words, exactly, but he

211

saw the door closing. His proud face turned white.

"Whose ghost are you?" he asked.

"Beware!" said Mark in a hollow voice. Whether or not the word was heard, the sense of it got across. Chauncey Cutlass shook.

"Your ship is adrift, and your men have mutinied," said Mark. "You are as good as shark-bait yourself!" And the shouts of the mutinying crew were heard outside the door to prove it.

Chauncey Cutlass showed that, whatever else he was, he had courage. He flung the door open and fired at Simon Sparhatch, who was in the lead. But a damp and perfumy puff of smoke was all that came out of the gun.

"Up with him to the deck and toss him over the rail," said Sparhatch.

The captain was pushed up, and villain though he was, the four children could not help feeling sorry for him. But they reckoned without the craft and courage of Chauncey Cutlass.

"Avast!" he cried, as the sailors lifted him to the rail. "If you drop me, I'll come back and haunt you worse than these others! You're letting some old ghosts ruin our whole cruise! If you do as I say, we'll be free of the pesky things sooner than you can box the compass! If we can feel their pinches, surely we can feel to *catch* them!"

The crew fell back and hesitated before him.

"Quick!" he went on, jumping lightly down from the rail. "Batten down all hatches so none may escape from the deck. Then form two parties, and all in each party join hands. Stretch out the width of the deck. Start at the stern and let one party stalk them to starboard and the other to port. When the two parties meet, you should have them trapped between you!"

Frightened by his fierce glance, the men obeyed. A sort of game followed. The pirates stalked the deck, feeling before them and hunting down the spirit-like children.

"Here's one," cried a pirate, laying hold of Jane. "A fierce female ghost, to judge by the hair and teeth."

"And here be another," said a second pirate, poking Martha. "A small fat one."

"Why, you!" said Martha, outraged.

Katharine was caught after that, and Mark last of all.

"Beware!" Mark cried as before, but this time Chauncey Cutlass was beyond being frightened.

"I don't care whose ghosts you are!" he said. "I'll teach you to come haunting *me*!

Fetch a plank and let them walk it. Then we'll see whether ghosts can swim!"

A plank was fetched, and the four children pushed onto it by the feel-and-grab method.

"Will we drown, do you suppose?" said Jane.

"Now, if ever," said Mark, "is time to call the turtle. It said not unless it was absolutely necessary, and it is."

"Here, turtle," said Martha.

"That's no way," said Mark. "It's not just some old pet. You want to be respectful, and flatter it. O turtle," he began. But at that moment Chauncey

214

Cutlass signaled to the men to tilt the plank, and his words ended in wetness.

There was a moment of doubt, and struggling, and lost courage. Then a familiar voice sounded in Mark's ear.

"Well?" it said. "Pirates were what you asked for. I hope you're satisfied."

Mark opened his eyes. A familiar figure was swimming beside him. But there seemed to be three more figures just like it, only smaller, swimming there, too. Suddenly Mark realized that he felt very peculiar and stiff in the middle and small in the arms and legs.

"What happened?" he said.

"Didn't you ever hear of turning turtle?" said the turtle. "It was the only thing I could think of at the time."

Mark looked down at himself. It was true. He had a shell on top and below, and little fat arms and legs stuck out from the corners.

"Now," said the turtle, "you can see how the other half lives."

"Thanks," said Mark.

They went on swimming for what seemed like forever, for turtles are not the quickest of creatures. But at last they came into shallow water and up over the sand and pebbles of their own beach.

"There," said the turtle. And it swam away, leaving the other four turtles on the shore, waiting to change back to their real selves.

You can read about other adventures of Martha, Katharine, Jane, and Mark in Magic by the Lake *and in* Half Magic, *another book by Edward Eager.*

Questions

1. Why did the pirates come ashore on the island where the children were?
2. Why were the pirates unable to see or hear the children?
3. Do you agree with Martha, who said it wouldn't be right to play tricks on the pirates, or with Jane, who said pirates ought to be preyed on? Explain your answer.
4. If you could have a wish granted by the turtle, what would your wish be?

Applying Reading Skills

Number your paper from 1 to 4. Choose the answer choice that best completes each sentence about "Magic by the Lake." Write the complete sentences.

1. After the pirates had buried the treasure, the children ____.
   a. dug it up   b. hid in the long boat   c. ran away

2. The story takes place ____.
   a. in the future   b. in the Caribbean
   c. on a lake and an island

3. The mood of the story could best be described as ____.
   a. suspenseful   b. comical   c. serious

4. The theme of the story is ____.
   a. the evils of piracy   b. fun in the water
   c. magic can sometimes lead to unexpected problems

CAPTAIN KIDD

This person in the gaudy clothes
Is worthy Captain Kidd.
They say he never buried gold.
I think, perhaps, he did.

They say it's all a story that
His favorite little song
Was "Make these lubbers walk the plank!"
I think, perhaps, they're wrong.

They say he never pirated
Beneath the Skull-and-Bones.
He merely traveled for his health
And spoke in soothing tones.
In fact, you'll read in nearly all
The newer history books
That he was mild as cottage cheese
—But I don't like his looks!

Stephen Vincent Benét

TREASURE
AT
BLUE
BEACH

SCOTT O'DELL

California went through many changes during the 1800s. Spain ruled the land for many years. Then Mexico took control in 1822. As more and more Americans began to settle in California, Mexican rule was threatened. Finally, in 1846, the United States and Mexico went to war over California.

While the war was being fought, the de Zubarans family and other California landowners tried to keep their ranches running. During the troubled times, however, even the best cattle had to be sold for low prices. With little money coming in, many ranchers went into debt. But Carlota de Zubarans and her father have discovered a secret that may help them survive.

My father and I had been coming to Blue Beach for two years, but we never told anyone our secret.

There was no way to find the Blue Beach except by following the river, either down from the mountains or up from the sea. From the sea no one would ever find it because of a series of lagoons. From the direction of the mountains you would need to be very lucky, as lucky as we had been in the beginning.

The river at this point, where it fanned out into the deep lagoons, ran narrow, between two sheer walls of granite, where even a mountain goat would be lost. At the bottom of these cliffs were two beaches, one facing the other across a distance of a hundred steps.

The beaches were strips of fine sand, finer than the sand you find on the sea beach itself. Both had a bluish cast, like pebbles you see through clear-running water. But they also had another color, a lighter blue that had a look of metal, as if there were copper deposits in the cliffs that had been washed down by the river and the rain and had mixed with the lighter color.

Someone might call the beaches green or the color of turquoise, but to us they were blue and that is what we called them—the Blue Beaches, more often, the Blue Beach.

On this day, as on the three other journeys we had made to the Blue Beach, we tied our horses and climbed up from the stream to a towering rock. This was where we took our second precaution. From this high place we could survey the trails, one coming along the river, and one from the sea.

We sat for an hour, to make sure that we had not been followed. When the sun was overhead, we crawled down from the pinnacle. We reached the Blue Beach and took off our boots and stepped out into the middle of the stream. We made our way for a distance of some fifty paces, leaving no tracks behind us. A clump of willows grew amidst a pile of driftwood and boulders at this place. Here the river divided and ran in two smaller streams on both sides of the willows.

The boulders could not be seen at high tide. But the tide was low now and they stuck up in two crescents, facing each other and leaving a clear space between them. The water was cold, both the sea water

that met the river at this point and likewise the river water itself.

I splashed water on my legs, on my arms and chest. I had found that the best way to approach cold water was by small shivers, suffered one at a time.

Throwing out my arms, I took in a great gulp of air, held it for a minute, counting each second. Then I let out all the air in a quick whoosh. Then I raised my arms again and took in a greater gulp.

This air I held for two minutes, still counting the seconds in my mind—one second, two seconds, and so forth. I repeated this three times. The third time I counted up to four minutes.

It had taken me two years to build up to where I could hold my breath for this length of time. My father had heard of pearl divers in La Paz who could hold their breath for five minutes and even longer. I had tried this but had fainted.

Carefully we stepped into the wide pool between the two crescents of stone, beneath the willows. We inched our way to the center of the pool.

As my foot touched a smooth slab of stone, I stooped down, lifted it with much care, and set it to one side. Beneath it was a rock-lined hole filled with water, the size of my body and twice its height.

At the bottom of this hole was something that, when we first saw it, seemed to be the trunk of a tree—a tree washed down from the mountains. Undoubtedly, it once had risen above the water, but over the years floods had worn it away to a stump.

It had been the mainmast of a ship, which my father said was some seventy feet in length. It had the

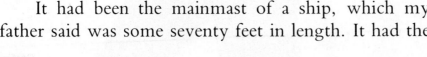

wide beam, the high stern, of the galleons that two centuries before had sailed the seas between China and the coast of California and Mexico.

These ships, my father said, came on favorable winds and currents to northern California, then along the coast to Mexico. They carried treasures so great that they became the prey of American and English pirates.

Some of these treasure ships had been captured. Others had run aground through careless navigation. Others were driven ashore by storms. Still others had sought refuge from their pursuers by hiding in lagoons such as the one at Blue Beach.

Hidden in the galleon's hold, near the stump of the mainmast, were two chests filled with coins. The coins were of pure gold. They showed three castles and the two flying doves that meant they had been struck in the mint at Lima, Peru. The date marked upon each coin that we carried away on the trips we had made was the year 1612.

The two chests—each made of hard wood banded with iron straps and sealed with a hasp that had rusted and fallen off—were well beneath the surface of the water, whether at low tide or in the summer, when the stream ran low.

There were many things to do before the chests could be reached. Usually it took me half a day to bring up a pouch of coins from the sunken ship.

The place where I dove, which was surrounded by jagged rocks and driftwood, was too narrow for my father. He had tried to squeeze through when we first discovered the galleon, but partway down he got stuck and I had to pull him back. It was my task, therefore, to go into the cavelike hole. My father stood beside it and helped me to go down and to come up.

I buckled a strong belt around my waist and to it tied a *riata* (rē ä′ tä) that was ten *varas* (bä′ räs) long and stout enough to hold a stallion. I fastened my knife to my wrist—a two-edged blade made especially for me by our blacksmith—to protect myself against spiny rays and the big eels that could sting you to death. In the many dives I had made, I never had seen a shark.

Taking three deep breaths, I prepared to let myself down into the hole. In one hand I held a sink-stone, heavy enough to weigh me down. I let out all the air in my chest, took a deep breath, and held it. Then I began the descent.

The sink-stone would have taken me down fast, but the edges of the rocky hole were sharp. I let myself down carefully, one handhold at a time. It took me about a minute to reach the rotted deck where the chests lay. I now had two minutes to pry the coins loose and carry them to the surface. We had tried putting the coins in a leather sack and hoisting them to the surface. But we had trouble with this because of the currents that swept around the wreck.

The coins lay in a mass, stuck together, lapping over each other and solid as rock. They looked, when I first saw them, like something left on the stove too long. I always expected to find them gone, but now as I walked toward the chests, with the stone holding me down, I saw that they were still there. No one had come upon them during the seven months since our last visit.

The first time I had dived and brought up a handful of coins, I said to my father that we should empty both the chests and take the coins home.

"Then everyone would talk," he said. "As soon as they saw the gold coins the news would spread the length of California."

"We don't need to tell anyone. I can hide them in my chest at home."

"The news would fly out before the sun set. At the ranch there are many eyes."

I still thought it was a better idea to empty the chests before someone else did, but I could see that my father enjoyed these days, when the two of us went to the Blue Beach, so I said no more.

The sun was overhead and its rays slanted down through the narrow crevice. With my knife I pried loose a handful of coins. They were of a dark green color and speckled here and there with small barnacles. I set the coins aside.

My lungs were beginning to hurt, but I had not felt the tug of the *riata* yet, the signal from my father that I had been down three minutes. I pried loose a second handful and put my knife away. Before the tug came I dropped my sink-stone and took up the coins.

Gold is very heavy, much heavier than stones of the same size.

Fish were swimming around me as I went up through the hole of rocks and tree trunks, but I saw no sting rays or eels.

On the third trip down, I hauled up about the same number of coins as the other times. The pouch we had brought was now full.

"Are you tired?" he said.

"Yes, a little."

"Can you go down again?"

"Yes."

"Then go."

I dived twice more. It was on the last dive that I had the trouble. The tug on the *riata* had not come, but I was tired, so I started away from the chest with one handful of coins. Close to the chests, between them and the hole, I had noticed what seemed to be two pieces of timber covered with barnacles. They looked as if they might be part of a third and larger chest.

I still held my knife and I thrust it at a place where the two gray timbers seemed to join. It was possible that I had found another chest filled with coins.

As the knife touched them, the two timbers moved a little. Instantly, I felt pressure upon my wrist. I drew back the hand that held the knife. Rather, I tried to draw it back, but it would not move. The tide had shifted the timbers somehow and I was caught. So I thought.

I felt a tug upon the *riata* fastened to my waist. It was the signal from my father to come to the surface. I answered him with two quick tugs of the leather rope.

Now I felt a hot pain run up my arm. I tried to open my fingers, to drop the knife, but my hand was numb. Then as I stared down into the murky water I saw a slight movement where my hand was caught. At the same moment I saw a flash of pink, a long tongue sliding along my wrist.

I had never seen a burro clam, but I had heard the tales about them, for there were many on our coast. Attached to rocks, or timbers, they grew to half the height of a man, these gray, silent monsters. Many fishermen had lost their lives in the burro's jaws.

The pain in my arm was not so great now as the hot pains in my chest. I gave a long, hard tug on the *riata* to let my father know that I was in trouble. Again I saw a flash of pink as the burro opened its lips a little, and the fat tongue slid back and forth.

I dropped the coins I held in my other hand. The burro had closed once more on my wrist. But shortly it began to open again, and I felt a sucking pressure, as if the jaws were trying to draw me inside.

Putting my knees against the rough bulge of the shell, as the jaws opened and then began to close, I jerked with all my strength. I fell slowly backward upon the ship's deck. My hand was free. With what breath I had I moved toward the hole. I saw the sun

shining above and climbed toward it. The next thing I saw was my father's face and I was lying on the river's sandy bank. He took my knife in his hand.

After I told him what had happened, my father said, "The knife saved your life. The burro clamped down upon it. See the mark here. The steel blade kept its jaws open. Enough to let you wrench yourself free."

He pulled me to my feet. "Here," he said, passing the reins of his bay gelding to me, "ride Santana. He goes gentler than Tiburon."

"I'll ride my own horse," I said.

"Good, if you wish it."

"I wish it," I said, knowing that he didn't want me to say that my hand was numb.

"Does the hand hurt?"

"No."

"You were very brave," he said.

My father wanted me to be braver than I was. I wanted to say I was scared, both when the burro had hold of me and now, at this moment, but I didn't because he expected me to be brave.

"It was good fortune," I said.

"Fortune and bravery often go together," Don Saturnino said. "If you do not hurt, let us go."

I got on the stallion and settled myself in the saddle. "Yes, let us go," I said, though I could not grip the reins well with but one hand.

On the way home we talked about the pouchful of coins and my father decided to sell them in San Diego. The first coins he had sold in Los Angeles to a *gringo* trader.

"The *gringo* was curious about where I got them," he said. "Too curious to suit my fancy."

"What did you say to him?" I asked.

"I said that the coins had been in the family for many years. He looked at them for a long time. He turned them over and over. He was curious about the green spots on the coins. He said the coins must have been in the sea at some time. I told him that it was likely, since my grandfather was a captain of the sea."

"I didn't know that my great-grandfather was a captain of the sea."

"He was not," Don Saturnino said, and laughed. "We will try San Diego this time."

UNIT THREE

LEVEL 12

PATTERNS OF FLIGHT

PREPARING FOR READING

Learning Vocabulary

1. The winged horse Pegasus created an enchanted spring at the <u>summit</u> of Mount Helicon.
2. A young man named Bellerophon longed to <u>tame</u> this wonderful <u>steed</u>.
3. He gazed in <u>awe</u> at the marvelous creature who could soar through the air.

summit   tame   steed   awe

Developing Background and Skills
Encyclopedia

Sometimes when you are reading a story, you may come across a subject or topic that you would like to know more about. Where can you look for more information?

A good place to look would be in an encyclopedia. An **encyclopedia** is a reference work in one or more books, or volumes. The information in an encyclopedia is presented in a series of articles.

The articles in an encyclopedia are usually arranged in alphabetical order. The spine, or back, of an encyclopedia volume is usually marked with a letter or letters and a numeral. Look at the "encyclopedia" on the next page.

234

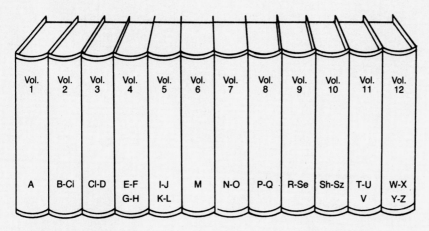

Suppose you wanted to find out more about Pegasus. In which volume would you look?

The article about Pegasus might end with a cross-reference. A cross-reference tells you where to look for more information about a topic or where to find other articles related to the topic.

At the end of the Pegasus article, you might find these cross-references:

See Bellerophon See also: myths, Greek

If you wanted to learn more about Pegasus, the articles about Bellerophon and Greek myths would help you.

As you read the next selection, think about what subjects or topics you might want to learn more about by using an encyclopedia.

THE WINGED HORSE

Krystyna Turska

In far-off days, there roamed the land a wonderful creature, Pegasus, the winged horse. He could fly as swiftly as an eagle and outrun any living thing. Indeed Pegasus was a wonder horse. He had created an enchanted spring at the summit of Mount Helicon when he struck the dry ground with his hoof.

In the city of Corinth lived a young man named Bellerophon (bə lãr' ə fon'). He was as strong and brave as he was fair to look upon. But Bellerophon, for all his good fortune, was not satisfied. He had heard many tales of Pegasus and longed to own the great white horse.

"Tell me," he asked a wise man, "how can I tame the winged steed Pegasus? I will not rest until I have done so."

The wise man told Bellerophon to go to the temple of Athena (ə thē′ nə) and sleep there. This Bellerophon did.

In the night he had a strange dream. The goddess Athena came to him, carrying in her hands a golden bridle. She held the bridle out to Bellerophon.

"Take this," she said. "With it you can win your heart's desire."

Bellerophon woke with a start and leaped to his feet. The goddess had vanished, but the golden bridle lay before him on the ground. Bellerophon looked at it with wonder. It was more beautiful than anything he had seen before.

Now Bellerophon was full of hope. He journeyed to Mount Helicon. He knew that Pegasus was often to be found drinking at the enchanted spring. So he lay down wearily beside the spring and waited.

Suddenly there came a rush of wings. Out of the clouds flew the magnificent Pegasus.

Bellerophon gazed at the huge beast in awe. He knew that there was no more wondrous creature in all the earth.

With one bound Bellerophon reached the horse's side. He slipped the golden bridle over his head, and mounted him.

Pegasus pawed the ground, trying to shake off his rider. Then he sprang into the air. His mane and tail were streaming behind him. His wings were outstretched. Bellerophon could feel the beast's panic lessen. Horse and rider became one, each accepting the other as an equal and a friend.

Bellerophon's heart filled with joy as he flew with Pegasus high over the countryside. He felt that all the world was his. He believed that he could accomplish any deed now that Pegasus was tamed. Together he and his horse soared and swooped. They raced as swiftly as the wind. They flew again and again into the air until both were exhausted and came down to earth to rest.

Now began a glorious time for Bellerophon, for Pegasus was truly his. The horse returned to Corinth with him and the two of them were the wonder and envy of all.

As Bellerophon's fame spread, his pride grew. One day he decided to challenge the gods themselves. Springing on to the back of Pegasus he shouted that he was as great as the gods. He would fly to Olympus, the home of the gods, to prove it.

Zeus (züs), king of the gods, was angered by the pride of Bellerophon. He made a fly sting Pegasus as he flew upwards. Startled, the horse reared. Bellerophon was thrown and fell to his death far below.

Pegasus was not blamed by the gods, for he had only been doing his master's bidding. Instead, the noble beast was welcomed in the stalls of Olympus. He was cared for along with the steeds of Zeus. It is said that he became the messenger of Zeus, carrying for him thunder and lightning across the heavens.

Later, Zeus decided to reward Pegasus for his devotion. He turned the horse into a constellation. The beauty of Pegasus still lights the night sky.

Questions

1. Why did Bellerophon sleep in the temple of Athena?
2. How did Bellerophon tame Pegasus?
3. Why was Bellerophon punished by Zeus?
4. Do you think the story of Pegasus and Bellerophon has a moral or teaches a lesson? If so, what is it?

Applying Reading Skills

Number your paper from 1 to 4. Use complete sentences to answer each question below.

1. If you wanted to find more information about the goddess Athena, what topic or subject would you look under in an encyclopedia?
2. Corinth is a city in Greece. If you wanted to find out where in Greece the city is located, what topic would you look for in an encyclopedia?
3. If you wanted to find out what the constellation Pegasus looks like and where it can be found in relation to other constellations, what topic would you look under in an encyclopedia?
4. Would you expect to find a cross-reference to Zeus if you looked up the topic *Olympus* in an encyclopedia? Why or why not?

PREPARING FOR READING

Learning Vocabulary

1. Charles and Uncle Coot went to <u>investigate</u> the report of a colt with wings.
2. Charles thought the colt might be a <u>descendant</u> of a horse in Greek <u>mythology</u>.
3. Uncle Coot tried to <u>assure</u> Mrs. Minney that there could not be a colt with wings.
4. When he actually saw the colt, he began to feel <u>dazed</u>.

investigate   descendant   mythology
assure   dazed

Developing Background and Skills
Encyclopedia

You know that an **encyclopedia** is a reference work in one or more volumes that contains articles about many different subjects or topics. An encyclopedia is a good place to look for more information about subjects that interest you.

Like the entry words in a dictionary, the articles in an encyclopedia are arranged in alphabetical order. The articles in a particular volume are indicated by the first letter or by the first several letters of their titles on the spine of the volume.

An encyclopedia can be like a dictionary in another way. Some encyclopedias have guide words at the top of each page. The guide words tell the names of the first and last articles on the page.

Locating information in an encyclopedia can be easy if you use the letters and numbers on the spine of the volumes and the guide words on each page. Cross-references at the end of some articles will direct you to other articles that are related to the topic you are interested in. The words *See* and *See also* often come before cross-references.

In the next selection, you will read about a boy who is very interested in reading and research. Notice the topics he refers to. Think about where you would look in an encyclopedia to find out more about them.

Texas Pegasus

Betsy Byars

Going to visit Uncle Coot was the most exciting thing that had ever happened to Charles. Charles's visit wasn't exactly what Uncle Coot had expected. As Uncle Coot tells it, that summer had more than its share of unexpected events.

This lady, Mrs. Minney, was another unexpected thing that had happened. She and her husband had come to Texas from New York and had bought an old worn-down place across the road. They had come, Mrs. Minney told me, because she was writing a book about the cliff dwellers who used to live in the mountains around here, and she wanted to investigate the caves. Her husband was an artist who was tired of painting buildings and subways and was going to paint horses and cattle and mountains for a change. The Minneys had had a good bit of trouble getting settled because neither of them was a practical person. I don't think a day went by without Mrs. Minney's driving over in her truck to ask me about one thing or another. As soon as I saw her coming, I said to Charles, "Well, something's wrong at the Minneys' again."

Charles turned his head to watch the truck. "Who are the Minneys?"

"That's Mrs. Minney now."

Mrs. Minney stopped her truck and got out. Her shirttail was flapping, and her hair was rising, and she came running over so fast Charles and I backed up a few steps. Even when she came to a halt, she still seemed to be going somewhere.

I said politely, "Mrs. Minney, this is my nephew Charles."

She said, "Mr. Cutter! Mr. Cutter! Do you know anything about cutting the wings off a colt?"

I said, *"What?"*

She repeated it. "Do you know anything about cutting the wings off a colt?"

"What?"

She sighed. "Wings! Little wings about that long on either side of his shoulders." She shook her head. "I just don't know what to do about it. I've never seen a colt with wings before."

"I haven't either, Mrs. Minney," I said. "But whatever those things turn out to be, I can assure you that they won't be wings."

"Why not?"

"Because they *couldn't* be."

"But they *could* be," Charles said. His eyes had gotten big with interest. He stepped right in front of Mrs. Minney.

I said calmly, "I beg your pardon, Charles, but I have seen horses and known horses since the day I was born. And there never has been such a thing as a horse with wings."

"A vase in the National Museum in Greece has a winged horse on it. Some people say that it's a scene from mythology, but others, including me, believe that there actually *was* a winged horse and—"

"Charles!"

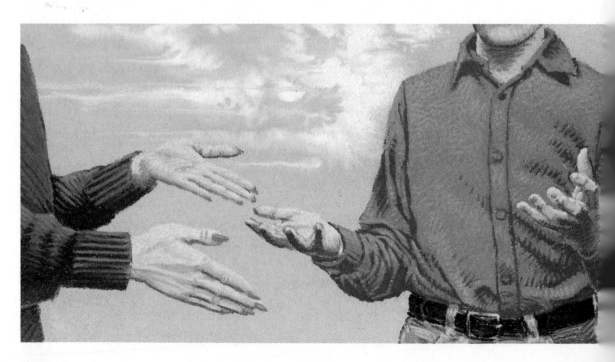

"And then there are the horses painted in a cave in France," he continued.

"I am familiar with that cave," Mrs. Minney said. She was far more impressed with Charles's knowledge of horses than with mine.

"And there are horses painted on the wall"—Charles went on—"and above the horses are handshaped marks like wings."

"That's true!" Mrs. Minney said. "I never thought of it, but those marks *are* like wings."

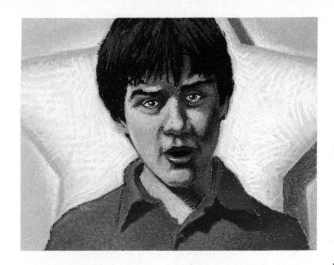

"And do you remember the skeleton found in the diggings at—"

"Charles!" He shut up long enough for me to say, "Now that is enough! Mrs. Minney doesn't want to hear you trying to prove something that is impossible."

"I do," Mrs. Minney cried.

I ignored her. "Mrs. Minney is worried enough without your adding to it. She doesn't care what's been painted on vases and cave walls and—"

"I do!" Mrs. Minney cried again.

"No, you don't!" She stepped back for a moment. "What the three of us are interested in right now"—I continued as calmly as I could—"is what has been on

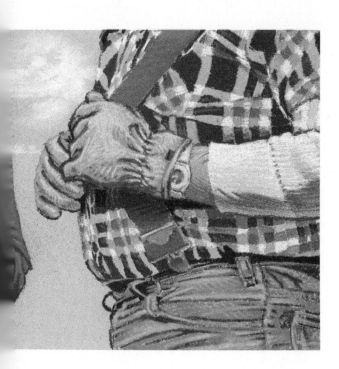

247

this earth, actually been on this earth. And there has never been a horse with wings and never will be. Never!"

They both looked at me without speaking. Then Mrs. Minney sat down on the porch steps. She said, "Well, actually, it is a relief, Mr. Cutter, to hear that." She sighed and patted her face with her shirttail. "Nobody knows what a relief it is to think you have a horse with wings and then find out you have a horse with—" She broke off and looked at me. "What would it be that the horse has?"

I did not want her to get excited again so I said, calmly,

"Well, since it's not wings, it will have to be something else. I think we can all agree on that." I glanced from Mrs. Minney to Charles.

"Well, if it's *not* wings," Charles said, "then of course it *will* have to be something else, but I still think—"

I rested my hand on his shoulder so firmly that he choked down the rest of his words. "What I am going to do, Mrs. Minney," I continued, "is come over to your place

now, look at the colt, and tell you what he has."

"Could I come too, Mrs. Minney?" Charles asked. "I'd like to see this for myself."

"Of course you can come." Mrs. Minney took a deep breath and sighed. "I feel better now. My trouble is that I get excited too easily. Another woman, seeing she had a colt with wings, would probably have the wings removed in a sensible way and go about her business."

We climbed into the truck, and she said, "Still and all, I will feel easier in my mind when I know what those things on the colt are."

I thought I heard Charles say "Wings" under his breath. I wasn't sure, but I nudged him again anyway. That kept him quiet for the rest of the drive.

We stopped in front of the barn and got out. Mr. Minney stuck his head out the back window of the house, and Mrs. Minney called to him, "Don't worry, those aren't wings on the colt after all."

"They looked like wings to me," he called back.

"Mr. Cutter says no."

"What are they then, Mr. Cutter?" he asked, still leaning out the window.

"I'll let you know as soon as I see the colt."

Mrs. Minney said, "Frank and I don't like this, Mr. Cutter. We don't like it at all."

"I got that feeling, Mrs. Minney."

"We had such happy visions of the grandchildren riding around the ranch. Come on in the barn." She took me and Charles in an iron grip and led us down to the last stall. We stood there for a moment because it took our eyes a while to see in the dim barn.

Peggy, the mare, was a fine chestnut with a white mane and tail. I reached over and scratched her muzzle and said, "Good girl." I couldn't see the colt—nothing but the spindly legs because he was on the other side of his mother, drinking her milk. Then Peggy shifted to the side, and there was the prettiest little palomino colt you ever saw. The sun was coming through the window behind us, and it

shone down on the colt. He was pale gold like wheat, and his mane and tail were silver. There was a white spot on his forehead.

I opened the door of the stall, went in, and rubbed Peggy's neck. You have to move gently with a colt that's a few hours old. I usually try to handle them from birth to get them used to me. I knelt down and ran my hands over

the colt. I turned to see him in a better light.

"Well?" Mrs. Minney said.

I put my hands on the colt's sides, and the wings came out and fluttered against my hands. I couldn't say anything because I felt like I had a wad of cotton rammed down my throat. I stood up slowly.

"Well?" Mrs. Minney said, louder.

I took off my hat and ran my hand over my hair. I shifted my pants up an inch or two and jammed my hands in my back pockets. I looked down at the colt and still I couldn't speak.

"Well?"

"Mrs. Minney." I swallowed and the sound of it was like a gun going off in the quiet barn. "Mrs. Minney, I don't know why and I don't

know how, but you have got a colt with wings."

As soon as I said that, Mrs. Minney took the leather pocketbook and brought it down hard on my head. It was like getting hit with a saddle. Then she started saying, "I knew it, I knew it," and "You're not getting away with this. You're not, you're not, you're *not*."

"Mrs. Minney," I said, "what is it you want me to do? Whatever it is—just tell me and I'll do it."

"That's more like it," she said. "I want one of two things. Either you remove those wings and leave no trace they were there—and frankly I don't think you can do that—or you take the mare and the colt back and refund my money."

I looked down at the little Palomino nuzzling against his mother. I wanted the colt all right. I wanted him a lot.

"Well?" she said.

"I would be pleased to take the colt and mare back."

"And no *forcing* this animal to fly either," she said. "I

don't want to turn on the television some night and see you forcing him to fly."

"No'm."

"I want you to be good to this horse. He'll fly if he wants to."

"Yes'm."

"Shake on it."

I put out my hand and we shook. Then she got a firmer grip on my hand and leaned over and said, "And there better not be any tricks."

"There won't be."

We hesitated a minute, but she didn't say anything about driving us home in the truck, so Charles and I began walking. I was too stunned to talk, but Charles plowed right in.

"You know, I thought of something else," he said. "There's a statue in one of the French museums of a horse with wings and also—"

"There is no such thing as a colt with wings," was all I could manage to say.

"Also there was Pegasus—he was the most famous flying horse in the world—and do you know how they tamed him, Uncle Coot?"

"There is no such thing as a—"

"With a golden bridle. And I also remember reading an article in *Time* magazine about this man who believes that mythical creatures like Pegasus really did exist, that they were super beings from other planets. So maybe there *was* a winged colt at one time, and this colt is a descendant!"

"There's no such thing as—"

"And there's another statue— I think it's Egyptian—and—" Charles kept talking about flying horses all the way to the ranch. I thought he never would run out of things to say. I thought he must have spent the biggest part of his life reading books. Finally I interrupted and said, "Wait a minute. How do you know all this stuff, Charles?"

"I read."

"Well, sure, everybody reads, but they don't know all that stuff."

"Well I read a lot. I once decided to read every book in the school library." He looked up at me. "But anyway, getting back to the statues, if there *was* no such thing as a flying horse, well, then why doesn't *one* of those countries have a flying bear or a flying dog? You never see statues of flying dogs."

"I don't know, Charles. The only place I ever saw anything about a horse with wings was on a gas station sign, and I can't even remember which one it was now." The truth was I was starting to feel dazed. I had seen that colt. I had looked right at him. The

wings had touched my hands. I still couldn't take it in.

"I wish," Charles was saying, "that I was close to a really good research library, because I would like to look into this matter in my spare time." He stumbled in his excitement. "Hey, you know what I'm going to do? I'm going to start a record of the colt and keep notes on everything he does. Tomorrow I'll take pictures with my camera, and—what time can we get the colt?"

"Afternoon."

"He'll be walking by then?" He looked up at me. His eyes were as round as quarters.

"He'll be walking," I said. "He may even be flying."

You can read more about the colt and Charles and Uncle Coot in **The Winged Horse of Casa Mia**. *The colt really does learn how to use his wings, but that's just the beginning!*

Questions

1. Why was Mrs. Minney so excited and upset?
2. Why did Mrs. Minney go to Uncle Coot with her problem?
3. What information did Charles give to support his belief that the colt could have wings?
4. If you had a chance to observe the winged colt with Charles, what information would you keep notes about?

Applying Reading Skills

Number your paper from 1 to 3. Use complete sentences to answer each question below.

1. If you wanted to find out about palomino colts, what topic would you look for in an encyclopedia? What cross-reference might the article have?
2. Mrs. Minney was writing a book about the cliff dwellers, a group of North American Indians. What topics might she look for in an encyclopedia to find out more about them?
3. Charles mentioned paintings of horses with handshaped marks like wings. He said they were found in caves in France. What topics might you look for to find more information about these paintings?

I, Icarus

There was a time when I could fly. I swear it.
Perhaps, if I think hard for a moment,
   I can even tell you the year.
My room was on the ground floor at the rear of the house.
My bed faced a window.
Night after night I lay on my bed and willed myself to fly.
It was hard work, I can tell you.
Sometimes I lay perfectly still for an hour before I felt
   my body rising from the bed.
I rose slowly, slowly until I floated three or four feet
   above the floor.
Then, with a kind of swimming motion, I propelled
   myself toward the window.
Outside, I rose higher and higher, above the pasture
   fence, above the clothesline, above the dark,
   haunted trees beyond the pasture.
And, all the time, I heard the music of flutes.
It seemed the wind made this music.
And sometimes there were voices singing.

Alden Nowlan

WRITING ACTIVITY

WRITE A COMIC STRIP STORY

Prewrite

The winged colt in "Texas Pegasus" was a surprise to Uncle Coot, Charles, and Mrs. Minney. Imagine what will happen when the colt grows up and learns to fly. Imagine you are Charles. You can fly anywhere on the winged horse and have any adventure. You are going to write a comic strip story about an adventure with the winged horse. If you don't want to draw the comic strip alone, perhaps you and a friend can work together.

An adventure comic strip story is like any other story. There are characters, setting, and a plot. To get ready to write your comic strip story, think about the pictures. Remember, the setting and much of the action will be shown in the pictures. You will tell the story by the conversations among the characters. You may wish to use "balloons" to show what the characters say.

You must plan the characters, setting, and the events in the plot of your story. Plan the pictures for each part of the plot. You may want to do a story board to plan your comic strip story. A story board has a sketch of each picture in the comic strip and notes about what the characters will say.

Write

1. Read your story board notes and look at the sketches.
2. Write the sentences the characters in each picture will say. Remember to tell the events in a sensible sequence.
3. Your audience will want to predict the outcome of the story as they read. Therefore, you must make sure you give clues about what might happen next without giving away the ending of the story.
4. Make sure the details in your pictures are clear. The pictures in a comic strip story tell much about the action, setting, and plot of the story. They also show how the people feel by the expressions on their faces and their actions.
5. Use your Glossary or dictionary for spelling help.

Revise

Read your comic strip story. Did you tell the story in a sensible sequence? Do the pictures match what the characters say? Do your pictures show the feelings of the characters as well as the actions? If you need to rewrite to make your story more exciting or interesting, do so now.

1. Did you spell words correctly?
2. Did you use verbs that explain the action of the story clearly?
3. Did you use correct end punctuation for each sentence?

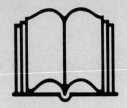

PREPARING FOR READING

Learning Vocabulary

1. Birds have <u>mastered</u> the <u>ability</u> of true flight.
2. A bird's body has a <u>streamlined</u> shape.
3. A feather may look simple, but it is actually very <u>complicated</u>.
4. A feather is a <u>structure</u> made up of many parts.

mastered   ability   streamlined
complicated   structure

Developing Background and Skills
Main Idea

Suppose you wanted to know what makes birds different from other animals. You might look up an article on birds in an encyclopedia. The first paragraph you read may be similar to the one below.

What exactly is a bird? You might say that a bird is an animal that flies. But not all birds fly. There are also other animals, including some insects and mammals, that fly. Birds, however, are the only animals that have feathers. Feathers, not flying, make birds different from all other animals. All birds have two legs and, whether they fly or not, they have a pair of wings.

The writers of the paragraph had an important point to make. The most important point in a paragraph is called the **main idea.**

The main idea of a paragraph is often found in a single sentence. The sentence may be found at the beginning, in the middle, or at the end of the paragraph.

Which sentence states the main idea of the paragraph about birds?

1. Birds are animals that may or may not fly.
2. All birds have wings.
3. Birds are different from all other animals in having feathers.

The third sentence states the main idea. It presents the most important information in the paragraph. The writer presented the main idea in the middle of the paragraph.

The other sentences present supporting details, or information that explains the main idea.

As you read the next selection, look for the main idea of each paragraph. Find the details that support the main idea.

A BIRD'S BODY

Contour Feather

Down Feather

Ornamental Feather

Joanna Cole

A bird's body seems to have been designed by nature as a living flying machine. Birds can cruise easily at speeds of twenty to fifty miles an hour. They can fly for a thousand miles or more without stopping. No other animals alive today except insects and bats have mastered the ability of true flight.

One feature sets birds apart from every other animal: they are the only creatures in the world that have feathers.

Except for its beak, feet, and legs, a bird is completely covered with feathers. There are different kinds of feathers for different uses.

Smooth contour feathers cover a bird's body, wings, and tail. These feathers give the bird its streamlined *contour*, or shape. A contour feather has a stiff shaft in the center and a flat *web*, or vane, on each side.

Beneath the contour feathers, many birds have a layer of fluffy down feathers for warmth. Some birds have special ornamental feathers for decoration.

Of all the feathers, the most important for flying are the contour feathers on the wing. They are known as the *flight feathers*. The flight feathers are attached to the

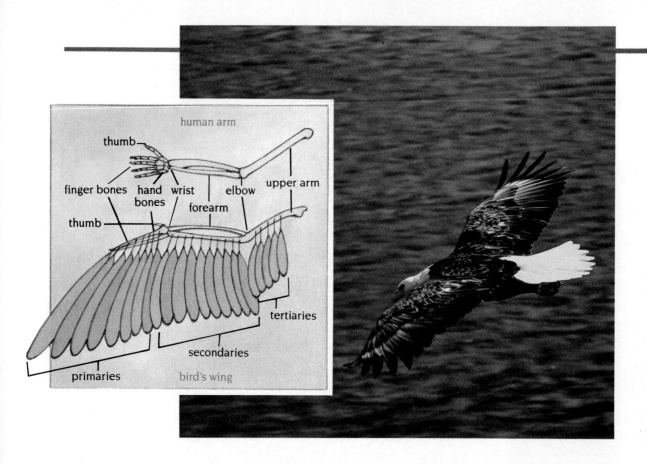

bird's wing bones by a *membrane,* or thin layer of skin. Because the bird's ancestors did not fly, the origin of the wing was a foreleg, or arm. The inner part of the wing is made up of the arm bones. The outer tip is supported by the hand bones. Many of the hand and finger bones are fused together, but the thumb bone is still separate.

There are three kinds of flight feathers. The ones at the outer edge of the wing are attached to the hand bones. These long feathers are very important for flying. They are called *primaries,* or first feathers.

The feathers that attach to the forearm bones are called *secondaries,* or second feathers. Those that attach to the upper arm bone are called *tertiaries* (tėr′ shē ãr′ ēz), or third feathers.

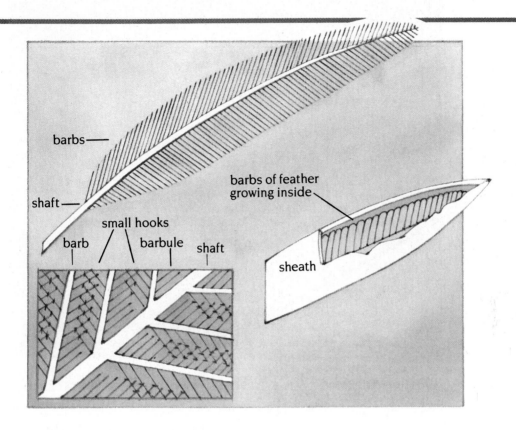

barbs—

shaft—

small hooks

barb   barbule   shaft

barbs of feather
growing inside

sheath

These feathers may look simple, but each one is actually a complicated structure. A single flight feather can have more than a million parts!

On each side of the feather's central shaft is a flat web. The web is made up of hundreds of smaller shafts called *barbs*. Branching out from each barb are hundreds of still smaller shafts called *barbules*. On each barbule are hundreds of tiny hooks that can be seen only through a microscope. These hooks hold the barbules together and keep the feather in shape.

As the bird moves around, the barbs may be pulled apart. When this happens, the bird "zips" them up again by drawing the feather through its beak. This is known as *preening* the feathers. A bird works hard to keep its

feathers in good flying order. It may spend several hours each day preening.

Once or twice a year birds *molt*, or shed, the old feathers. When feathers become worn, they are pushed out a few at a time by new ones. A new feather grows inside a horny *sheath*, or covering. When the new feather is fully formed, the sheath splits open.

The heavier a flying machine is, the more energy it uses to fly. To save energy, a flying machine is built to be as light as possible. A bird is also built for lightness. Its bones are extra thin. Many of them are hollow. Its feathers have hollow shafts. Instead of heavy jawbones and teeth, a bird has a lightweight beak made of thin, horny material.

Once in the air, a bird is a lightweight, fuel-efficient, feathered flying machine. Even more than that, it is beautiful to see.

Questions

1. How many kinds of flight feathers does a bird have? What are they called?
2. What advantage does being lightweight have for a bird?
3. Why is molting important for birds?
4. If you were designing a flying machine, what would it be like? How would you make it lightweight and fuel efficient?

Applying Reading Skills

Number your paper from 1 to 5. Find the paragraph from which each of the sentences below was taken. Read the paragraphs. Then decide whether the sentence is a main idea or a supporting detail. Write your answers.

1. Birds can cruise easily at speeds of twenty to fifty miles an hour.
2. Of all the feathers, the most important for flying are the contour feathers on the wing.
3. On each side of the feather's central shaft is a flat web.
4. On each barbule are hundreds of tiny hooks that can be seen only through a microscope.
5. A bird is also built for lightness.

PREPARING FOR READING

Learning Vocabulary

1. The cranes waded in the marsh grass ready to <u>strike</u> for food.
2. They <u>pierced</u> their prey with their sharp beaks.
3. A feeling of <u>trust</u> can develop between people and some animals.
4. The injured crane kept its <u>distance</u> from the girl.
5. The girl's body was <u>rigid</u> with fear when she saw the snake.

strike   pierced   trust
distance   rigid

Developing Background and Skills
Cause and Effect

When you read, you find out how things are related to one another. One way in which things or events are related to one another is called **cause and effect**. In a cause-and-effect relationship, one event or action, the cause, results in another event or action, the effect.

Sometimes a writer uses signal words such as *because*, *so*, *in order to*, or *since*, to help you recognize cause-and-effect relationships.

The girl screamed because she saw a snake.

In the sentence above, a cause-and-effect relationship is signaled by the word *because*. The effect, the girl's screaming, was caused by her seeing the snake.

The girl saw the snake moving across the floor. Suddenly she began to scream.

The two sentences above are also related by cause and effect. You must figure out the relationship because no signal word is used. In the example above, the cause and effect are the same as they are in the first example. However, they are stated in two separate sentences.

To figure out cause-and-effect relationships, you should ask yourself "What happened?" The answer will tell you the effect. Then ask yourself "Why did this happen?" The answer will tell you the cause.

As you read the next selection, think about how the events and actions are related. Look for cause-and-effect relationships.

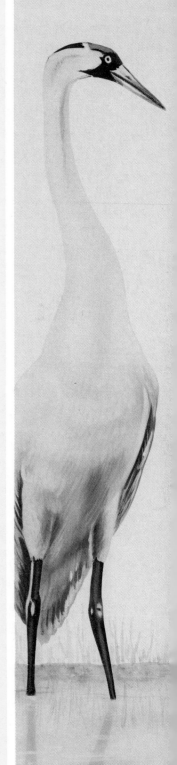

269

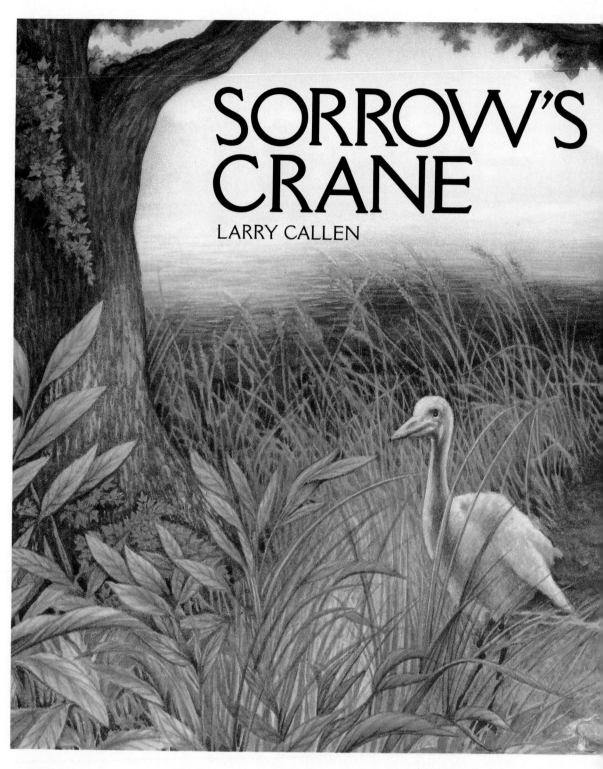

SORROW'S
CRANE

LARRY CALLEN

Sorrow is an unusual name for a girl, but Sorrow was an unusual girl. She couldn't speak, but she had ways to make herself understood. One way was writing, and she carried pencil and paper wherever she went. Drawing was another way she used to communicate. At times Sorrow also used a willow whistle.

Sorrow's best friend also has an unusual name—Pinch. When Sorrow discovers a small crane with an injured wing, she takes Pinch to Blind River. She and Pinch watch as the crane tries to fly, but fails. They both realize that winter will soon make it hard for the crane to find food. They decide to capture the bird and care for it until it is well.

No one followed Sorrow and me down the road toward Blind River after school. When we got close, we stopped by a big oak tree and waited. I looked behind and to all sides. We seemed to be alone, but there were so many other trees and shadows, someone could be watching from anywhere.

The small brownish crane was down the shoreline a ways, feeding in some marsh grass. We put a trail of corn on the shore and I ducked behind some bushes. Sorrow put on wading boots and moved slowly out into the water behind the crane. It saw her coming and stopped feeding. Then Sorrow started chasing it to shore. When the crane saw the corn it slowed down and I flipped the sack.

That was it! We had a squawking, unhappy bird in a sack. It weighed about as

much as a watermelon so it wasn't too hard to carry. At least not for the first quarter mile. Then, before my arms fell off, Sorrow stopped me and grabbed hold of one part of the sack. We made a kind of hammock out of it.

We snuck around behind Sorrow's house and strung chicken wire around some trees in the woods. We checked the bird's wing before turning it loose. There wasn't anything broken. One wing was bent kind of funny. I was thinking maybe this bird just wasn't meant to fly.

Sorrow thought differently.

"The wing will mend," she wrote me. "I know it."

She tried being friendly with the crane. She threw it a handful of corn, but it didn't pay one bit of attention to the corn. It just stood there, watching.

It wouldn't eat. It wouldn't let us come near. That's the

way it stayed for about three days. Then one morning early we came up on it scratching in the dirt for grubs. Sorrow threw it a handful of acorns. It gobbled them so fast, you could almost count the acorns slipping down its long neck. After that we had to work hard to feed it. Most evenings Sorrow put me to work catching little fish and crabs with a net. She figured the crane needed a treat once in a while.

Things were nice. The crane was safe. Sorrow was happy. That lasted for a week.

We took good care of the crane. The trouble is, that's all we did. Find acorns and catch little fish! That's all Sorrow wanted to do. I had really started to like the crane, but chores are chores, even when you're doing them for Sorrow's crane.

"Sorrow, let's take a walk to Red Bluff and see if we can find some arrowheads?" I asked her. She picked up the bent bucket we kept the little fish in and put it in my hand. But I put it down on the ground.

"I'm not going to do it!" I told her. "I'm tired of messing with that crane. It was fun for a little while, but it's not fun anymore."

She tilted her head kind of sideways, like the crane did when it was puzzled. I stared straight at her, but I never could say no to Sorrow. So I pretty quick stopped staring.

"I'm going to see if Charley wants to find some arrowheads," I told her. And I left.

I didn't want to find arrowheads. I mean, maybe I did, but that wasn't the main thing. It's not doing things. It's who you do things with. Charley is pretty nice. At least some of the time. But it's not the same hunting arrowheads with Charley and hunting arrowheads with Sorrow. I don't know why that is.

Three days later I went back to Sorrow's house. Sorrow was sitting on the cold, damp ground, staring at the crane. The crane wasn't paying her one bit of attention.

I walked over and picked up the fish bucket and started toward the road and Blind River. I hadn't gone ten feet before I heard her running after me. Her hand touched my arm and I turned and gave her a little bit of a grin.

"A fellow can get pretty tired of playing with Charley," I told her.

Her eyes twinkled. She reached over and took hold of the wire handle so we could carry the bucket together.

In the few days I had been away, the bird had changed.

The brown splotches were melting away. The crane was slowly turning pure white, except for the black mittens on the tip of its wings.

Other things had changed, too. Sorrow wanted to cuddle the bird but it wasn't about to let her do it. It wasn't interested in being anybody's friend.

I watched Sorrow trying to touch the crane. She turned quickly and saw me looking at her. She dug out her pencil and paper and wrote me a note.

"I think it's a girl crane," she wrote. "She's beautiful."

The bird kept its distance, staring at Sorrow every once in a while. She went in the pen and held out a handful of corn, standing perfectly still for the longest time. But the crane didn't seem interested at all. It was getting very late. When the cold air got to me, I stood up.

"I'm going home, Sorrow."

She looked out at me and nodded, but kept standing there, hoping for the crane to come to her.

"Why does it stare at us like that?" I asked her. She shrugged her shoulders.

When I got home I asked Mom the same question. She was fixing one of Dad's socks.

"Suppose there was an animal and it was sick and you tried to take care of it and it wouldn't let you come close. All it would do is stare at you."

"What kind of animal are we talking about, Pinch?"

"Just any old animal."

"Well, son, if it was a dog that would be strange, 'cause there's a certain trust, say, between a man and a dog. But if it was a fox, or a rabbit, or maybe a skunk, well, that would be a pretty regular thing for it to do."

"Suppose it was a big bird?"

"I think big birds would feel like rabbits do, son."

I told her how the crane would only stare at us.

"It doesn't really bother me much, but it does Sorrow. She would like to touch it."

"That's just the way things are, Pinch. That's the way love is. Love doesn't work the way Sorrow wants it to."

She put away her sewing and stood up.

"Sorrow ought to get a puppy. Puppies know how to give love back," she said.

When I went outside, Dad was working on the gate. He had a brand new hinge in his hand and was about to nail it on when he saw me. He stopped working.

"Been waiting for you, Pinch. I want to get a good look at that big crane from close up." Mom was watching from the porch. She took off her apron and said she would like to go too. We headed down the road, talking while we walked.

"Listen to that mockingbird sing," Mom said. "I guess I like birds 'cause I like music." She smiled at me. "I'm not talking about roosters, now, Pinch. A rooster barely makes it as a bird. More like a loud-mouthed lizard with wings and bad manners. You write down your ten favorite birds, nobody in his right mind will write down a rooster."

"You are right, Victoria," my dad said, smiling. "But if I was writing down my ten favorite dinners, chicken would be right at the top."

"It's fried chicken tonight, Will Grimball, so you can quit your hinting about what I ought to fix."

We moved away from the road and into the woods before we got to Sorrow's house. She was at the chicken wire pen. She had the bucket of acorns and was trying to feed the crane. It had been eating from her hand, but moved off when we got there.

"Look at that big bird!" Dad said. "It's bigger than you are, Pinch."

"Does it sing?" Mom asked. She went inside the pen and took a handful of acorns to help feed the crane. Sorrow nodded that it did. But the crane's bugling sound always sent a chill through me.

There were too many people around, and the crane walked slowly away to the other side of the pen. Mom switched her attention to the Rhode Island Red and her chicks that Sorrow had brought as company for the crane. Mom walked over toward them.

There was something on the ground!

"Here, little chick-chick." Mom knelt down on the ground near the chicks. She stuck her hand in her dress pocket and pulled out a piece of white bread. She had come prepared to feed a bird, crane or otherwise.

Something brown near the fence!

One chick came near and poked at the bread. It was a pretty little yellow ball of fur. It started peeping, and in a minute a half-dozen little chicks were pecking away only touching distance from Mom as she knelt on the ground.

Something was slithering along the ground!

"Here, little chick-chick," Mom said. She reached out and carefully lifted one up. She put it to her face and nudged its beak with her nose. She was having the best time of her life.

I looked at Sorrow, wanting to see her smile.

She was standing rigid, her fists clenched. Her eyes were on the ground, watching. Her mouth was open to scream but no scream came. My eyes jerked to where Sorrow was staring.

There was a copperhead slithering slowly across the yard! It was after one of those baby chicks!

My mom's back was turned to the snake. She was cooing to the chicks. Dad was busy watching her have her fun. He smiled. He didn't see the snake coming.

Sorrow saw it! She couldn't yell. She couldn't even whisper a warning. The yell was screeching from my chest for Dad to help when the willow whistle sounded.

"Whhhhhooooo!"

Dad looked to Sorrow. The whistle was still in her mouth. She stabbed her arm toward the snake. The copperhead had crawled to the edge of Mom's skirt and stopped.

"Victoria," Dad said softly.

Her head came up slowly. There had been a warning in

his voice and she had heard it in the single word.

"Don't move. Not an eyelid." He ran as he spoke. "There's a copperhead after the chicks and it's close enough to you to strike. Don't move."

The copperhead sat still, tongue darting out. Then it started to slide. The rustle of the snake on the cloth drove all the other sounds away. Mom heard. It was the loudest noise in the whole, wide world.

The crane watched the snake's every move. The crane's long black legs carried it slowly across the yard.

"Hssssssssss!" It was the crane that hissed, not the snake.

It was over terribly fast. The crane lifted both its huge black-tipped wings and hopped in the air. The snake faced the crane and struck. The crane hopped again, dropping down, wings flapping, beak stabbing.

The long, sharp beak pierced the head of the copperhead again and again. By the time Dad dashed through the gate there was no life left in the snake.

Mom trembled. She stood up slowly. Dad was at her side. She held onto him for a minute. The little chicks kept pecking away at the bread. The crane moved to where Sorrow had thrown the acorns and pecked at one.

I walked Sorrow home. When we got to her house, there was a worried look on her face. She took out her pencil and paper and we talked.

"I saw the copperhead. I wanted to scream," she said. "If it had bit your mom, it would've been 'cause I didn't warn her in time."

When I got home, Mom had already put the fried chicken on the table. Dad was out back, fixing something.

"Wash up, Pinch, and help me finish setting the table."

I put out the plates and the knives and the forks. I mashed the warm potatoes and mixed in the butter and the cream. Mom carried over the plate of steaming fried chicken.

"Pinch, I was never so proud of Sorrow as I was this afternoon. If she hadn't warned us with that whistle when she did, no telling what would've happened."

After supper Dad and I sat on the front steps and talked about it.

"Son, a bird doesn't go after a snake unless it can't do much else. I would've figured the crane to hop out of the way. Why did it attack? It didn't know your mom, and it sure wasn't worried about those little chicks. It's a strange bird, Pinch."

A brave one is what it is. It was protecting Sorrow is what it was doing.

Questions

1. How did Sorrow and Pinch capture the injured crane?
2. Why do you think the crane wouldn't eat at first?
3. Do you think Pinch was right when he said that the crane attacked the snake to protect Sorrow? Explain your answer.
4. Have you ever cared for an injured animal? Describe your experience.

Applying Reading Skills

Number your paper from 1 to 5. Then complete each sentence below by writing a cause or an effect. Write each sentence on your paper. Underline the cause once. Underline the effect twice.

1. Sorrow carried pencil and paper with her because she _____.
2. Pinch was tired of finding food for the crane so he _____.
3. Sorrow put a Rhode Island Red and its chicks into the pen with the crane because she _____.
4. When Pinch's Mom and Dad came to see the crane, it _____.
5. In order to warn Pinch's mother, Sorrow _____.

BE LIKE THE
BIRD

Be like the bird, who
Halting in his flight
On limb too slight
Feels it give way beneath him,
Yet sings
Knowing he hath wings.

Victor Hugo

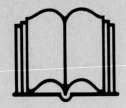

PREPARING FOR READING

Learning Vocabulary

1. When an airplane takes off, it climbs upward at an angle.
2. Then it levels off to fly on a horizontal path.
3. Pilots can reduce the speed of a plane by making slight adjustments.
4. They must often vary their flight pattern based on directions given by the ground crew.

angle   horizontal   reduce
slight   vary

Developing Background and Skills
Follow Directions

Before an airplane leaves the ground, the flight attendants ask for the attention of the passengers on board. They explain some important information. Part of that information is a set of **directions** for fastening seat belts.

The attendants check to make sure that the passengers have followed their directions. They know that if seat belts are not properly fastened, passengers could be hurt by an unexpected jolt or bump.

You will follow directions better if you know a few facts about them. Directions can be written or oral. They may be presented with pictures or diagrams. All directions are organized into a series of steps that are in a certain sequence. One step must be done before you move on to the next step.

To help you understand the sequence, the steps in directions are often numbered, as 1, 2, 3, and 4. Some directions are lettered in alphabetical order, as A, B, C, and D. Sometimes directions have clue words such as *first*, *second*, *then*, *next*, or *last* to show the sequence.

As you read the next selection, "Paper Airplanes," you will find many directions. One set of instructions, or directions, tells you how to make a paper airplane. Other directions tell you what to do in order to see certain effects. As you read the selection, think about how the directions help you.

P·A·P·E·R AIRPLANES

Seymour Simon

Have you ever flown a paper airplane?
Sometimes it twists and loops through the
air and then comes to rest, soft as a feather.
Other times a paper airplane climbs straight
up, flips over, and dives headfirst into the
ground.

What keeps a paper airplane in the air?

How can you make a paper airplane go on a long flight? How can you make it loop or turn? Does flying a paper airplane on a windy day help it stay aloft? What can you learn about real airplanes by making and flying paper airplanes? Let's experiment to discover some of the answers.

HOW TO CONSTRUCT

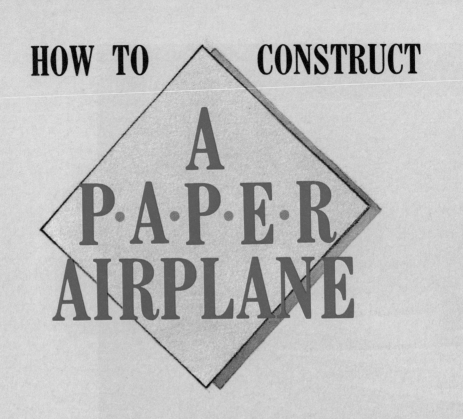

A P·A·P·E·R AIRPLANE

Let's make a paper airplane. Use a sheet of 8½-by-11-inch paper. For this plane you can also use heavy art paper or construction paper.

1 Fold the paper in half lengthwise (A). Run your thumbnail along the fold to crease it sharply. Open the paper and fold one corner down toward the center (B). Fold the other corner down in the same way (C).

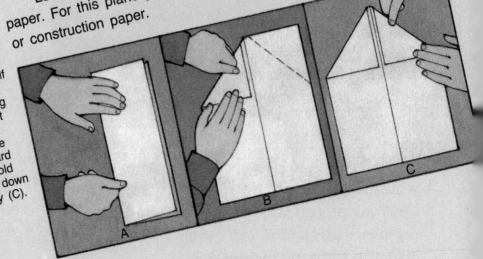

2 Fold one side again toward the center (E) along the dotted line shown in drawing D. Fold the other side (F) along the other dotted line. Make sure the folds are sharply creased.

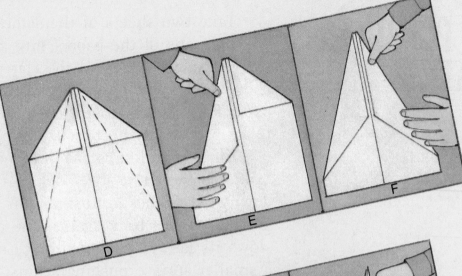

3 Turn the paper over. Fold one side over (H) along the left-hand dotted line shown in drawing G. Open the paper. Fold the other side over (I) along the right-hand dotted line in drawing G. From the bottom your plane should look like the one in drawing J.

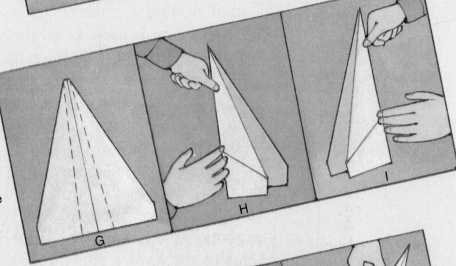

4 Use a piece of tape to hold the body of the plane together and to give the wings a slight upward tilt (K).

P·A·P·E·R AIRPLANES

Take two sheets of the same-sized paper. Crumple one of the papers into a ball. Hold the crumpled paper and the flat paper high above your head. Drop them both. Which paper falls to the ground first? What seems to keep the flat sheet from falling quickly?

Air is a real substance even though you can't see it. A flat sheet of paper falling downward pushes against the air in its path. The air pushes back against the paper and slows its fall. A crumpled piece of paper has a smaller surface pushing against the air. The air doesn't push back as strongly against the crumpled sheet as it does against the flat piece, and the ball of paper falls faster. Like the flat paper, the wings of a paper airplane keep it from falling quickly. We say the wings give a plane *lift*.

You want a paper airplane to do more than just fall slowly through the air. You want it to move forward. You make a paper airplane move forward by throwing it. Usually the harder you throw a paper airplane, the farther it will fly. The forward movement of an airplane is called *thrust*.

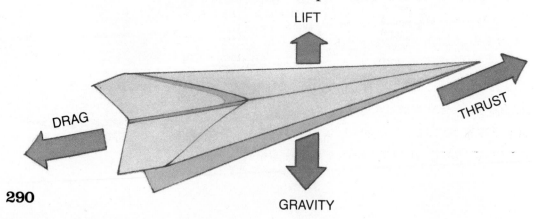

The front edges of the wings of a real airplane are usually tilted slightly upward. The air pushes against the tilted underside of the wings, giving the plane lift. If the angle of the tilt is too great, however, the air slows down the forward movement of the plane. This is called *drag*.

Drag works to slow a plane down, as thrust works to make it move forward. At the same time, lift works to make a plane go up, as gravity tries to make it fall down. These four forces are always working on paper airplanes just as they work on real airplanes.

Launch your plane in a large room or out-of-doors. Make sure that there are no easily broken objects it can hit and knock over. Hold the *fuselage* (fū′ sə läzh′), or body, of the plane between your thumb and forefinger a few inches back from its nose. Raise your hand high over your head and throw the plane gently forward. Throw the plane at a slight upward angle to the ground. If the plane climbs steeply and then dives into the ground, adjust the angle of thrust a bit downward. If the plane just dives into the ground, adjust the angle upward. Which angle of launch gives you the longest flights?

Try making some slight changes in the design of your paper airplane. With a pair of scissors, make two ½-inch cuts (about 1½ inches apart) in the back edge of each wing.

P·A·P·E·R AIRPLANES

Fold the paper between the cuts at a slight upward angle. This will form flaps on the back of each wing.

Launch the plane with the flaps at this upward angle. How do the flaps seem to change the way the plane flies? Fold the flaps flat again and see how the plane flies without them.

Try flying the plane with the flaps folded at a slightly downward angle. How does this flight compare with the others?

The flaps change the direction of the flight. As the plane moves through the air, the flaps push against the air. With an equal force, the air pushes back against the flaps.

Fold the flaps downward and push against them with your fingers. Now launch

the plane. The back end of the plane is pushed up. The front end points down, and the plane dives.

Change the angle at which you bend the flaps. Try flying the plane now. Does the angle of the flaps seem to make a difference in the plane's flight? Using flaps can add to the plane's lift.

Fold one flap very slightly upward and the other flap very slightly downward. Fly the plane to see what happens. If the plane spins around, reduce the angle of the folds. Reverse the direction of the folds of each flap. Which way does the plane turn now?

Most real airplanes have flaps on their wings and on the *horizontal stabilizers* in the tail of the plane. The flaps on the wings

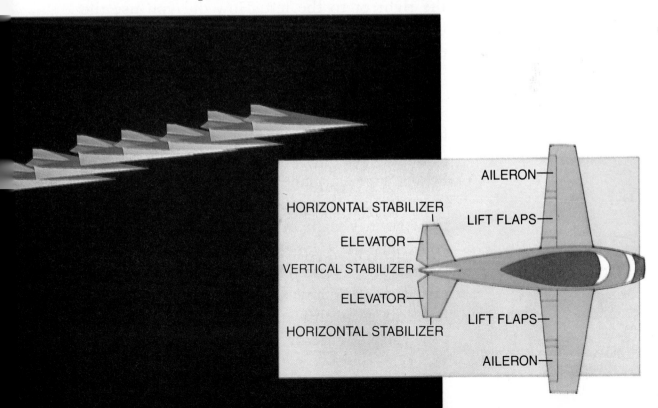

AILERON

HORIZONTAL STABILIZER

LIFT FLAPS

ELEVATOR

VERTICAL STABILIZER

ELEVATOR

HORIZONTAL STABILIZER

LIFT FLAPS

AILERON

P·A·P·E·R AIRPLANES

are used to increase the lift during take-offs and landings, when the plane is moving at its slowest speeds. Remember that the slower the plane moves through the air, the less lift it gets. The pilot can vary the angle of the flaps to change the amount of lift.

The flaps in the back edge of the horizontal stabilizers are called *elevators*. Just like the flaps in the wing of a paper airplane, they make a real plane's nose point up—or down. This allows the pilot to reach the right altitude and to adjust this height during flight.

Set alongside the lift flaps on the wings of a real plane is another set of flaps called *ailerons* (ā′ lə ronz′). These are tilted in opposite directions to make the plane roll to the right or to the left. How did you use the flaps on your paper airplane in these different ways?

Building and flying paper airplanes is fun for young people and adults too. Several years ago the magazine *Scientific American* held a paper-airplane contest. It received almost twelve thousand entries. Entries came from twenty-eight different countries. Maybe you can hold a contest among your own friends or in your school. You might be surprised at the many different models entered. It seems as if almost everyone has a favorite paper airplane he or she likes to fly.

Questions

1. What four forces are always working on paper airplanes and real airplanes as they move through the air?
2. What happened when you launched your paper airplane with the wing flaps at an upward angle?
3. How do the elevators on a real airplane allow the pilot to reach higher altitudes during flight?
4. Would you like to be an airplane pilot or a flight attendant? Why or why not? What other jobs can you think of that would involve working with airplanes?

Applying Reading Skills

The following directions tell you how to reach the center of the maze below. Follow the directions and use your fingers or the eraser end of a pencil to trace the route to the center of the maze.

ENTRY

1. Enter maze and turn left; continue until there is a choice of ways.
2. Turn right; continue past next three openings on right; at next choice of ways, turn left.
3. Continue past next opening on right; at next choice of ways, turn left; continue to next choice of ways.
4. Turn left and continue to center of maze.

PREPARING FOR READING

Learning Vocabulary

1. When the field of <u>aviation</u> first began to boom, women <u>aviators</u> weren't taken seriously.
2. Harriet Quimby was a <u>competent</u> pilot who decided to attempt a <u>feat</u> that was daring at the time.
3. As she flew over the Channel's <u>notoriously</u> rough, choppy waters, she began to feel the damp, <u>penetrating</u> cold.

aviation	aviators	competent
feat	notoriously	penetrating

Developing Background and Skills
Main Idea

You know that the **main idea** states the most important information in a paragraph. Read the paragraph below and find the main idea.

In 1911, the field of aviation was booming. Only eight years had passed since the Wright brothers' first flight. Flying schools were opening in Europe and America. Crowds flocked to air races. New flight records were being set every month. Improved flying machines were being designed and built.

Which of the sentences below best states the main idea of the paragraph?

1. The Wright brothers made the first flight in 1903.
2. By 1911, new and improved flying machines were being built.
3. In 1911, the field of aviation was booming.

A good writer does more than make an important point in a paragraph. A good writer also provides details that support, or tell more about, the main idea. What details support the main idea in the paragraph?

You should have found four supporting details.

1. Flying schools were opening.
2. Crowds went to air races.
3. New flight records were being set.
4. Improved flying machines were being built.

When you read, you should try to figure out the main idea of each paragraph. You should also try to identify the details that tell more about, or support, the main idea.

As you read the next selection, you will learn more about Harriet Quimby and the history of aviation. What important information are you given? What details help support the main ideas you read about?

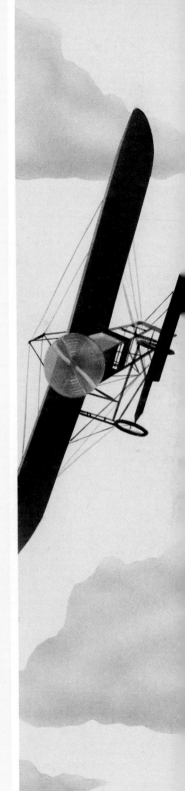

Harriet Quimby
Pioneer Aviator

Sherwood Harris

On December 17, 1903, two men stood on the sand dunes near Kitty Hawk, North Carolina. They were tossing a coin. Nearby rested a machine that was part bicycle and part kite.

The men were Orville and Wilbur Wright. The machine was *The Flyer*. Wilbur lost the toss. Orville climbed into the airplane and started the engine. The airplane picked up speed and slowly rose into the air. For 59 seconds *The Flyer* stayed in the air. When Orville touched down, the age of aviation had begun.

In 1911, just eight years after the Wright brothers' first flight, the new field of aviation was booming. Flying schools opened in the United States and Europe. Air races drew enormous crowds. Records were being set almost every month as better flying machines were built.

The first men who took to the air were thought of as heroes. But a woman who wanted to fly was considered slightly odd. At that time, women were expected to stay at home. The Wright brothers would not teach women at all in their flying school in Dayton, Ohio.

Still, a small but determined group of women in France and the United States were among the first pilots. By the end of 1911, three American women—Harriet Quimby, Matilde Moisant, and Blanche Scott—had earned their licenses. "Flying seems easier than voting," said Harriet Quimby, and in fact it was. The Constitutional amendment guaranteeing women the right to vote was not passed until 1920.

While still in her twenties, Harriet was drama critic and editor for *Leslie's Weekly*, a New York magazine. One evening, as she was working on an assignment for the magazine, she met some pilots who were in town for a big air show. From then on she was determined to become a pilot, too.

In the summer of 1911, Harriet Quimby passed her tests and received the first official pilot's license issued to a woman in the United States. Miss Quimby flew in the New York area for a while and made a barnstorming trip to Mexico with Matilde Moisant.

But women aviators still weren't taken seriously. Most newspapers devoted as much space to their flying suits as to their flying skill. So Harriet Quimby planned a flight that would earn the respect of other pilots and show the world what women fliers could really do. She decided to fly across the English Channel.

It's hard for us today to imagine that a flight across the English Channel could ever be considered a daring feat. The distance from Dover, on the English side, to the French port of Calais is only 22 miles (35 km). A modern jet takes less than five minutes to make the trip.

It was different in Harriet Quimby's time. Those 22 miles looked like one great, wet graveyard to most early pilots. On a clear, calm day it might not be so bad. But the Channel is hardly ever clear enough of fog and mist to see from one coast to another. Calm days are very few. The Channel's water is notoriously rough, choppy, and cold. To pilots who had learned from experience that their engines could easily quit every time thay made a flight, the Channel was the last place they would choose for a forced landing.

By the time Harriet Quimby decided to try the flight, several men pilots had managed it successfully. But one very competent English aviator had disappeared without a trace on a Channel flight in 1910. Many more had simply decided there were better places to fly.

In early March 1912, Harriet Quimby went to Paris to arrange a plane for her flight. She picked out a new monoplane. It was one of the finest aircraft of its day, but far from ideal for a flight out to sea. The cockpit was open and not even protected by a windshield. The engine had so little power that the plane couldn't take off if the wind was more than five miles per hour. In the air, the controls were hard to use. It often took a pilot several tries before he could get a turn started.

Harriet Quimby tried to get in some practice before setting out across the water. Each day she woke before dawn and went to the field where the plane was kept. Day after day, high winds kept her from flying. She shipped the plane to Dover, hoping that the weather would be better for practice on the other side of the Channel.

Sunday, April 14, was a perfect day for flying. The wind was calm, and from the airfield near Dover Castle, the young American could see the French coast in the distance. Her friends urged her to take off at once, but she made it a rule never to fly on Sunday. Bad weather set in again on Monday, but at 3:30 on

Tuesday morning it seemed to the crew at the field that conditions were improving. They put in a call to Miss Quimby at her hotel. She raced to the field. It was just getting light when the plane was rolled from its hangar and warmed up. The wind was calm and the sky was clear. Patches of fog were still drifting in from the sea.

Experienced pilots advised that it would be cold crossing the Channel in the open cockpit so Quimby dressed warmly. She wore two suits of long underwear under her satin flying suit, two overcoats over the suit, and a stole over her shoulders. At the last minute, someone handed her a hot-water bottle, which she tied to her waist.

These were the *only* preparations she made for flying the Channel. At 5:30 A.M. Harriet Quimby took off for a coast she couldn't see through the fog, in a plane she had never had a chance to try out. She had no maps, no instruments—except a compass—and no life jacket.

She climbed to about 1,500 feet (450 m), then circled back over Dover Castle so that a movie crew could film her departure. The fog was thicker now. In an instant the Cliffs of Dover were behind. The fog was thinner over the water. Quimby spotted a tugboat that had been sent out by a London newspaper to follow her flight and help her if she was forced down. But up ahead, the French coast was hidden by another wall of fog that stretched as far as she could see in either direction.

She plowed right into it. Moisture from the cloud bank drenched her plane and dripped from every surface in the open cockpit. Her goggles fogged up and she had to remove them. The warmth of the hot-water bottle soon disappeared in the damp, penetrating cold. Unable to see anything, she flew on by instinct alone.

All great pilots seem to have a powerful inner feeling about flying. When the odds turn against them, they seem to make the right moves without even thinking about them. So when the Channel fog closed around Harriet Quimby, she simply flew on. She guided the plane as best she could until something told her she was near the coast of France.

Then she nosed over and began her landing descent. With the ground covered by fog and with no altimeter aboard, she had no way of knowing how close she was getting to the ground. Down, down she went. Then suddenly the fog parted and she saw a sandy beach below! She had arrived in France.

She flew back and forth for a while to find the best place to land, then landed on the beach. For a few moments she was all alone. Then an excited crowd rushed up. Someone gave Quimby a mug of hot tea and bread and cheese. The people pushed the plane beyond the reach of the rising tide. In crossing the Channel in a flight that lasted a little more than 30 minutes, Harriet Quimby had become the most famous woman pilot in the world.

Questions

1. Write three sentences telling about Harriet Quimby.
2. Why did Harriet Quimby decide to attempt a flight across the English Channel?
3. What disadvantages made Harriet Quimby's flight over the Channel more dangerous than it might ordinarily have been?
4. Do you think Harriet Quimby's success might have changed the attitude of people toward women aviators? Explain your answer.

Applying Reading Skills

Number your paper from 1 to 5. Find each of the sentences below in the selection "Harriet Quimby—Pioneer Aviator." Then decide whether the sentence is a main idea or a supporting detail. Write your answers.

1. At that time, women were expected to stay at home.
2. Still, a small but determined group of women in France and the United States were among the first pilots.
3. Those 22 miles looked like one great, wet graveyard to most early pilots.
4. In the air, the controls were hard to use.
5. She had arrived in France.

TO AN
AVIATOR

You who have grown so intimate with stars
And know their silver drippings from your wings,
Swept with the breaking day across the sky,
Known kinship with each meteor that swings—
You who have touched the rainbow's fragile gold,
Carved lyric ways through dawn and dusk and rain
And soared to heights our hearts have only dreamed—
How can you walk earth's common ways again?

Daniel Whitehead Hicky

PREPARING FOR READING

Learning Vocabulary

1. The starship set its <u>course</u> for a distant star.
2. As the engines roared into action, the ship began to <u>vibrate</u>.
3. When his panic <u>ceased</u>, the spaceman began his descent to Earth.
4. He would have to be careful of his <u>precious</u> air supply to prevent a <u>disaster</u>.

course   vibrate   ceased
precious   disaster

Developing Background and Skills
Cause and Effect

You know that in a **cause-and-effect** relationship, one event or action, the cause, results in another event or action, the effect. Conditions and feelings, as well as events and actions, can be causes and effects.

When he found himself falling through space, the spaceman became frightened.

In this sentence, the effect, the spaceman's becoming frightened, was caused by his finding himself falling through space.

You have also probably noticed that a single event, action, condition, or feeling can be both an effect and a cause.

When the starship took off suddenly, the spaceman fell off into space. He became frightened.

In the sentences above, three things are described.

1. The starship took off suddenly.	Cause ↓
2. The spaceman fell off into space.	Effect Cause ↓
3. The spaceman became frightened.	Effect

The second sentence is a cause *and* an effect.

As you read the next selection, look for cause-and-effect relationships. Ask yourself whether the causes and effects are events, actions, conditions, or feelings. Try to figure out what effect in one cause-and-effect relationship is also a cause in another cause-and-effect relationship.

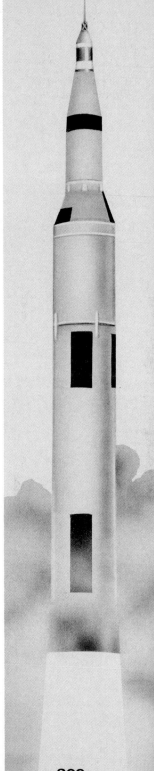

Lee Harding

The alien starship circled Earth many times before the spaceman fell.

The people inside the starship looked a little like us, but they were different in many ways.

They came from another world in a distant part of the galaxy.

They were small, like children, with tiny arms and legs. They had large eyes and pale faces and no hair at all, not even an eyelash. The tops of their heads were as smooth and as polished as apples.

Their voices were strange. To our ears their speech would sound more like music.

They moved around carefully. They were not very strong and their soft bones could be easily broken. They had made many clever machines to do most of their work. This gave them time to think and to play and otherwise enjoy themselves. In this way they were most like us.

They passed by our world on their way to another star. They were curious and decided to study Earth for a while. They swung their great starship into orbit and watched us through their powerful telescopes.

They could not be seen from Earth. They had a way of making their starship invisible, so they could carry out their work undisturbed.

They drew maps of our world and their powerful cameras made a valuable record of our way of life. After several long days, they finished their study and continued their journey.

They set course for a distant star. The whole ship began to vibrate as the mighty engines roared and pushed them away from Earth at a tremendous speed. In a matter of hours they would be clear of the solar system and heading in the direction of another star cluster.

But they made a terrible mistake. They forgot that Tyro was outside, working on the hull. . . .

Tyro was repairing a broken camera when suddenly, without warning, he felt the great starship shake under his feet.

He instantly recognized the deep vibration of the atomic engines starting up. Puzzled, he wondered what the engineers were doing, and why he hadn't been called inside. It was dangerous to be working on the hull when the engines were being tested.

He looked at the enormous tail of the starship, where the great engines pointed at the stars. At that moment the hull shook underneath him and the rockets fired.

The stars blurred and spun about him. The shock of the starship taking off sent him spinning away into space, tumbling over and over like a wheel. He was knocked unconscious and could not stop his wild tumbling through the deep darkness of space.

In minutes, the starship was thousands of miles away. By the time they discovered one of their crew was missing, they would be in another part of the galaxy. Meanwhile, Tyro kept falling. Spinning and falling in no particular direction, while the bold blue Earth swam beneath him.

It was some time before he came to. He saw the stars spinning around outside his faceplate and knew that something terrible had happened.

He leaned forward in his safety harness and moved one of the control levers. Several small rockets fixed to the outside of his spacesuit fired for a few seconds. When they ceased, his wild tumbling had stopped. The stars had ceased their mad dance but there was nothing else for him to see.

Where was the starship? And why hadn't they come back for him?

Tyro shivered. Never before had he felt so completely alone . . . and afraid.

His spacesuit was enormous. It was as tall as a five-story building. He sat inside it, in the center, protected by his safety webbing, like a spider in his web.

He was small and weak, but his spacesuit had great power. It was built like a small starship. In front of him was a control panel with many dials and switches, and behind it was a small computer that helped him to control his movements.

His spacesuit was powered by a small atomic engine. It was strong enough to move a starship into orbit or push a mountain to one side. There were

small rocket motors built into the arms and legs. By firing them carefully, he was able to move around in space.

He moved another lever. Then another. The spacesuit began to turn around. The stars moved to one side and the great blue globe of Earth appeared in his faceplate.

An aching sadness crept over him when he realized he was lost. What would he do if the starship did not return? He could not stay up here forever! His air would run out in a few more hours.

He tried not to think about that. Instead he thought of himself, drifting idly around Earth, waiting for a rescue that might never come.

Better to take his chances on the unknown world below! If he could reach it in safety, he would be able to keep alive until the starship returned—if it ever returned.

What would the air be like down there, he wondered. If it was unsuitable for breathing he would die an equally painful death. But at least he would have tried.

His head was clear now. He studied the control panel carefully. He had made up his mind to go down . . . and take his chances. There was no time to waste—every moment that ticked away used up a little more of his precious air supply.

It was a long way down to Earth. The descent would take several hours, and there was much that worried him about the journey.

He would fall at a great speed—so fast that his spacesuit would be burned up like a meteorite if he didn't use his rockets carefully. At the very last moment the computer would reverse them and direct their energy toward the ground, breaking his fall. With luck he would make a safe landing with fuel to spare.

The computer plotted a safe downward course. Tyro sat back and waited while it took over the controls and got the strange journey under way.

The huge spacesuit dipped slowly toward Earth. The beautiful blue world swam out of view. All he could see were the solemn stars.

He felt his shoulder rockets fire, gently pushing him down. He began to fall very fast.

Tyro was frightened for the first few minutes. But after a while he got used to the strange feeling and relaxed in his safety harness.

He thought about the unknown world below. He didn't know much about Earth. He wasn't a scientist.

He would have to find somewhere to hide while he waited for the starship, and that might not be so easy. But for the moment all he was concerned with was a safe landing.

Faster and faster fell the spaceman. The Earth grew large beneath him and nudged into view outside his faceplate—blue and bold and beautiful.

Soon the Earth had pushed everything else aside and filled his view. He could see patches of white clouds racing around it. He could see land, green and brown, through the gaps in the fleecy clouds. The great oceans threw back the sunlight and dazzled his weak eyes.

The oceans worried him—he didn't want to come down there! What he needed was a deep forest, far away from any cities, where he hoped he would be safe.

He entered Earth's atmosphere at a terrific rate. Clouds rushed past his faceplate and it grew suddenly hot inside the spacesuit. He sped across oceans and mountains, forests and jungles, deserts and rain forests. Cities flashed by underneath his spacesuit's gigantic feet. He saw all the Earth, but too fast for his tired eyes to follow.

The computer saw and recorded everything. It sorted through this information, looking for a suitable place to land.

Tyro could not have made such a swift descent without its help, and he relied upon it now to choose the right place for him to hide from the people of Earth.

Faster and faster he fell. Inside the spacesuit it was like an oven. It was so hot he could hardly breathe. He glanced away from the controls and out through the faceplate. He was over land again, and falling at a steep angle toward a wooded mountain range.

Will I make it alive, he wondered. The heat was burning him up. His eyes stung and his skin had begun to dry up.

Two miles up and falling! The wind buffeted his spacesuit like an angry fist.

The forest, rich and green, raced up from below in his faceplate. The computer was guiding him to a small clearing in the trees.

The bare ground reached up for him. Tyro felt a warm glow of relief. He closed his eyes.

He was only a few hundred feet above the forest when the computer fired the braking rockets. Flashes of fire flared at the feet of the spacesuit, slowing its dangerous fall.

But something inside the computer slipped. It corrected too much. The blackened spacesuit came to a sudden halt in midair, jiggling around as though a giant, invisible hand were shaking it.

Tyro was thrown forward—only his safety harness saved him from dashing his head against the control panel. He looked about, wild-eyed with surprise. Whatever was happening?

The spacesuit danced across the sky like something gone mad, rockets blazing. The fall had been checked, but the powerful surge of energy had thrown the spacesuit wildly off course.

Tyro saw what was happening. He reached forward to take manual control, but the panel would not respond; the levers were stiff and lifeless in his tiny hands!

Gradually the spacesuit steadied as the dazed computer realized what had happened. But by then it was too late to avoid disaster.

Tyro almost made it. The topmost branches of the trees were level with his faceplate when the spacesuit finally straightened up. And then . . .

The rockets coughed and died. The last drop of precious rocket fuel had been used up trying to stop the wild tumbling of the spacesuit.

The spaceman fell.

The air screamed past his faceplate. Tyro pressed an emergency button, and a second safety harness snapped around him, pinning him down.

He closed his eyes and waited. The ground rushed up to meet him. The tearing, crashing noise outside rose to a dreadful roar.

The spacesuit slammed into the ground with its speed unchecked. The shock rattled every bone in Tyro's body. The spacesuit toppled over and buried its great helmeted head in the ground. Tyro passed out. His last thought was that he was down at last. And alive!

Questions

1. Describe the spacemen on the alien starship. How were they like us? How were they different?
2. Why do you think the spacemen might have forgotten that Tyro was outside the starship when they took off?
3. Do you think Tyro's decision to come down to Earth was a good one? What alternative did he have?
4. What do you think might have happened to Tyro after he landed on Earth?

Applying Reading Skills

Copy the chart below on your paper. Fill in the missing information about cause-and-effect relationships from "The Fallen Spaceman."

Cause	Effect
The spacemen were curious.	They decided to study Earth for a while.
	The spacemen could carry out their work undisturbed.
The starship took off.	
	Tyro was knocked unconscious.
Tyro moved two levers.	
	Tyro fell and slammed into the ground.

THE CREW OF
APOLLO 8

Elaine V. Emans

Shall we call them poets, for having observed
on their earliest times around
the moon that it appeared to be layered
with a grayish white beach sand
with footprints in it? Or geologists
for having reported to us
the six or seven terraces leading down
into crater Langrenus?

Or shall we call them some new breed of bird
for having swiftly flown
weightless and unfearing and sharp-eyed
into the dark unknown?
Yet words to tell their skill and valiancy
are as weak as water—
and their return, and being earthlings with us
again, are what most matter.

WRITING ACTIVITY

WRITE A FRIENDLY LETTER

Prewrite

Tyro had a frightening experience in the story "The Fallen Spaceman." He made it to Earth alive, but he's not sure what will happen next. Imagine that Tyro keeps notes about his visit to Earth. He uses his notes to write a letter to his friend Yako. What do you think he would say?

Read the story again. Think about how the Earth and Tyro's planet compare. What things may be different and what things may be alike? The atmosphere must be the same or Tyro would have died at once. Space travel must be different. Tyro came on a starship from a distant part of the galaxy. We on Earth do not travel that far yet.

You will write Tyro's letter to Yako. As Tyro, you will want to compare things on Earth and things on your planet. The chart below can help you organize your thinking. Write sentence notes for each item on the chart.

	Tyro's planet	Earth
1. People and animals		
2. Transportation		
3. Homes and food		
4. Language and communication		

Write

1. Read the sentence notes from your chart.
2. You may want to begin Tyro's letter by telling Yako about all the ways Earth is like your planet. Then you can tell about all the ways the two planets differ.
3. Remember, Yako knows nothing about Earth. Try to use a clear main idea sentence in each paragraph. Your detail sentences should give facts about that main idea.
4. Because you are pretending to be Tyro, you will write in first person. You will use pronouns such as *I*, *me*, *mine*, *we*, and *ours*.
5. Look at a language book for the correct form for a friendly letter.
6. Use your Glossary or dictionary for spelling help.

Revise

Read your letter. When Yako has read your letter, will she have a clear picture of Earth and how it compares to your planet? If you have left out information or need to explain something more clearly, rewrite now.

1. Did you use correct punctuation and capitalization in each part of your letter?
2. Did you use the correct form for a friendly letter?

PREPARING FOR READING

Learning Vocabulary

1. Students need a teacher's <u>recommendation</u> to go to Space Camp.
2. They learn to use computers to make <u>calculations</u>.
3. Space suits help astronauts <u>survive</u> the <u>extremes</u> of temperature in space.
4. The zero-gravity machine gives a camper a floating <u>sensation</u> <u>similar</u> to being weightless.

recommendation	calculations	survive
extremes	sensation	similar

Developing Background and Skills
Main Idea

Most paragraphs you read have an important point that is called the **main idea**. Sometimes the writer states the main idea directly in a sentence that may be found at the beginning, in the middle, or at the end of the paragraph.

Read the paragraph on the next page. Look for the main idea.

Campers exercise every day. They use computers to build model rockets. They sample freeze-dried food. They try on space suits and use a zero-gravity machine. They train for recovery at sea. They learn how to use a robot arm. Kids at Space Camp train and learn just as real astronauts do.

In the paragraph above, the main idea is stated in the sentence at the end. The other information in the paragraph helps support the main idea. These details also add interest to the paragraph.

Supporting Details

exercise
use computers
eat freeze-dried food
try on space suits
use zero-gravity machine
train for recovery at sea
use robot arm

Kids at Space Camp train as astronauts do.

Main Idea

Look for the main ideas and supporting details as you read the next selection.

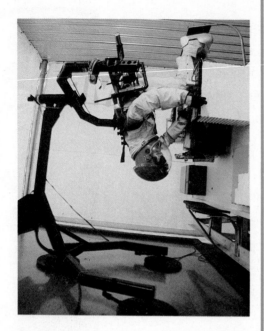

One of the devices campers discover at the Alabama Space and Rocket Center is called the Five Degrees of Freedom, or 5DF (right). The 5DF lets campers experience the feeling of weightlessness.

The 5DF is also used by campers involved in Extra Vehicular Activities, or work done outside the space capsule. The camper above is working upside down to repair the film canister loader on the outside of the capsule. His feet are in restraints that keep him in position.

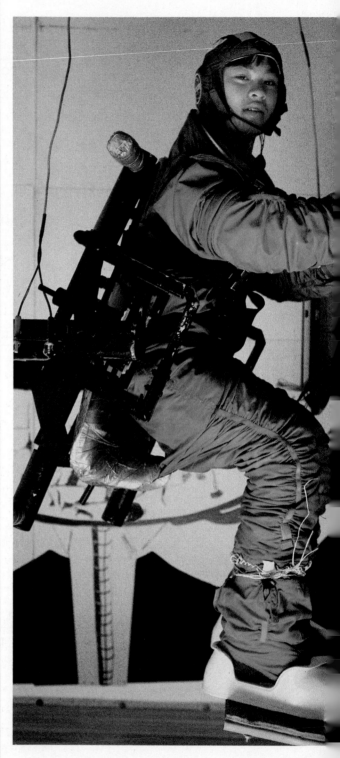

3-2-1 BLAST OFF!

William Teal

Imagine that you are a crew member on the space shuttle. You are zooming through space at thousands of miles an hour. Suddenly, the cockpit computer screen flashes—DANGER! A damaged container in the cargo bay is releasing a dangerous fluid. Should you end the mission and return to earth? Or should you see if the damage must first be repaired? To find out, you have to take a space walk. Your heart is racing as you put on your space suit and step out of the cabin. But you are not in space at all.

You're at Space Camp, in Huntsville, Alabama. It's at the world's largest space museum, the Alabama Space and Rocket Center. You're taking part in a training course for kids who want to know what it takes to survive in space.

A FAR-OUT EXPERIENCE

Kids ages 12 to 14 come from all over the United States to the Space Camp. They have a special interest in science and need a teacher's recommendation to join.

At the camp, kids use the equipment that was once used by NASA astronauts. Learning how to survive in space is not just something you can read about. Most of

Campers use the PLATO computer every day to learn more about the principles of space flight. If they touch a picture on the screen, the computer will explain what the picture shows.

Campers inside the space capsule (bottom right) communicate with Mission Control through headphones.

the equipment imitates the kind of action that would take place in space.

One machine imitates a space capsule. Another teaches astronauts how to walk on the moon. By practicing on such equipment, astronauts are ready when it's time for the real thing.

At the space center, campers start with some basic training. Day one is *rocketry day*. After morning exercises—the same kind the astronauts do—campers separate into groups of 10-member teams. Now they are ready to work with PLATO, the camp computer.

Without computers, space flight would be impossible. Even some of the calculations needed to get off the ground would take weeks to complete with only pencil and paper. Soon, campers use PLATO to figure out how to build model rockets. Of course, the model rockets that the kids build, and launch later in the week, don't have nearly as much power as space rockets. But they work the same basic way.

331

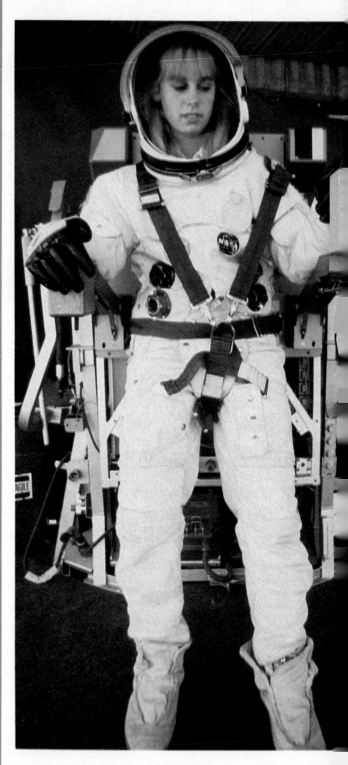

The Apollo Lunar Rover or moon buggy (above) is displayed in front of the Apollo Lunar Landing Module which is covered with gold heat-reflective foil.

Campers have a chance to try on the 21-layer space suit which is like the ones worn by astronauts on the Apollo 11, 12, and 14 missions (right). The suit provides protection in temperatures that range from −145 C (−290 F.) to 156 C (310 F.).

LIVING IN SPACE

On the second day of camp, the kids get a taste of space life. They sample the same freeze-dried food the astronauts eat. But kids planning to go to the moon will have to know more than how to add water to freeze-dried food. For instance, they'll have to know how to drive a moon buggy. Campers try out the space car on a model of the moon's landscape. The buggy moves along at 10 miles (16 km) an hour. Even though you can't quite zoom around, it's fun.

But life in space can also be dangerous. To survive the lack of air, for example, astronauts count on an important piece of equipment—a space suit. Campers try on suits similar to those worn by astronauts who visited the moon. The space suit's 21 layers did a great job of protecting astronauts from the hot and cold temperatures. Today's space shuttle suits are much less bulky, but they protect astronauts just as well from the temperature extremes of space.

Besides getting used to wearing a space suit, astronauts have to get used to feeling weightless. On day three, *gravity-no gravity day*, campers get the chance to feel what it's like, too. The action takes place on a zero-gravity machine. It looks like a giant see-saw, with a seat at one end and heavy weights at the other. When a camper is in the seat, the weights are used to counterbalance her weight. She pushes off the ground with her feet and—hold on!—she feels a floating sensation. It's almost like being weightless, but not quite!

Later that day, the kids take out their swim suits. It's time to train for recovery at sea, just in case of an

Campers practice for an emergency splash-down. The team of pilot and co-pilot must help each other into a NASA "Bird Cage." One camper holds a weight at the bottom of the cage to keep it steady so the other camper can climb in. A similar cage was used in the early Apollo missions (above).

Mission Control specialists direct camper astronauts during simulated space flights (top right).

Campers learn how to operate robotic arms that can carry out many operations such as inserting or removing bolts (bottom left).

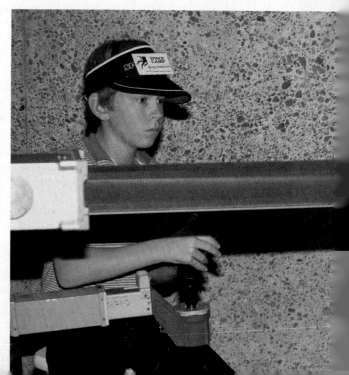

emergency shuttle splashdown. In a pool they try to climb from the water into a rubber raft without turning it over. From the raft they climb into a cage hung over the pool. It feels as if it were hanging from a rescue helicopter at sea. The exercise isn't easy, even in shallow water. For astronauts, it would be harder during a real emergency in the ocean. But with enough practice, astronauts can be ready for anything.

ROBOT HELPERS

To give the astronauts a hand, there are robots. These mechanical helpers make it easier for the space crew to do their work. If you watched the space shuttle missions on television, you may have seen the astronauts guide a robot arm to lift equipment out of the cargo bay. On day four, *technology day*, campers learn how to use the same kind of robot arm.

When the campers finish their basic training, they're ready for day five, *mission day*. It's time for the

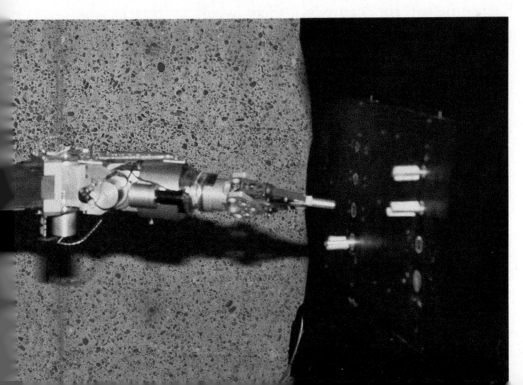

campers to simulate sending their own shuttle flight into space. The 10 members of each team work hard to complete this final test at Space Camp.

Five members of each team act as mission control—the people who guide the flight from the ground. Five campers are given positions in the make-believe shuttle cockpit. Each camper has a job to do. On a real shuttle team, some astronauts are pilots and some are scientists with their own experiments to complete.

Shortly after the simulated shuttle's lift-off, PLATO the computer signals that a container in the cargo bay is damaged. Campers must walk in space to solve the problem. After they do, the mission is over.

THE END OR THE BEGINNING?

Finally, the crew comes down to earth. They meet to discuss the flight. When it's all over, the kids receive certificates of graduation. And they each get a pair of Space Camp wings.

For some of the campers, their week at Space Camp could be just the beginning. Maybe one day they will live in colonies on the moon. Or maybe they'll live in huge space stations orbiting the earth. But whether they ever live in space or not, their week at Space Camp was out of this world!

3-2-1 BLAST OFF!

Questions

1. Name one of the special days at Space Camp and describe what happens on that day.
2. Why do you think the campers do morning exercises every day?
3. How do you think the experiment at Space Camp might help a student decide whether he or she wants to become an astronaut?
4. Would you like to attend Space Camp? If not, why not? If so, what activities would interest you most?

Applying Reading Skills

Number your paper from 1 to 4. Use complete sentences to answer the questions below.

1. What is the main idea of the first paragraph on page 333?
2. What are two supporting details in the same paragraph?
3. What is the main idea of the third paragraph on page 333?
4. What are two supporting details in the same paragraph?

338

UNIT FOUR   LEVEL 12

SOUNDS
OF
MUSIC

PREPARING FOR READING

Learning Vocabulary

1. The <u>audience</u> waited eagerly for the piano <u>recital</u> to begin.
2. The name of each player was announced, along with the name of the piece and its <u>composer</u>.
3. Just as the audience began to grow <u>impatient</u>, an <u>intermission</u> was announced.
4. Hilary was nervous when she began to play, but as she continued, she grew more <u>confident</u>.

audience   recital   composer
impatient   intermission   confident

Developing Background and Skills
Summarize

Read the paragraph below. It is from the front page of a newspaper.

LOCAL NEWS IN BRIEF
Piano Finalists Chosen

The winners of the district piano competition for students ages 10–14 were announced last evening. The six local winners will compete against other regional winners in the state-wide competition to be held in the capital next month. Said Madame St. George, organizer of the competition, "We are very proud of the talent shown by these promising young musicians." (See story on page 5.)

The paragraph you just read is a summary of the story that appears on page 5 of the paper. A **summary** is a brief account of something. The summary presents only the important facts. If you wanted to know more about the competition, you could read the story on page 5 of the paper. The story would probably tell you when and where the competition was held, who the winners were, and the date of the state-wide competition.

When you give a summary of an event or happening, you don't give every detail. You tell only the most important points and leave out unimportant or repeated information. You select a topic sentence or write one of you own. Reporting and organizing information in this way is called summarizing.

The next selection tells about a piano recital and the feelings of one of the performers. As you read, look for the important information that is presented. Think about how you might summarize this information.

PLAY THE BACH, DEAR

Judith Groch

Hilary slid into her seat just in time. The recital hall was quiet, the audience alert. "And now," Madame St. George was saying, "we shall open our little show. Let me see . . ." She reached for her glasses. "Ah, yes," she said, looking at the program, "Marcia Joy Miller will play the 'Moonlight Sonata' by Ludwig van Beethoven (lŭd′ wig van bā′ tō′ vən)." Madame St. George always gave a composer's first name as if there could be another Beethoven—Jack Beethoven?

The audience buzzed, coughed, shifted. Madame St. George went back to her seat. Marcia Joy Miller ran onto the stage as if chased by a ball of fire. Once safely seated at the piano, she plunged into the "Moonlight Sonata." After a bumpy start, Marcia Joy settled down, and the "Moonlight Sonata" flowed on. When the last notes of the music died away, Marcia Joy bolted back to her seat.

Next, Harold Mendelssohn played "Venetian Boat Song, No. 2," by Felix Mendelssohn. In his second piece, he had to play several sections with his hands crossed, so that he looked like he was hugging himself. Once, he reached high into the treble keys and almost fell off the seat. Finally, he untangled himself and, to everyone's relief, finished the piece.

When Lyra Lyons was called, Madame St. George paused to announce that Lyra had been chosen to appear on a television program for talented young musicians.

Everyone gasped. Madame St. George said that the school was honored. Then Lyra mounted the stage, bowed, and seated herself. She waited for what seemed like a year until the audience was completely quiet. Slowly, she lifted her hands to the keyboard and waited again. Hilary admired her nerve. Then, at some inner signal, she pounced. Away she flew, ripping through a sonata like a flash of lightning. When Hilary tried to play that fast, all the notes crumpled together and mashed into a lump.

The girl sitting beside Hilary was next. She played a gooey piece, mooning over the slow passages and swaying in her seat. Serena Lang (who had played first last year) tossed off a sonatina by a composer Hilary couldn't pronounce. She kept speeding up and slowing down. Hilary's stomach plunged and pitched.

Up onto the stage, be seated, play, APPLAUSE, back to your seat . . . next. Just like last year. The audience grew restless. It was going to be a long concert.

Hilary sat frozen in her seat. Each player brought her one step closer to . . . She didn't dare think of it. She was trembling. It was exactly like last year, she groaned to herself.

Pink Frills was climbing onto the stage, skipping out toward the piano, flipping ribbons and flounces as she went. A murmur passed through the audience. Pink Frills reminded Hilary of last year's Little Creep. Little Creep had gone to a professional music school. Hilary sighed. Pink Frills . . . Little Creep . . . it made no difference. There was one at each recital. Pink Frills was worse, though. She was probably ten, but she looked about four and a half. The audience loved it when you looked too little to play. It wasn't a piano recital, Hilary decided. It was a contest for the parents. The winner had the smallest, cutest, loudest, fastest, best-playing child.

Hilary clutched her hands in agony. She tried to think of how the Bach (bäkh) went. *This is the way it goes— Up-Down, Up-Down.* She searched for the opening notes. Nothing came. NOTHING! Shaking with fright, she tried to think of something simple: her own name. When she finally found the words—Hilary Banister—she wondered who *that* was!

The audience was getting impatient. Just in time, Madame St. George announced a brief intermission.

"Hilareee! Over here!"

344

It was her mother calling. Hilary turned in the crowd and saw her parents trying to make their way over to her.

"Well, dear, just a little more to go and we'll be hearing *you*," said her mother with a smile. "I'm certain we'll all be very proud of Hilary this after-noon," said Mrs. Banister to her sister-in-law. "In the past two weeks, Hilary's hardly been away from the piano. Isn't that true, Hilary?"

"You can say that again." Mr. Banister spoke up. "It even surprised me. To be quite frank," he laughed, "I'd kind of written you off for music." He put his hand on her shoulder.

Hilary was dying—slowly, quickly, all at once.

People were chattering, laughing, and calling, "Here, HERE . . . over here." For some, the intermission was a celebration. For others, it just extended the agony. Uncle Archer pushed a glass of lemonade into Hilary's hand.

"Here, Hilary, old girl. You look pale . . . ha ha . . . have a swig of lemonade . . . ha ha . . . maybe it will help."

Hilary put up her hands in protest. She didn't want anything. Her mouth was so pasty, she couldn't even swallow. But Uncle Archer kept shoving the glass at her. Well, maybe, after all, the lemonade would help. She took the glass from her uncle and thanked him with a sick smile.

"Well, it looks like intermission's over," boomed Uncle Archer, patting Hilary on the head, messing up her hair, and practically knocking her unconscious. "Time to face the music, ha ha!" Hilary ducked another pat.

Mrs. Banister said, "Oh, dear, I'm getting nervous myself. It's Hilary's turn next."

Mr. Banister said, "Come, let's get back to our seats and get it over with."

Time was running out. Hilary sat in her seat, waiting in a state of controlled terror. She couldn't believe it was really happening to her. Oh, but it was. Her breath came sharp and fast, sometimes not at all. She tried to calm herself by playing a little game. She would imagine The Worst.

O.K., she would forget everything. O.K. People would break into wild laughter. She would be expelled from the school. Anything else? Hilary let her thoughts roam, searching, but nothing turned up. Now she forced her mind to return to the image of herself sitting at the piano while the audience sat there laughing. Horrible! She flinched and the image disappeared. Summoning courage, she made it come back again.

Then, suddenly, having taken a good, hard look at The Worst, she felt less frightened.

The audience had settled down—more or less. For those who had already played, the second half of the recital was a waste of time. Madame St. George arose to welcome her guests back. She consulted her program. Then she spoke again. "Hilary Banister will play the 'Mazurka in C Minor' by Frederic Chopin (fred' ər ik shō' pan), followed by the very lovely 'Invention in B-flat' by Johann Sebastian Bach."

Hilary felt the challenge of "very lovely." Very lovely until played by Hilary Banister.

"Hilary Banister!" Madame St. George announced.

"Hey, isn't that you?" Somebody gave her a poke. "It's *your* turn."

Like an arrow released from its bow, Hilary flew from her seat and up onto the stage. She found herself sitting in front of the enormous piano. She had no idea how she got there. A rustle of shifting seats and shuffling programs came from below in the audience. People coughed. She didn't dare look out at the sea of faces. The piano waited, its black and white teeth gleaming. The audience waited. Madame St. George waited.

Hilary drew a deep breath and began to play. To her surprise, she heard the opening measures of the Mazurka emerge from beneath her fingers. Thanks to her piano teacher, Miss Orpheo, the delicate grace notes went easily. The music flowed, winding and curving, a dance of the heart. After a while, Hilary realized she was holding her breath. She exhaled in little racking sighs. Her entire body

relaxed and immediately she felt better.

By the time she reached the second page, Hilary's stomach had stopped zipping up and down, and her hands had almost stopped trembling. She even dared let her fingers carry on for a split second while she listened to herself play. The audience grew quiet and attentive.

She was filled with a sense of uplifting joy and of great power. And a feeling, not exactly of love, but certainly of gratitude to Chopin who had provided the music. So this is what it was like to be talented, to be a concert performer, she thought. This is why they *wanted* to play! Armed with the magic of great music, you could *do* something to the audience, *give* them something—something they might not even know they needed. You could make them laugh; you could bring tears to their eyes or fill them with joy.

When the Mazurka came to a close, there was a rewarding

burst of applause. Instead of the usual spray of polite handclapping, this was real applause, concentrated and aimed: the solid response of people who had listened to her and who liked what they had heard.

The applause died down. Hilary lifted her hands and began the second piece. *This is the way it goes . . . Up-Down, Up-Down . . . This is the way it goes . . .* The two voices of the Bach Invention chattered back and forth, joyously answering and echoing each other. The piano bench, as usual, was a little too far out for comfort. She tucked her left foot around the bench leg, lifted herself slightly, and managed to wriggle the bench a little closer. There—that was better. The second theme entered, high-spirited and bouncy. The Invention sparkled and danced like water splashing in the sunlight.

Hey! That was close. She almost missed a note. Pay attention. Hilary concentrated on the music, tensing slightly as she approached the Horrible Spot. Was there that much good luck in the world? Yes. She emerged from the difficult stretch, smiling. Now that it was safely behind, she played on with a dash she had never dared before. She had to admit, practicing hadn't hurt. In fact, it had helped. For the first time, she had the feeling that she really had the music in her fingers. It had become part of her. She had worked so hard that by now the music was permanently stamped in her brain. Confident, almost enjoying herself, Hilary entered the concluding passage. Her fingers flew along. The worst was over. In a few seconds she would be home safe.

Trusting her fingers to finish their work, she let them bring the music to a close. A volley of applause burst from the audience. Hilary bowed and returned to her seat. She smiled to herself. She had done it!

Questions

1. Describe one of the performers at the recital as seen through Hilary's eyes.
2. How did Hilary feel as she waited for her turn? How did her feelings change as she began to play?
3. Do you think Hilary was overly critical of the other performers at the recital? Explain why she might have felt as she did.
4. Have you ever performed before a large group of people? How did you feel? In what ways were your feelings similar to those of Hilary? In what ways were they different?

Applying Reading Skills

Number your paper from 1 to 2. After each number, write the answers to the questions that follow.

1. In three sentences, summarize the last paragraph on page 346.
2. In two sentences, summarize the third paragraph on page 348.

WRITE A FIRST-PERSON NARRATIVE

Prewrite

In "Play the Bach, Dear," Hilary Bannister proved to herself that she could overcome her fear and play in the recital. At some time in life almost everyone has a scary experience. For Hilary, it was playing in a recital. For someone else, it might be shooting foul shots in a basketball game. What makes us able to do these things even though we are scared? For Hilary, practice helped her to be more confident. She also thought about the worst things that could happen and then the actual playing didn't seem so scary.

You are going to write a first-person narrative about something scary that happened to you. When you write in first person, you use pronouns such as *I*, *me*, *my*, and *mine*. In a narrative, the writer writes about the events in an experience in the order, or sequence, in which they happened.

Think of all the little events or steps that you must tell to help your readers understand your experience. Then write sentence notes to tell how you felt about each step as it happened. You may want to make a chart like the one below.

Steps	Feelings
1. Hilary waits while others play.	She feels panicky and can't remember her music.
2.	

When you have written your notes, read them and try to draw some conclusion. Hilary concluded that concert performers wanted to play for audiences because they could give something to those who heard them play.

Write

1. Read your notes and conclusion again.
2. Think about how many paragraphs you will have in your narrative. One or two paragraphs will probably be enough to tell what happened and describe your feelings.
3. In the third paragraph, you can draw a conclusion about your experience.
4. You may want to write a title for your narrative.
5. Remember to use the pronouns *I*, *me*, *mine*, and *my* to show first person.
6. Use your Glossary or dictionary for spelling help.

Revise

Read your first-person narrative. Did you tell the events that happened in your experience in a clear sequence? Did you draw a conclusion based on what happened and your feelings? Rewrite any parts of your narrative that are unclear.

1. Did you use pronouns correctly?
2. Did you use complete sentences?
3. Did you use correct punctuation and capitalization in your sentences?

PREPARING FOR READING

Learning Vocabulary

1. The students who <u>apply</u> to Fiorello H. LaGuardia High School will be <u>auditioned</u> for admission.
2. Every day, students can be found <u>rehearsing</u> music, dance, and dramatics.
3. An exceptionally talented student may perform as a <u>soloist</u> in one of the school productions.
4. The years at LaGuardia High are a <u>memorable</u> experience for many of the school's <u>graduates</u>.

apply	auditioned	rehearsing
soloist	memorable	graduates

Developing Background and Skills
Summarize

You know that a **summary** is a brief account of something. When you are asked to summarize a selection, you should think about what important facts or ideas are presented. A summary should include only the most important information.

Read the paragraph on the next page and think about how you might summarize it.

On every floor, there is evidence of the special nature of the Fiorello H. LaGuardia High School. This school is New York City's High School of Music and the Arts. Some people call it the *Fame* school, in reference to the movie that used it as a setting. Whatever name is used, it's a place where talented young musicians, actors, dancers, singers, and artists get outstanding training in their field and an education that will prepare them for college. Its name and reputation have become so widely know that LaGuardia has served as the model for other high schools of the arts.

Read the summary below. Find the topic sentence. What information was left out? What information was included?

Fiorello H. LaGuardia High School, New York City's High School of Music and the Arts, provides talented students with training in their artistic field and education preparing them for college. This outstanding school has served as a model for many other such schools.

"The Halls of Fame" presents a great deal of information. As you read the selection, think about how you might summarize each paragraph. Think about how you might summarize the entire selection.

THE HALLS OF FAME

ALICE BENJAMIN BOYNTON

From the outside, it looks like a modern, nine-story building. Bold letters announce that it is the Fiorello H. La Guardia High School. To most people who pass by, it looks like any other public high school in a city.

This is a special place, however. Each year almost 14,000 junior high students apply for admission. Visitors come from all over the world. The school has even been the subject of a success-ful movie and a popular weekly television series.

What's so special about this high school of 2,600 students? Why does it produce so much

interest and excitement? A walk down its hallways
provides some clues.

- In one room, a student is rehearsing his own
  arrangement of *We Shall Overcome* with the
  singers in a chorus.
- In a large studio with mirrored walls, a professional dancer is teaching a new dance to a
  group of students.
- In front of a wall of lockers, four students are
  working on a scene from a play.
- In a room with large windows, students are
  sketching a gigantic white sneaker which holds
  a large bunch of flowers instead of a foot.

On every floor, there is evidence of the special
nature of this school, for La Guardia is New York
City's High School of Music and the Arts. Some
people call it the *Fame* school, referring to the
movie that used it as a setting. Whatever name is

used, it's a place where talented young musicians, actors, dancers, singers, and artists can get outstanding training in their field and an education that will prepare them for college. Its name and reputation have become so widely known, that La Guardia has served as the model for other high schools of the arts around the country.

A DREAM COMES TRUE

Although the building is new, the school has a long history. In the early 1930s, New York Mayor Fiorello H. La Guardia dreamed of a school where the city's most talented students could develop their gifts in music or art while they completed an academic program. In 1936, the determined mayor saw his dream come true with the opening of the High School of Music and Art. Twelve years later, the School of Performing Arts was created to train talented students for careers as dancers, actors, or musicians. This was the school building in which *Fame* was filmed.

In 1984, the present building opened. The two schools were joined together under one roof and named in honor of Mayor La Guardia.

STUDENTS **WHO MADE IT TO THE TOP**

Over the years, students who have achieved fame helped to bring attention to the school. One-time students include Liza Minnelli, Billy Dee Williams, Janis Ian, Barbra Streisand, Tony Roberts, Dom DeLuise, Ben Vereen, and many more. Others whose names are not as familiar are active in every area of the arts, sciences, education, politics, and business.

**Clockwise:
Barbra Streisand,
Ben Vereen,
Dom DeLuise,
Billy Dee
Williams,
Liza Minnelli**

APPLICANTS **WHO WANT A CHANCE**

At La Guardia High School students can choose from many special courses in their field of interest. The music department, for example, has a large variety of offerings. A person interested in going on the stage can sample a workshop in singing and acting in musical-comedy or in opera. A pianist can study jazz and also get a taste of conducting an orchestra, learn to use the synthesizer to play electronic music, and even take up the trombone.

It's no wonder then that every year the number of students who want to attend La Guardia increases. Every one of the 14,000 applicants will be auditioned, but the school will have room to take only 650 of them! Choosing the most talented boys and girls from such a large number of candidates is no easy task.

A STUDENT **WHO BELONGS**

Liuh-Wen Ting, a girl born in Taiwan, was once one of the thousands of applicants to La Guardia's music department. To test Liuh-Wen's musical ability, the examiner played a number of melodies on the piano. At first, the melodies were short and simple. Then, they became longer and much more complicated. Each time, Liuh-Wen had to sing the melody back exactly as it had been played. Next, the teacher tapped out a series of rhythms which Liuh-Wen had to remember and tap back. Again, the rhythms became increasingly difficult. Liuh-Wen did well. One half of the test was over.

Liuh-Wen was then asked to play her instrument. She picked up her viola and played the piece she had prepared. The examiners seemed to like what they heard. She told them she also played the piano. Her judges were amazed by her performance on the keyboard, too! By that time it was very clear that Liuh-Wen belonged in La Guardia.

PREPARING FOR THE FUTURE

Liuh-Wen entered the school knowing what she wanted for her future—a career in music. Those who expect to become professionals in any of the arts must have enough time to learn and practice their craft many hours each day. How can you practice for many hours a day when you have to go to school? Usually, a student goes to school and takes lessons afterward. At La Guardia, school classes and music lessons are combined. As the assistant principal puts it, "Our biggest problem is trying to do what every other school does, PLUS three or four periods in the arts."

To make this goal possible, students start school at 8:10 A.M. They have to take a full academic program in addition to studio classes in their special area. For Liuh-Wen that means classes in English literature, French, science, and math. She is also required to take three or four classes in music. One of these must be a performance class.

Many high schools have an orchestra, a marching band, and maybe a jazz band. At La Guardia there are four orchestras, three bands, two jazz groups, and fourteen instrument classes. Some

groups are for beginners and others for advanced
players. Students are grouped according to their
level of ability. Every music student must perform
in at least one of these groups. Liuh-Wen plays
viola in the school's highest-level orchestra.

Liuh-Wen welcomes the many opportunities to
perform. "I was always very nervous about performing in front of an audience, even if I was well
prepared," she says. "It's very important for me to
get a lot of chances to play, so I can get used to
the feeling."

SACRIFICES AND REWARDS

To perform well, students spend hours rehearsing after school ends at 3:00 P.M. For those who
love what they're doing, this is a pleasure rather

than a forced choice. Most of the students at La Guardia seem to thrive on the pace. The assistant principal says that even after a long day, "We have to kick them out! They don't want to leave!"

Liuh-Wen is used to devoting many hours a day to her music. She started playing the piano when she was five years old, and the viola when she was ten. Although her family and her teachers urged her to concentrate on just one of the instruments, she couldn't choose. So she continued to study both. This meant sacrifices. "When I was in elementary school," she says, "I never had time to play with the neighborhood kids. I had to stay home and practice. But I enjoyed practicing."

One thing students should not sacrifice, Liuh-Wen says, is reading. "Music is not only playing," she explains. "You also have to think and feel. I think I should know about different kinds of people and different life styles. The more I know, the better I think my music will become. What I know will enrich my music."

Liuh-Wen, like many other students at La Guardia, seems to be able to cram two days' worth of activities into one. After a very full school day, she may rehearse with friends for a recital or act as a piano accompanist for a performing student. There may be private music lessons on the viola or piano. When Liuh-Wen finally gets home, she practices whichever instrument she feels like playing.

The hard work does have its rewards. Twice, Liuh-Wen had been selected to be the soloist with La Guardia's orchestra. One year she was chosen to play the piano, and the next year she performed on the viola.

SCHOOLWORK

"What about homework?" you may be wondering. Can there ever be enough time for math and English? Despite the heavy demands on their time, students at La Guardia are expected to keep up with their schoolwork. And they do. In each graduating class, 92% of the students go on to some kind of higher education.

Although the teachers expect the work to be done, they are understanding of the special demands on their students. Many of them are

graduates of the school, so they know the needs of their students. Others are professional artists, actors, dancers, and musicians as well as teachers. They know how much time is needed for practice and rehearsal.

HIGHPOINTS **IN THE YEAR**

Although all students are required to perform, the performances may be limited to their own departments within the school. Students are only allowed to appear in public presentations when they are considered trained and ready. For most, this does not happen until their senior year. The annual performances put on by the dance and drama departments are big productions. There are semiannual art shows and concerts. All require tremendous amounts of time for preparation. Rehearsals can run long hours after school. When these special events occur, no tests may be given one week before the actual performance.

The productions are high points in the year. They are not just the product of a few months of intense work, but of all the years of study and training each student has received at La Guardia.

The new building gives students a spectacular showcase for their talents. Words like "fabulous" and "magnificent" have been used to describe La Guardia's concert hall and theater. The concert hall used for dance and orchestra concerts seats 1,200 people. It has a stage large enough to be found in a Broadway theater. It is also equipped with computerized lighting.

Smaller than the concert hall, La Guardia's theater seats 600. It is a perfect setting for dramatic productions and recitals by soloists. The theater, like the concert hall, reflects the very latest in technology and design.

AN ALL-AROUND SCHOOL

With so many special classes and events, it is easy to lose sight of the other activities at the school. La Guardia has track, basketball, tennis, volleyball, and soccer teams. The school also has a student newspaper, magazine, and yearbook. No one seems to be surprised that the yearbook editor also manages to fit four periods of dance studio and four periods of academic classes into her day.

A feeling of cooperation and pride is very strong at La Guardia. Although most students agree that the movie *Fame* was not completely accurate, the film did seem to capture the spirit of the school. To Liuh-Wen Ting, the atmosphere is one of support and encouragement. "The school's like a family," she says.

In some schools, the competition can be fierce. Students try to out-do one another. Liuh-Wen says, "Here, if they like your playing, if you play well, they admire you for it."

The loyalty and devotion of students and staff does not end with graduation. A former student, now a college president, was the guest speaker at the school's graduation exercises one year. He summed up his years at the school this way: "This school was the most memorable experience of my life."

Questions

1. Where is the Fiorello H. La Guardia High School?
2. What kind of background and interests should a student have to apply to La Guardia High School?
3. What rewards does the hard work at La Guardia High School have?
4. If you had a chance to go to a school like La Guardia, would you take it? Why or why not?

Applying Reading Skills

Number your paper from 1 to 3. Follow the directions given below.

1. Write a two-sentence summary of the paragraphs on pages 359–360, "A Dream Comes True."
2. Write a three-sentence summary of the paragraphs on pages 362–363, "Preparing for the Future."
3. Read the summary below. Then find the two paragraphs in the selection that it summarizes. Write the number of the paragraphs and the pages on which they are found.

Despite the long hours of practice and rehearsal, students are expected to keep up with their homework. The teachers, however, are understanding of the demands on students' time.

PREPARING FOR READING

Learning Vocabulary

1. Jim Bridger tried to cheer up the people by <u>reporting</u> the <u>wonders</u> of Yellowstone Park.
2. The people were so glum that they didn't even <u>accuse</u> Jim of lying.
3. John Potter <u>tuned</u> up his fiddle to prove to Bridger that he was the <u>mightiest</u> fiddler who ever was.

reporting   wonders   accuse
tuned   mightiest

Developing Background and Skills
Summarize

Read the poster below.

N O T I C E !
BARN DANCE SATURDAY
May 14

Earl's Barn   John Potter,
Smithton   Fiddler

Dancing starts at 8:00 P.M.
Admission: $1.00

The poster summarizes the most important information about an event that is going to happen. It tells *what*, *when*, *where*, and *how much*. The poster doesn't give you all the details about the barn dance. It doesn't tell you exactly where Earl's Barn is. It doesn't tell you how good a fiddler John Potter is. But it does give the most important facts about the event.

If you wanted to tell a friend about the barn dance, you might summarize the information even more. You might say that there's going to be a barn dance Saturday night at Earl's Barn.

Remember that a **summary** is a brief account of important information. Follow these steps when you write a summary of a story or article.

1. Choose the most important information.
2. Leave out unimportant details.
3. Do not include information that is repeated in several places. If such information is important, include it only once in your summary.
4. Select or write a topic sentence for each paragraph in your summary.

If you are summarizing a longer article or story, your summary may have to be more than one paragraph.

The next selection, "The Fiddler Who Wouldn't Fiddle," is a tall tale. As you read, think about the information that is presented. Think how you might summarize the story.

THE FIDDLER WHO WOULDN'T FIDDLE

SID FLEISCHMAN

Jim Bridger was coming back from exploring Yellowstone Park when he bumped into a brand-new town.

Blue Horizon didn't amount to much, but it did have a general store, a stable, a blacksmith shop, and a funeral parlor.

Jim said his howdys, but everyone he met had the grumbles. Sitting around the stove in the general store, he tried to cheer them up by reporting the wonders he'd seen in Yellowstone.

"Durn my gizzard if steaming water didn't shoot up out of the earth. And boiling water flows out of the rocks into the prettiest lake full of trout you ever saw."

"Can't no trout live in boiling water," grumbled the mayor.

"You're exactly right," Jim answered. "Down below, the water's cold as a frog. The hot spring floats on top. Oh, I ate a mess of trout and never once had to build a cook fire and get out my pan."

"You eat your fish raw?" the blacksmith asked.

Jim shook his head. "No, sir. It was just a matter of hauling up that trout slowlike through the boiling top water. When I unhooked it, the trout was cooked and ready to eat."

Jim could see nobody gave a hoot about his hot-and-cold lake. They didn't even accuse him of lying.

"Something bothering you gents?" he asked.

The mayor nodded. "We got to call off the barn dance tonight. The fiddler won't fiddle."

Now Jim Bridger loved a party, and it had been a long time since he'd kicked his heels to a jolly tune.

"Who's the fiddler?" he asked.

"Buryin' John Potter, the undertaker. He's hornet-mad because folks didn't elect him mayor instead of me."

The more Jim Bridger thought about it, the more his feet hankered for fiddle music. So he walked across the street to the undertaker's parlor.

"You can't fool me, Buryin' John Potter," said Jim. "I see your fiddle on the wall, but that don't mean you can play a note. On purpose, I mean."

"Can, but won't," grumbled the undertaker.

"No, sir," Jim said. "If you was to saw your fiddling bow across those strings, I'll bet you couldn't hit two notes out of five."

"Haw," said the undertaker, smirking.

"Reckon you don't even know 'Chicken in the Bread Tray Pickin' Up Dough.'"

"By heart," said the undertaker sourly. "But I'm

not fiddlin' tonight. Don't think you can sweet-word me into changing my mind.''

"Wouldn't think of it,'' Jim replied. "But I'm a powerful fine judge of fiddle music. Once heard Jingle-Bob Earl play back in Missouri, and I guess you'll agree he's the mightiest fiddler who ever was.''

"Faw,'' snorted Buryin' John Potter. "He couldn't play high C if he was standing on a stepladder. I'm the mightiest fiddler who ever was—but I'm not fiddlin' tonight.''

Jim said, "I brought a gourd plugged full of hot steam from Yellowstone, and it's still hot. That Yellowstone steam takes years to cool off. I figured to use that gourd as a foot warmer—the nights are turning chilly already, wouldn't you say? Buryin' John, that Yellowstone foot warmer is yours if you can play as well as Jingle-Bob Earl. Come outside and prove it.''

The undertaker took down his fiddle, and the two men rode out to a distant spot west of town. Buryin' John tuned his strings and began beating time with one foot as if he were pounding a stake into the ground. He ripped out "Turkey in the Straw."

Jim thought he'd never heard it played so sweet, but he said, "Won't do. Jingle-Bob Earl played louder'n that. His fiddling rattled windows for miles around. Do you know 'Scooping Up Pawpaws'? Or 'Have You Seen My New Shoes'?"

"Both," Buryin' John said, and began sawing away twice as loud as before. The music raised the sap in Jim's feet. It was all he could do to keep from leaping to his heels and raising dust.

Then the undertaker lifted his chin from the fiddle. "Reckon that gourd foot warmer is mine," he declared.

"Not so fast," said Jim. "You call that a contest? Why, Jingle-Bob Earl could fiddle all night without playing the same tune twice."

The undertaker tucked the fiddle back under his jaw and scraped away. Hour after hour the bow cut wild figures in the air. Jim had never heard such fiddling. It was an ear-quivering wonder.

Finally the sun began to dive for home. Jim jumped up and said, "Buryin' John, you win! You're the mightiest fiddler that ever was! The Yellowstone foot warmer is yours."

When Jim got back to the general store, it was falling dark. "Head for the barn!" he exclaimed. "The dance is about to begin."

The barn filled up in no time. Folks stood around waiting for Buryin' John. They'd heard him practicing his fiddle all day long. A mule began to bray, but they couldn't dance to that.

Finally, the mayor, who was there to do the fiddle calling, said, "Can't be a dance without a fiddler. We might as well go home."

"Keep your hair on, Mayor, and the barn doors open. All the windows, too," said Jim, cupping an ear. "Coming this way is the grandest, mightiest fiddling you ever heard. Caller, clear your throat!"

Suddenly, bouncing back from Echo Mountain, came the first notes of "Turkey in the Straw."

"Right on time," said Jim. "I figured it would take Buryin' John's echo about four hours to bounce back."

Then Jim leaped to the center of the floor with hours of stored-up dancing in his feet. He kicked his heels and the dance was on. The fiddle caller aired his lungs.

Grab your partners, make a square,
Music's comin' from I don't know where!

The rafters shook with a romping and a stomp-
ing. The mayor took off his coat and kept calling.

Suddenly the undertaker appeared in the doorway.

"Durn my gizzard, if it ain't Buryin' John!" Jim
called out.

"That's my fiddlin'!"

"Oh, you're a sly one," Jim laughed, thinking
fast. "That was clever of you to echo your fiddling
so you could kick your heels to your own music.
Had everybody fooled, you did! They thought you
were hornet-mad. Don't just stand there. Grab a
partner, Buryin' John, and lift your feet to the mightiest fiddler that ever was."

Questions

1. What story did Jim Bridger tell the people of Blue Horizon to try to cheer them up?
2. Why were the people of Blue Horizon glum?
3. What three things in the story could *not* be true?
4. People often exaggerate for effect. They say things such as "I waited for ages" and "I'm so hungry I could eat a horse." What are two or three expressions you use that are exaggerations?

Applying Reading Skills

Summarize the entire selection "The Fiddler Who Wouldn't Fiddle" in three or four paragraphs. Each paragraph should have at least two or three sentences. Reread the steps for writing a summary that are given on page 371.

A Fiddler

Once was a fiddler. Play could he
Sweet as a bird in an almond tree;
Fingers and strings—they seemed to be
Matched, in a secret conspiracy.
Up slid his bow, paused lingeringly;
Music's self was its witchery.

In his stooping face it was plain to see
How close to dream is a soul set free—
A half-found world;
And company.

His fiddle is broken
Mute is he.
But a bird sings on in the almond tree.

Walter de la Mare

PREPARING FOR READING

Learning Vocabulary

1. The popularity of the musical group Menudo continues to grow.
2. The group spends much time rehearsing dance routines and song lyrics.
3. Menudo has gained much publicity, and members are often interviewed by television, radio, and newspaper reporters.

popularity   routines   lyrics
publicity   interviewed

Developing Background and Skills
Graphs

Writers sometimes include **graphs** in their books or articles. Graphs help readers to make comparisons and see relationships more clearly than words alone.

One kind of graph is called a circle graph. Sometimes circle graphs are called pie graphs. The sections of a circle graph look like pieces of pie.

Each section of a circle graph stands for a percentage of the whole graph. All the sections together add up to 100 percent.

Look at the circle graph below.

Favorite Music of Students at Bowden School

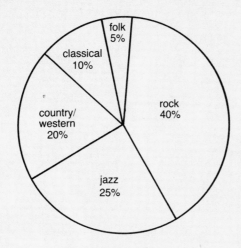

What kind of music is most popular among the sixth graders at Bowden School?
What kind of music is least popular?
What percentage of students enjoys country/western music?

You will find two graphs in the next selection. Think about what each graph shows. Think about how the graphs present information and how they help you make comparisons and reach conclusions.

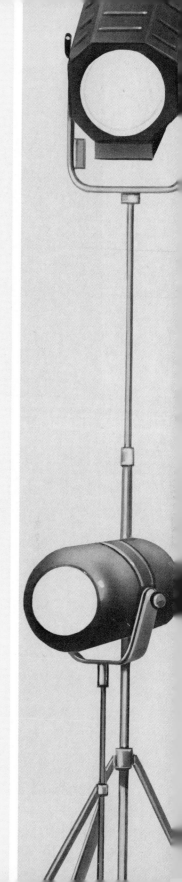

Meet Menudo

Deborah Kucan Witkowski

If you had Menuditis, would you have to stay home from school? What if someone called you *fanático*? Should you get angry?

You could answer both questions if you knew that Menuditis is the feeling shared by thousands of fans *(fanáticos)* for their favorite musical group—Menudo.

Edgardo Díaz started the group in 1977. He wanted to create an act that would remain young forever. He chose five Puerto Rican teenagers, all under the age of fifteen, and trained them to sing and dance. He called them Menudo (which means "small change"). The original group members were Fernando and Oscar "Nefty" Salaberry, and Oscar, Carlos, and Ricky Meléndez.

In the early days, the boys wore jeans and tennis shoes. They performed only in Latin America and sang all songs in their native language, Spanish.

Since 1977, there have been many different members. But membership isn't the only change for the group.

Their jeans and tennis shoes have been replaced by flashy outfits. They have had to learn forty-six separate dance routines for their stage show. They've also learned English so they can understand and answer the questions of reporters. The group is often interviewed for magazines, newspapers, radio, and television. Their popularity continues to grow, not only in Latin America where they got their start, but around the world as well. They even have computers for their fan club mail and membership information.

Even with all the changes, however, some things have stayed the same. Edgardo Díaz's idea of a group that would stay young has not changed. The group rules make sure of that.

Roy Rosello

Charlie Rivera

Ray Reyes

Johnny Lozada

Ricky Meléndez

1. A Menudo must be at least twelve years old and be able to speak Spanish.
2. A Menudo must be a talented singer and dancer.
3. A Menudo must be healthy. (Remember, they rehearse most of the time when they are not performing.)
4. A Menudo must study hard and get good grades. (Private tutors go along on the tours so the boys can keep up with their classes.)
5. A Menudo must have no bad habits and must get along well with others.
6. A member of Menudo must leave the group when he turns sixteen or if his voice changes.

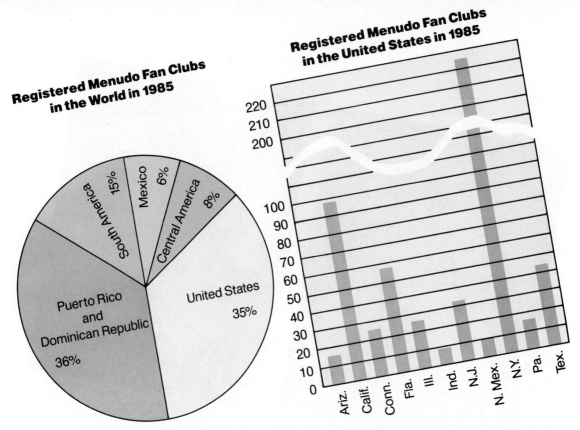

Registered Menudo Fan Clubs in the World in 1985

Puerto Rico and Dominican Republic 36%

United States 35%

South America 15%

Mexico 6%

Central America 8%

Registered Menudo Fan Clubs in the United States in 1985

The boys know the importance of following the rules. After all, there are thousands who would like the chance to take their place.

What about Menudo's music? It is pop rock with a dance beat. The lyrics are positive and uplifting. They do not write their own songs nor do they play instruments. On stage they sing and dance to pre-recorded music.

Since 1977, Menudo has recorded twelve albums. They have sold millions of copies. In 1984, they released their first album recorded in English, *Reaching Out*. It features Robbie Rosa, the first member of the group who was not born in Puerto Rico. Robbie was born and raised in Long Island, New York. At thirteen, along with hundreds of other teenage boys, he auditioned for the group. He knew he could keep the job for only a few years, but he also knew he would remember it for his whole life.

How do the fans feel about the boys when they leave the group? Most of them enjoy the change in membership, but still keep track of where their past favorites go. Some have gone to college. Others have found jobs in a variety of fields, including music. It takes time to get used to a normal lifestyle. The publicity and travel are hard to forget. It's a sad time for the boys when they leave. Menudo was like their family for a few years. But they knew the rules when they started. They feel glad that those who come after them will have so much to experience.

The *super cinco* (fabulous five) used to make only $75.00 for a performance. That amount has increased many times over. A whole line of products including t-shirts, jeans, key chains, buttons, and posters has

become available. There is even a store in New York City called "Menuditis." It sells nothing but Menudo products.

Menuditis seems to be spreading as more and more people get to see the group. They have made two films in Spanish: *Menudo La Película* (Menudo The Film) and *Una Aventura Llamada Menudo* (An Adventure Called Menudo). The group has released music videos, like many other musical groups. They also have a weekly television show, seen in thirty-three countries.

Menudo members learn a valuable lesson from their experience in the group. Edgardo Díaz told the boys, "From our example, kids see that if you work hard you can get what you desire." It certainly seems to be true for the boys in Menudo.

Menudo congratulates Michael Jackson at the Grammy Awards ceremony.

Questions

1. What is Menudo?
2. How has the group changed since it first began performing in 1977?
3. Why do you think one of the rules for the group has to do with getting good grades?
4. Are you a fan of a particular musical group? What is it? What makes you like this group?

Applying Reading Skills

Number your paper from 1 to 4. Refer to the graphs on page 388 to answer the questions below.

1. What state has the largest number of Menudo fan clubs? About how many fan clubs does New Mexico have?
2. What country has the largest percentage of Menudo fan clubs? Can you tell from the graph you used how many fan clubs there are in this country?
3. What two countries or regions together have half of the Menudo fan clubs in the world?
4. How could you figure out the total number of Menudo fan clubs in the United States? What is this number?

PREPARING FOR READING

Learning Vocabulary

1. Recently, doctors have begun to realize the many benefits of music to good health.
2. Sounds that are soothing have positive effects on patients.
3. On the other hand, loud noises or constant sound can contribute to stress.
4. A doctor may prescribe music with the same tempo as the ideal heart beat rate for patients with high blood pressure.

benefits	soothing	stress
prescribe	tempo	

Developing Background and Skills
Graphs

Graphs can help you to see relationships and make comparisons. A bar graph is one kind of graph. On bar graphs, bars of different lengths are used to show and compare information.

Look at the bar graph on the next page.

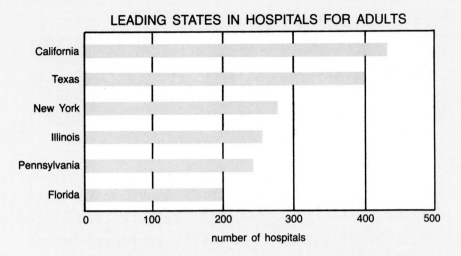

LEADING STATES IN HOSPITALS FOR ADULTS

number of hospitals

Look at the title of the graph. What does the graph show?

Look at the states listed on the left. What are the six leading states in number of hospitals for adults?

What state leads in number of hospitals for adults?

How many states have more than 200 hospitals for adults?

The next selection includes a graph. When you have finished reading the selection, study the graph and think about what it shows. Think about how the graph helps you to understand what you have read.

MUSIC AND HEALTH

DEBRA DESIDERI

Have you ever sat through a movie with tears rolling down your cheeks while the star sang a sad song? Does a favorite song make you want to get up and dance?

Studies have shown that music can affect our moods. Scientists have found that the human body itself is affected by music.

RELAXATION IS THE KEY

More and more doctors are making use of music in their work. Many doctors and dentists agree that having music in their office helps calm nervous patients. The patient concentrates on the music and not on the needle or drill. Some dentists even give their patients head-phones and a choice of tapes.

Some doctors prescribe a tape of harp music and a relaxation guide. The tapes and guides help patients relax before surgery. The tapes also help patients during their recovery.

Music is also used to regulate blood pressure, or the flow of blood pumped from your heart through your arteries. The ideal heart rate is 60 beats per minute. One doctor suggests to her high blood pressure patients that they listen to music with a 60-beat-per-minute tempo. The goal is to let the heart relax to the same rhythm as the music's.

STRESSFUL AND SOOTHING SOUNDS

Certain sounds we hear every day contribute to stress. Loud noises such as car horns or constant sounds like the humming of a refrigerator are examples.

Doctors also believe that there are certain sounds that have more positive effects. The sound of a flute, an electric piano, and bells have been described by patients as being soothing. If you listen to enough soothing sounds, you could help to reduce stress.

DON'T JUST SIT THERE, SING!

There is also much to be said for the effect that participating in music has on your health. You don't have to play an instrument to experience the joy and benefits of music. Your own body is a ready-made instrument. Singing is a good way to start making music. Jack Thorpe, a collector of cowboy songs, once wrote, "Singing songs, and making them too, seem as

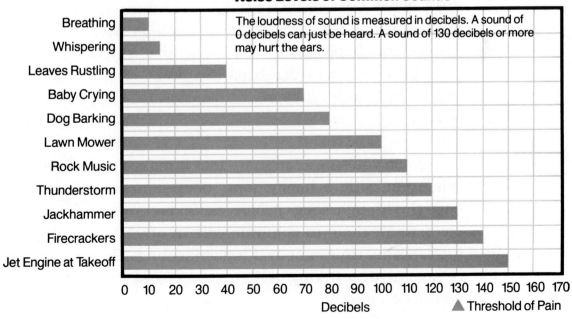

Noise Levels of Common Sounds

The loudness of sound is measured in decibels. A sound of 0 decibels can just be heard. A sound of 130 decibels or more may hurt the ears.

Decibels — ▲ Threshold of Pain

natural to human beings as washing is to a cat." Thorpe knew what he was talking about. Tension is released while singing because the body itself is used as the instrument. It has also been found that singing helps your breathing and digestion. So don't sing for your supper, sing after supper!

SPECIAL CHILDREN AND MUSIC

When you sing a sad song, does it make you feel sad? When you sing a happy song, does it make you feel happy? Through song, people can express feelings that are hard for them to communicate in other ways. Singing can sometimes uncover hidden feelings. This makes it helpful in working with retarded and emotionally disturbed children.

Music can also help blind people develop listening skills. Since the blind rely heavily on sound, music helps them tune in to sounds in the environment.

A deaf child is also helped through music. A child who cannot hear is unaware of rhythm, or sound patterns. Music can help the deaf child understand rhythms. Vibrations from musical instruments or records can be felt. The child can use these patterns to bring order to his or her speech and movement.

MUSICAL BODY BUILDING

Singing or playing an instrument is also good exercise. Playing a flute or trumpet helps to strengthen the lip and mouth muscles. People who have been hurt in accidents often have to work hard to build up their

injured muscles and bones. Playing an instrument can make that work more fun. Playing the piano can strengthen fingers, wrists, and shoulders. The neck and back are also exercised when playing the piano. Playing the violin can help the elbow, wrist, and shoulder.

A PERSONAL NOTE

Doctors tell us that every body has its own special inner rhythm. Every atom, cell, and muscle in your body will respond to certain notes. There is a special note for your liver, another one for your heart, and so on. All those notes combine into one biosymphony that is yours, and yours alone.

So turn on the record player or sing a song. Flip on the radio or fiddle around with a fiddle. Relax, listen, and feel the music of a healthy, happy you.

Questions

1. What kinds of music or sounds seem to have a good effect on health? What kinds of music or sounds seem to be harmful to health?
2. How does soothing music or music of a certain tempo affect how people feel?
3. Do you think that there are sounds and music that have no effect on our health? Explain your answer.
4. What kind of music helps you relax? What sounds are annoying to you?

Applying Reading Skills

Number your paper from 1 to 5. Refer to the graph on page 395 to answer the questions that follow.

1. What kind of graph is the graph on page 395? What does it show?
2. What is the decibel level of a dog barking?
3. What noise has a decibel level of about 100?
4. What noises listed on the graph have a decibel level about the threshold of pain?
5. About how many times louder than the sound of leaves rustling is the sound of a thunderstorm?

400

Ourchestra

So you haven't got a drum, just beat your belly.
So I haven't got a horn—I'll play my nose.
So we haven't any cymbals—
We'll just slap our hands together,
And though there may be orchestras
That sound a little better
With their fancy shiny instruments
That cost an awful lot—
Hey, we're making music twice as good
By playing what we've got!

Shel Silverstein

401

WRITING ACTIVITY

WRITE A SUMMARY

Prewrite

"Music and Health" is the kind of article that is helpful to read if you are writing a report. Suppose you have to write a report called "The Effect of Music on People." First, you need to find and read information about the subject. You might read books and magazine articles. As you gather your information, you will take notes that summarize the information you have read.

When you write a summary, you choose and write the important facts about a subject in your own words.

You can follow these steps to write a summary.

1. Read the material.
2. Think of questions to ask about the information as you read.
3. Using the information in the article, write sentence notes as answers to your questions.
4. Read your notes and choose the most important facts for your summary.
5. Write these facts in a summary of one or two paragraphs.

Read the article "Music and Health" again. You are going to write a summary of this article. Look at the headings for each part of the article. One way to think of questions for your summary is to turn each heading in the article into a question. For example, a question for the heading "Relaxation Is the Key" could be: "How is music a key to relaxation?"

When you have written your questions, write answers in your own words. Use the facts from the article.

Write

1. Read your questions and answers.
2. Write a main idea sentence for your summary. This is an example.

   Music can have positive effects on a person's health.

3. Then write the most important facts from your notes to support your main idea sentence.
4. Use your Glossary or dictionary for spelling help.

Revise

Read your summary. Did you write a clear main idea sentence? Are your detail sentences based on facts from the article? Have you left out an important fact? If so, rewrite your summary now.

1. Did you use complete sentences?
2. Did you use correct capitalization and punctuation in your sentences?

PREPARING FOR READING

Learning Vocabulary

1. Sizzle, Splat, and their <u>colleagues</u> played with the Pirelli Youth Orchestra.
2. Mr. Pirelli made a <u>motion</u> for the players to begin.
3. Pirelli thought that two tubas might <u>overpower</u> the rest of the orchestra, so he asked the players to <u>alternate</u>.
4. The young musicians were being provided with a good <u>foundation</u> on which to build their musical education.

colleagues   motion   overpower
alternate   foundation

Developing Background and Skills
Context Clues

Many times when you read, you come across words that are not familiar to you. How do you find out what these words mean? Of course you can always look for them in the dictionary. There is another way, however, in which you can find out the meaning of unknown words.

You can often use **context clues** to figure out the meaning of unfamiliar words. Nearby words, sentences, and phrases may provide clues to the meaning of unknown words. You can use the words you do know to figure out the meaning of the words you don't know.

Read the paragraph below. See if you can figure out the meaning of the underlined words by using the other words, phrases, and sentences.

Mr. Pirelli, the conductor, picked up his <u>baton</u> and stepped quickly up to the <u>podium</u>. He looked down at the open music lying on it, then rapped the baton against the side three times. He then raised it in the air and held it for the attention of the orchestra members.

What clues do you have to the meaning of *baton*? You know it is something an orchestra conductor uses. You know Mr. Pirelli picked it up, rapped it, and held it in the air. You can probably guess that a baton is a stick or wand.

What about *podium*? You read that Mr. Pirelli stepped up to the podium, looked at the music lying on it, and rapped his baton against it. You probably figured out that a podium is some kind of stand.

You may want to check the meaning of a word you guess by using context clues against the dictionary definition.

As you read the next selection, you may come across words that are unfamiliar to you. Try to figure out their meaning by using context clues.

Sizzle and her friend Splat have more in common than their odd nicknames. They both enjoy and play classical music. Sizzle is the star trumpet player for the Pirelli Youth Orchestra. Splat becomes the new tuba player. Their love for music and their understanding of its meaning grow as they rehearse with the orchestra's conductor, Vidor Pirelli.

THE MEANING BEHIND THE MUSIC

RONALD KIDD

"Ladies and gentlemen, we begin please at letter P. This is coming into the last movement."

Vidor Pirelli moved nervously about the podium. He used any small motion to pass the time, which moved so much more slowly than he did.

I opened the first trumpet part of the Sibelius (sə bāl′ yəs) Second Symphony and turned to letter P. It was one of many key points in the music marked with a letter for rehearsal purposes. As I did, I looked down the row of brass players, the trumpets, trombones, and tubas. Splat was sitting there. His instrument was sitting in its case several feet away. Pirelli, afraid that two tubas playing at once might

407

overpower the rest of the orchestra, had asked him to alternate with the regular tuba player, Eddie Greenbaum. Since Eddie was playing the first half of the rehearsal, Splat was resting.

Pirelli tapped his baton on the podium. "Before we begin to start," he said, "we must know the meaning behind our music. Mr. Jean Sibelius wanted freedom for his Finland peoples, and in this Second Symphony he shows them the way. At letter P we can hear the peoples calling for freedom, and then rumblings of excitement grow as they see it far away. It gets close and close, and then at letter R freedom is here. It is so happy. Now come on."

He turned to his left. "Young people of the violins," Pirelli said, "your beautiful notes here are the rocks on which your colleagues in woodwinds and brasses build. Please to rehearse it now."

"Mr. Pirelli," came a voice from the back of the room, "he's pulling my hair!"

"She started it!"

"Please, Jerry and Sandra, please! Act right. We are in the cathedral of music. Mr. Jean Sibelius is trying to speak to us." Jerry and Sandra glanced at each other, then turned back to their music.

Pirelli had the violins play their part, warning them not to slow down in the difficult passages. Next he combined the violins with the violas, cellos, and basses. Satisfied with the strings, he turned to the woodwind section.

"My young friends the woodwinds, your turn now comes. While the violins sing out their hearts

408

in a steady beat, you run along with shouts of
excitement. 'Look!' you are saying. 'Look, it is
coming, it is coming! Freedom, isn't it lovely!' All
right, letter P, we now try it."

He gave them the downbeat, and there it was,
just as he said. You could hear the excitement and
see it in the faces of the clarinet and flute players.

Finally Pirelli looked up at the brass section.
"You are so lucky, you peoples, because Mr. Jean

Sibelius has given the greatest honor to you in this symphony. You are freedom itself, shining bright. Please now to play your part, and let us listen to freedom."

It was the kind of part brass players love, the kind that keeps you going when you're sitting there counting rests, wondering why the violins get all the fun parts. We must have done a good job playing it, because when we stopped there was a

moment of silence before Pirelli murmured, "Ah, yes, my young friends."

"And now," he went on, "we ask the drums and other percussion to join in, and we put all the sections together at the same time. Come on now, letter P."

The music began. The strings swirled and throbbed, then came the cries of the woodwinds, and finally, soaring above it all, the brass. As we launched into the fanfare at the beginning of the last movement, the feeling started. It was a dizzy sort of feeling, as if suddenly I was way up in the sky looking down. It was a feeling of rightness, of everything being just as it should be. Along with it there was what Pirelli meant when he talked about the cathedral of music.

"All right, peoples," Pirelli said when we had finished rehearsing the Sibelius. "Please now turn to *Pictures at an Exhibition*, by Mr. Moussorgsky (mu̇ sôrg′ skē). As you play, pretend you be walking very nice through a museum, with many paintings hanging on the walls. As you stop and look at each one, you sing out how it makes you feel. Some are happy, some are angry. Listen closely to the music and you see what I mean. We begin, please, at letter T. This picture is an old man pushing his cart steady down the old cobbled street. We have a tuba solo, which we shall play on baritone horn. Carl, please to get your instrument."

The baritone horn is similar to the trombone in range and tone, so it is usually played by one of the trombonists. But as Carl Freidlander, the first trombonist, reached for his baritone, a voice came from the end of the row. "Why don't we play it on the tuba?" It was Splat. "We can do it, can't we?" He asked Eddie Greenbaum. Eddie shook his head. "Well, then, I'll give it a try," said Splat. He rose from his chair and went over to take his tuba out of its case.

"You are Arthur, isn't this true?" asked Pirelli. They had met before the rehearsal.

"That's right."

"Well, Arthur, I must thank you extremely," said Pirelli, "but this solo plays too high for the tuba."

"Not for my tuba." Splat lifted his instrument and carried it over to his chair. "Ready when you are, maestro," he said.

Pirelli smiled uncertainly and raised his baton. "Ladies and gentlemens, please, letter T."

With the downbeat, the string basses began a sad tune, and Splat started in. To my amazement, the tone that came out was full and round and golden. Heads turned and eyebrows rose as the solo went on. As Splat played it, you could imagine every aching muscle on the stoop-shouldered old man in the painting. I guess you might say Splat was doing what Pirelli constantly asked us to do in our music: Tell a story.

When the last phrase died away, Pirelli made a motion I'd never seen him make before. He laid down his baton and started applauding. Everyone else joined in. "Bravo, young tuba friend," he called. "Bravo, Arthur."

In the second half of the rehearsal, the brass section sounded better than I'd ever heard it. With Splat playing tuba, our chords were fuller and richer because we had a strong foundation to build on.

At noon, Pirelli stopped us. "That's finish for today, ladies and gentlemens. You play lovely for me this morning. Keep that safe in your heart for next week, and we will do this again."

Questions

1. Who was Mr. Pirelli?
2. How did Mr. Pirelli feel when Splat had finished the solo?
3. Do you think that Mr. Pirelli's comments on the music and the composers helped to inspire the orchestra members? Why or why not?
4. Has a teacher or another person in your life influenced your feelings about something you were interested in? Describe the person and tell how he or she affected you.

Applying Reading Skills

Number your paper from 1 to 3. Read the following sentences. Use context clues to choose the meaning of each underlined word. Write the word and its meaning on your paper.

1. Sandra's hands fairly flew over the keys of the piano without missing a note. Her dexterity was amazing!
   a. skill   b. speed
   c. strength   d. smoothness

2. The trio was made up of a flutist, a pianist, and a guitarist.
   a. orchestra   b. group of two
   c. group of three   d. musical group

3. The musicians played the same notes over and over. The monotony of the music made Carl sleepy.
   a. soothing quality b. sameness
   c. softness   d. speed

How to Sing or Read

Robert Louis Stevenson

Mark the note that rises, mark the notes that fall.

Mark the time when broken, and the swing of it all.

So when night is come, and you have gone to bed,

All the songs you love to sing shall echo in your head.

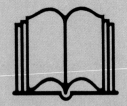

PREPARING FOR READING

Learning Vocabulary

1. Instrumentalists, or people who play musical instruments, were the first stars of jazz.
2. Later, vocalists, or singers, entered the jazz scene.
3. Many famous jazz musicians have made appearances for many, many years.
4. Some of the best jazz performances were improvised, or made up at the moment.

instrumentalists   vocalists

appearances   improvised

Developing Background and Skills
Context Clues

You know that one way to find out the meaning of unknown or unfamiliar words is to use **context clues.** You can use nearby words, phrases, and sentences to help you learn the meaning of words that you don't know. Sometimes clues in more than one or two sentences may be needed to help you be sure about a word's meaning.

Read the paragraph on the next page. What clues can you find to the meaning of the underlined word?

Bob "Buttons" Brown <u>devoted</u> his life to music. He began singing at an early age, and before he was 20, he had become famous. Later, he started working out his own arrangements and composing his own music. For years he contributed articles on jazz to leading magazines. He always gave encouragement to young musicians and set up several scholarships to help them in their careers.

All the sentences in the paragraph after the first one give you clues to the meaning of devoted. They are examples of the ways Bob "Buttons" Brown was involved in music. They should help you figure out that *devoted* means "gave or applied time, effort, or attention to some purpose."

As you read the next selection, you may come across words that are unknown or whose meaning is not clear. Try to figure out their meaning by using context clues. You may want to check your definitions of the words against those found in the dictionary.

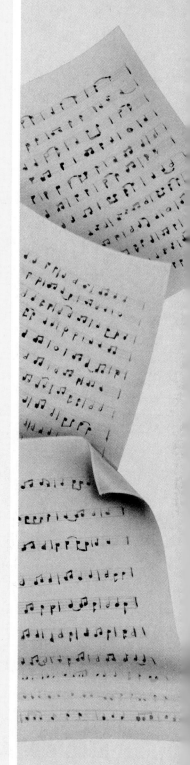

Jazz

Langston Hughes

Jazz started with people singing. It came from church songs and from music that people sang to express their feelings about work and love and life in general.

We don't know the names of the earliest jazz singers. They were not very famous people. Instrumentalists like Buddy Bolden and King Oliver were the first stars of jazz. As time passed, talented singers, or "vocalists," appeared. They took the old church songs and shaped them into something quite new.

Some instrumentalists were almost as well known for their singing as they were for their playing. Louis Armstrong would often play one chorus of a song with his trumpet and then sing the next chorus. One time Louis dropped his sheet music. He was recording a song called "Heebie Jeebies." Since he couldn't read the words, he made up nonsense phrases like "skee-bee-da-bee-dip" to go with the melody. It sounded good on the record, so Louis and other singers tried it on other songs. This was the start of what we call "scat" singing.

Jelly Roll Morton, Roy Eldridge, and Jack Teagarden were other jazzmen who were best known

Left to right:
Jack Teagarden (top), Jelly Roll Morton (bottom), Louis Armstrong, Roy Eldridge

Jazz

for their playing but had almost as much talent at singing. Roy Eldridge, a short man, came to be known as "Little Jazz." In 1981, in his seventies, "Little Jazz" was still playing and singing. Ray Charles and the late Nat "King" Cole were both pianists. They are examples of instrumentalists who became even better known for their singing.

But it was women who took the spotlight when jazz singing first began to build a public following. In 1920, a blues singer from Cincinnati named Mamie Smith made a record of a song called "Crazy Blues." It was the first jazz vocal ever recorded and one of the first jazz recordings of any kind by a black artist. It caused a sensation among black people. It was their kind of music, and they had never had a chance to hear it on a record before. Mamie Smith became a star almost overnight. She made many more records and toured the country for several years with small bands. Mamie became known as the "Queen of the Blues."

Bessie Smith was a woman from Mississippi with a voice so powerful she could shout down

Left to right:
Ray Charles, Mamie Smith and the Jazz Hounds, Bessie Smith

the loudest instruments in a band. During the 1920s and early 1930s, Bessie made hundreds of records and appeared with the best musicians of the day. If Mamie Smith had been "Queen," Bessie Smith was truly "Empress of the Blues." That's what she was called.

These early blues stars were not sweet singers. Their songs were mostly loud. The melodies were simple and so were the words. This music was very different from the kind of music most Americans were listening to at the time.

That started to change when jazz was played on the radio. It spread around the country. Some of the country's best songwriters, like George Gershwin, Harold Arlen, Jerome Kern, and Duke Ellington began to work the rhythms and the blue notes of jazz into their songs. Other com-

posers picked up the idea. In the 1920s and 1930s, American songwriters poured out a flood of songs with a jazz "feel." Songs like "Stardust," "On the Sunny Side of the Street," and "Stormy Weather," were some of the most popular.

You can't draw a clear line between "jazz" and "pop" music. Jazz is a way of playing rather than a kind of song. A "popular" song is any song a lot of people want to hear. But great songs like these helped bring jazz into the mainstream of American music, and so did the people who sang them.

Mildred Bailey, a big woman with a small, delicate voice, made her reputation singing pop songs with genuine jazz phrasing.

She was the first great "band singer" of the big band era.

Another great singer was Billie Holiday, the beautiful "Lady Day." She had a hard life as a child. She expressed the hurts of those years in her singing. Billie could do things with her voice that seemed to make every song she sang belong to her alone.

Ella Fitzgerald was competing in a singing contest when drummer Chick Webb spotted her in a Harlem theater. He signed her up for his band. When Webb died five years later (in 1939), Ella was a star. She took over the leader-

ship of the band for a while. The "First Lady of Swing" was still making club and television appearances more than forty years later. No other jazz vocalist has been able to swing so well for so long.

The most famous singers appeared with the big bands. Frank Sinatra became one of the most popular. Sinatra wasn't known as a "jazz singer" at first. But later, after he left the band and went on his own, he made some of the best jazz vocals ever recorded. He had a real jazz sense for the beat, but

Left to right:
Billie Holiday (top), Ella Fitzgerald (bottom), Mildred Bailey, Frank Sinatra

Jazz

paid attention to the words, too. Sinatra set a standard for all jazz singers who followed.

You could say that Sinatra's singing started something. American popular music has just about been taken over by singers in the last thirty years. Sinatra, Ella Fitzgerald, Mel Torme, Peggy Lee, and other singers who sang with the big bands continued to perform the kinds of songs the bands made popular. They stayed on top long after the bands themselves had gone.

New kinds of singers came along, too. Aretha Franklin blended gospel and blues styles into something that came to be called "soul." Ray Charles took gospel music and filled it with an emotional charge that could make people jump from their seats and shout with excitement. Sarah Vaughan echoed the swoops and swirls of bebop and "progressive" music played by jazz instrumentalists in the 1950s.

Then came rock. By the 1960s, rock music was pushing even the best jazz singers into the background. Rock is not jazz. You listen to it in a different way. Rock 'n roll started as an offshoot of the old rhythm and blues

Left to right:
Aretha Franklin, Lionel
Ritchie, Olivia Newton-
John (top), Sarah Vaughan
(bottom)

music, but with a heavier, more regular beat. The excitement came from the heavy beat and the loud sound. Rock groups also used lighting and costumes to make their acts more dramatic.

Rock has produced many talented and original singers. Groups like the Beatles, Hall and Oates, and the Go-Gos, and individuals like Lionel Ritchie, Olivia Newton-John, and Billy Joel use more interesting harmonies along with simple rock 'n roll chords. They often write and sing lyrics that make people want to listen to the words as well as feel the beat of the music. Some of their best performances are improvised. In the tradition of jazz, they make up their music as they play it.

Questions

1. Choose two of the musicians discussed in the selection and write a sentence about each.
2. Explain how jazz originated.
3. Do you think recordings helped make jazz popular more quickly than it might otherwise have become? Explain your answer.
4. Have you ever listened to jazz music? Tell how it is different from other music you have heard.

Applying Reading Skills

Number your paper from 1 to 3. Read the sentences below, then use context clues to choose the meaning of each underlined word. Write the word and its meaning on your paper.

1. The song began slowly, then its tempo increased. The acceleration made the music very exciting.
   a. mood   b. time
   c. speeding up   d. enlargement

2. As Cummins began to listen to the other jazz musicians of his day, their styles began to influence his own.
   a. affect   b. improve
   c. control   d. help

3. The saxophonist played the same notes over and over. This constant repetition seemed to bother the audience.
   a. repeating   b. noise
   c. beat   d. vibration

SWEETWATER

LAURENCE YEP

The galaxy is an awfully big place so I don't expect you to know about my home world, Harmony. My ancestors came from Earth. If you go out some cold winter night and look for your constellation Virgo, you might be able to see the tiny pinprick of light on her left side where her heart ought to be. That's my star. Even if you strained your eyes, you wouldn't be able to see the fifth planet around that star, which is my world.

The first thing you ought to know is that our colony here was split into two groups, the ones we call the Mainlanders and my own group, the Silkies. You see, the original colony built a city on what they thought was the coast; but Harmony has a fifty-year cycle of tides and they built Old Sion during the lowest time of the tides. When the sea rose, it submerged half the city. Many colonists gave up and moved to the mountain ranges where they knew it would be dry. They built a new city, called New Sion.

But my ancestors stayed on in the city. They learned to adjust to the new kind of life, and traveled in the flooded streets in boats. They took so well to the half-flooded city that the other colonists began to call my ancestors Silkies. The Mainlanders meant it as an insult because the mythical Silkies were so ugly on the land. My ancestors adopted the name with pride because the Silkies were beautiful in their own mysterious sea.

From the very day the colony was founded, my ancestors had never gotten along with the other colonists. My ancestors had been the crews of the starships that had brought the colonists here. They had never meant to stay, but when their starships broke down, they were stranded.

These lonely people fell in love with a city no one else wanted. Each family of Silkies took a house, salvaging more than enough to make their homes comfortable. A lot of the former residents just left things—like chairs and tables. They meant to come back for them later. Then they just forgot about them.

My ancestors took their food from the sea. They turned the flooded streets into sea gardens by damming them with rubble and then stocking each alley with oysters, clams, and seaweed.

For two weeks of each winter, the whole community would do nothing but eat and sing and dance. The only time I saw Pa dance in public was at the winter party two years ago, when I was eleven. The marvelous sight of Pa dancing was what got me so interested in music. A master fiddler by the name of Jubal Hatcher came to that party, and his bow work could have matched Great-Great-Grandpa's.

Jubal Hatcher was an old friend of Pa's. During the winter, he and his wife Poppy came up north in their boat. They play music all around the country just for the fun of it.

Jubal raised his fiddle and shouted out, "Gonna play 'Sweetwater,' neighbors." It was an old hymn from Earth and Pa's favorite. It put him into just the right mood.

When Jubal started the next song, Pa couldn't take it anymore. He got up out of his chair. Then he turned to Ma with a grin.

Ma was a tall woman with a solid frame, but she could move real light and easy. She was smiling now. She did love music.

She let Caley, my sister, slide off her lap and she stood up, gracefully brushing the wrinkles from her formal dress. She let Pa take her in his arms and they danced out there on the floor—No, not danced, they floated out there with hardly any effort.

I wanted that music so bad. You might call it
hillbilly music and even a mainland foolishness, but
that's all right. There was never any kind of music
that wouldn't catch you as long as it was done
right before you. Music is music. I don't care what
type, be it free jazz or a child's off-key singing.
It's music if it reaches inside and makes you want
to keep time right along from the tappings of your
toes to the nodding of your head because you want
to be part of that rhythm.

After that night when I saw what music could
do, there was nothing for me to do but carve out

a flute. I just had to be a musician. What with school in the morning and chores in the afternoon, I only had an hour of spare time every day before dinner, but I was determined to make the most of it. I found out that while it may be hard to listen to a beginner learning how to play an instrument, it's twice as bad to be the beginner and know that you're playing badly. I wanted to find someplace where no one could hear me play.

I knew there was one place in Old Sion where no Silkie would hear me, because no Silkie would go there. I was willing to go there to find a place where I could practice. I planned to go to Sheol.

We still called the area by its old name, given when Sheol was the most elegant and expensive area in Old Sion. Now the mansions were occupied by the Argans, the only intelligent race native to Harmony. The Argans were a strange race, and they liked to keep their secrets.

There were some humans who had never forgiven the aliens because they didn't warn the colonists about the tides, but then we weren't asked to come to their world.

Later when the city, Old Sion, was abandoned, the Argans drifted back from the wastelands, claiming that the land was still theirs. By that time it didn't matter who Old Sion belonged to legally, because the sea had already filled most of the city.

Sheol didn't look like it belonged to people anymore. The elegant houses looked like ancient monsters. Their great stone faces were covered with delicate beards of green seaweed.

It was really scary, but I thought like a human in those days. I figured that whether the Argans liked it or not, I was going to practice there. I picked out the finest and biggest mansion, which had been built on a hill. I tied my boat to one of the pillars and splashed up the steps. I checked the rooms on both floors for the acoustics until I found one that satisfied me. Then I practiced my scales until I heard something strange.

At first I thought it was the wind but then I realized it was music, and the more I listened, the more I felt that I had never heard anything more lovely. The song was at once sad and yet beautiful. The echoes floated up the street over water, past the empty apartment houses. It bounced and danced past walls that slowly spilled stone after stone into the sea. It was a song for Old Sion.

I had to find the musician and I searched the entire mansion until I found him sitting by my boat. It was an Argan, an old one, sitting there calmly. The bristly fur on his back and arm-legs was a peppery gray. He looked very much like a four-foot-high Earth spider, though you would never suggest that to an Argan.

He put down his reed pipes when he saw me. He seemed surprised and walked around me. He walked delicately on two arm-legs like a ballet dancer imitating an old man. His six other arm-legs stretched out to balance his overpuffed body. He stepped back in front of me and examined me boldly.

"What can I do for you, Manchild?" he asked.

I shifted uncomfortably from one foot to the other. I told myself that it was silly to feel like I had invaded this Argan's home. In those days I believed I had as much right to this place as the Argans did. "I heard you playing," I said finally.

"My nephews and my neighbors heard your free concert," the old Argan said. "They found me and told me so I could come home and hear my competition."

"There's no competition," I mumbled. It was

easy enough to get embarrassed about my playing in those days. "Well," I added, "I guess I'll be moving on. I don't want to drive folk away from their homes."

"What do they know? It's the song that counts, not the singer." He pointed at the flute. "That's a mighty nice flute. Did you carve it?"

I turned my flute over in my hands. "I'm afraid I spent more time carving pictures into it than I did playing it."

"Do you like music?"

"More than anything," I said. "But there's no one to teach me."

"Of course." The old Argan was thoughtful for a moment. "What did you think of my song? It was just a little night music."

"I thought it was beautiful," I said and added truthfully, "it was the most beautiful thing I've ever heard."

I don't know what he was looking for, but he studied me for a long time.

"Would you like me to teach you?" the old Argan said.

I felt a warm rush of gratitude inside me. "I would like it an awful lot if you would teach me, Mister . . ." I realized that I had almost made a bad mistake. Argans don't believe in giving their true names. They feel that gives the listener power over the person named. Argans have what they call use-names, which they change every so often.

"My use-name is Amadeus (ä′ mə dā′ əs). Come back tomorrow night and I'll see if I can teach you that you have only two thumbs and not ten."

I knew that I had met one of the aliens' songsmiths, and all the way home I felt warm and good inside. I knew what a privilege I was being given. If there is one thing the Argans love, it's their music.

The Argans don't think of music as we humans do. An Argan song seems skimpy by human standards. It just has a basic story line—like how the three moons were created—and a theme of music which represents the song. It's up to the musician to combine established themes which the audience recognizes as representing a castle, or a feast, or a heroic battle, or anything like that.

In Argan music, songs keep on evolving and changing as they are played. The Argans think that the human style is the mark of a mediocre musician. Only mediocre musicians play a song in the same way all the time. In human music, since you usually have a song sheet, the musician is limited to a fixed pattern of themes. His performance is judged by his skill in playing the song. But in Argan music, the best musicians have to be not only skilled players but also geniuses at finding new and original patterns.

Of course, Argan music isn't really that loose. When I first started to play it, I wondered how a musician knew what to play next, since you had to choose while performing at the same time. Now I know that there's a kind of logic to it—like know-

ing the ending to a story halfway through the telling. For example, if two Argan heroes meet, you have to describe both of them, and their battle.

Amadeus was very patient about explaining things like that about music. He really earned his title, the Ultimate Uncle—which was his social position among the Argans. He hated to talk about himself and Argan affairs, but about music there was almost no stopping him. I took to visiting Sheol three times a week, and Amadeus would listen patiently. Whenever I tried to apologize for a particularly clumsy performance, he would encourage me by telling me that my song and I had not found one another yet. According to Argan belief, it's the song that finds the singer and not the other way around.

After a while, though, not even that belief could satisfy me. "It's no use, Amadeus. I'm never going to be a musician."

Amadeus sighed and shook his head. "Manchild, you have everything that a person needs to make music. You have the talent, you have the skills now, but you still hold your soul back from the music. You can't forget you're a human playing Argan music. You just have to remember that it's the music that counts—not the one who plays it."

With that he put the reed pipes to his mouth and began to play the human song, "Moonspring." I sat in astonishment as he slipped next into "Shall We Gather by the Stars" and "These Happy Golden Years."

"Amadeus, where did you ever learn to play human songs?" I asked in amazement.

He made a disappointed noise. "Manchild, didn't I just tell you that a musician can play both 'human' and 'Argan' music? I'm not an Argan playing human songs. I'm a musician making music. The only thing that matters in this changing universe is the song, the eternal song that waits for you."

"Yes, but—"

"Play," Amadeus angrily ordered, so I played. It was strange. Amadeus wouldn't talk about himself and he wouldn't let me talk about myself. Yet I felt closer to him than I had to anyone else. And in the moments when I doubted myself, Amadeus somehow always managed to keep me looking for my song.

Anybody who thinks Argan music is easy to learn has never really tried to master it. A lot of it was boring work when I had to master all the themes so I would have a variety to choose from. After a year's work, I could play two songs well. Even Amadeus had to admit I was a good backup man—though I had yet to be found by my own song. But then one night he sat for a long time and smoothed the hair down on his arms thoughtfully before he finally looked up at me again. "I don't know what to do, Manchild. You're not going to develop any more unless you listen to others play— and you play for others."

"Amadeus," I said, "have they been staying away because of me or have you been keeping them away so I wouldn't be nervous?"

"A little of both," Amadeus said.

"The Argans don't like the idea of your giving me lessons, do they?"

"Who told you?" he asked angrily. "You pay those fools no mind. They've heard you play but they just won't believe."

"Believe what?" I asked.

"That an Argan song will ever find a human," Amadeus was forced to admit.

I gave up asking any more questions and just thought for a while. After all he had done for my sake I could hardly do less. "If you can get some of them together, I'll play for them," I said. "We'll show them."

Amadeus made sure I wanted to go through with it before he named the next night for my test. That night there must have been some twenty Argans sitting on the porch. The moment I sat down to warm up they began to crack jokes in the

clicking language of the Argans. I did not know the words but their jokes were obviously about me.

"You just start whenever you like, Manchild. Don't you mind the noise." If I had been Amadeus, I would have been jumping up and down with anxiety, but Amadeus had a quiet kind of strength. He was like a calm pool of water that you could have dropped anything into and it wouldn't have disturbed the pool besides a momentary ripple. Just having Amadeus there gave me confidence.

"I'd like to play now, Amadeus," I said.

"Well," and Amadeus nodded to me approvingly, "well, go on."

I shut my eyes against all the furry faces and I tilted my head up toward the night sky, toward the stars. Suddenly my song had found me. It was "Sweetwater," the song Jubal had played at that winter party—but now I made it my own. I took the melody and I played it like an Argan, modeling my song after an Argan song about a lost child looking for its mother. All the months of frustration poured out of me. I played like I was the lost, lonely child calling across the empty light-years of space to Mother Earth.

When I felt the song was finished, I put the flute down to see Amadeus laughing to himself. The other Argans looked a little stunned. Amadeus started to play a theme, this time an Argan song, "The Enchanted Reed Pipes." I played backup man but he was the master, sending his song ringing and echoing up the empty streets, the two of us gone mad with music.

Glossary

This glossary can help you to pronounce and find out the meanings of words in this book that you may not know.

The words are listed in alphabetical order. Guide words at the top of each page tell you the first and last words on the page.

Each word is divided into syllables. The way to pronounce each word is given next. You can understand the pronunciation respelling by using the key below. A shorter key appears at the bottom of every other page.

When a word has more than one syllable, a dark accent mark (′) shows which syllable is stressed. In some words, a light accent mark (′) shows which syllable has a less heavy stress.

The following abbreviations are used in this glossary:

n. noun   *v.* verb   *adj.* adjective   *adv.* adverb   *pl.* plural

The glossary entries were adapted from the Macmillan *School Dictionary.*

PRONUNCIATION KEY
Vowel Sounds

/a/	bat	/ō/	rope, soap, so, snow
/ā/	cake, rain ,day	/ô/	saw, song, auto
/ä/	father	/oi/	coin, boy
/är/	car	/ôr/	fork, ore, oar
/ãr/	dare, hair	/ou/	out, cow
/e/	hen, bread	/u/	sun, son, touch
/ē/	me, meat, baby, believe	/ù/	book, pull, could
/èr/	term, first, worm, turn	/ü/	moon
/i/	bib	/ū/	cute, few, music
/ī/	kite, fly, pie, light	/ə/	about, taken, pencil,
/ir/	clear, cheer, here		apron, helpful
/o/	top, watch	/ər/	letter, dollar, doctor

Consonant Sounds

/b/	bear	/s/	city, seal
/d/	dog	/t/	tiger
/f/	fish, phone	/v/	van
/g/	goat	/w/	wagon
/h/	house, who	/y/	yo-yo
/j/	jar, gem, fudge	/z/	zoo, eggs
/k/	car, key	/ch/	chain, match
/l/	lamb	/sh/	show
/m/	map	/th/	thin
/n/	nest, know	/th/	those
/p/	pig	/hw/	where
/r/	rug, wrong	/ng/	song

A

ab·a·cus (ab′ ə kəs) *n., pl.*
ab·a·cus·es, ab·a·ci (ab′ ə sī). a
device made up of a frame with balls or
beads that slide back and forth on wires,
used especially for adding and
subtracting.

a·bide (ə bīd′) *v.* **a·bode** or **a·bid·ed,**
a·bid·ing. put up with; tolerate. **to**
abide by. to obey.

a·bil·i·ty (ə bil′ ə tē) *n., pl.* **a·bil·i·ties.**
the power to do or act.

a·bun·dance (ə bun′ dəns) *n.* plentiful
supply.

ac·a·dem·ic (ak′ ə dem′ ik) *adj.* relating
to general education, especially to that
which prepares the student for college.

ac·com·pa·nist (ə kum′ pə nist) *n.* one
who plays or sings a musical background
for the principal part.

ac·com·plish (ə kom′ plish) *v.* to carry
out; perform.

ac·cuse (ə kūz′) *v.* **ac·cused,**
ac·cus·ing. to find fault with; blame.

a·cous·tics (ə küs′ tiks) *n., pl.* the
qualities of a room, theater, auditorium, or
the like that determine how well sound is
carried and heard in it.

a·drift (ə drift′) *adj.* moving freely with the
current or wind; not tied or anchored;
drifting.

ag·ate (ag′ it) *n.* a type of quartz, usually
having layers or bands of different colors.

ag·o·ny (ag′ ə nē) *n., pl.* **ag·o·nies.**
great pain or suffering of the mind or
body.

ai·le·ron (ā′ lə ron′) *n.* a moveable flap
along the back edge of an airplane's
wing, used to move the airplane to the
right or left.

al·ien (āl′ yən, ā′ lē ən) *n.* **1.** a being from
another planet. **2.** a person who is not a
citizen of the country in which he is
living.—*adj.* of or belonging to another
country, place, or people.

al·ly (al′ ī, ə lī′) *n., pl.* **al·lies.** a person,
nation, or group united with another for a
common purpose.

al·ter·nate (ôl′ tər nāt′) *v.* **al·ter·nat·ed,**
al·ter·nat·ing. to take turns.

al·ter·na·tive (ôl tėr′ nə tiv) *n.* a choice
between two or more things.

al·tim·e·ter (al tim′ ə tər, al′ tə mē′ tər) *n.*
instrument for measuring height above
sea level or ground.

al·ti·tude (al′ tə tüd′, al′ tə tūd′) *n.* the
height that something is above the
ground or above sea level.

am·e·thyst (am′ ə thist) *n.* a purple or
violet quartz. Amethyst is often used as
an ornament or jewelry.

a·mi·go (ə mē′ gō) *n.* the Spanish word
for friend.

an·ces·tor (an′ ses tər) *n.* a person of
one's family who lived long ago.

an·chor (ang′ kər) *v.*
1. to fasten in
place; fix firmly.
2. to hold a boat or
ship in place by an
anchor.

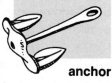

anchor

an·cient (ān′ shənt) *adj.* **1.** very old.
2. having to do with times long past.

an·gle (ang′ gəl) *n.* the space between
one surface and another, usually
measured in degrees.

an·nu·al (an ū əl) *adj.* occurring or
returning once a year.

anx·i·e·ty (ang zī′ ə tē) *n., pl.*
anx·i·e·ties. a feeling of worry or fear
about what may happen; uneasiness.

ap · pear · ance (ə pir′ əns) *n*. a public performance.

ap · ply (ə plī′) *v*. to make a request; ask.

ap · point (ə point′) *v*. to name or select for an office or position.

ar · ter · y (är′ tər ē) *n*., *pl*. **ar · ter · ies.** one of the tubes carrying blood away from the heart to all parts of the body.

artery

as · sist · ant (ə sis′ tənt) *n*. a person who assists; helper.

as · sure (ə shür′) *v*. **as · sured, as · sur · ing.** to guarantee; tell with confidence.

A · the · na (ə thē′ nə) in Greek mythology, the goddess of wisdom and the arts.

at · om (at′ əm) *n*. the smallest particle of a chemical element that has all the qualities of that element. An atom has a central nucleus of protons and neutrons that is surrounded by electrons.

at · ten · tive (ə ten′ tiv) *adj*. paying attention; listening closely.

au · di · ence (ô′ dē əns) *n*. a group of people gathered to hear or see something, such as a recital.

au · di · tion (ô dish′ ən) *v*. **au · di · tion · ing, au · di · tioned.** to test the abilities of a singer, musician, actor, or other performer.

av · er · age (av′ rij, av′ ər ij) *adj*. ordinary; usual.

a · vi · a · tion (ā′ vē ā′ shən, a′ vē ā′ shən) *n*. **1.** the science or art of flying heavier-than-air aircraft. **2.** the design and production of heavier-than-air aircraft.

a · vi · a · tor (ā′ vē ā′ tər, av′ ē ā′ tər) *n*. a person who flies an airplane or other heavier-than-air aircraft; pilot.

a · void (ə void′) *v*. **1.** to keep from happening. **2.** to keep away from.

awe (ô) *n*. great wonder, fear, or respect.

B

Bach, Jo · hann Se · bas · tian (bäk, yō′ hän sə bas′ chən) 1685–1750, German composer and organist.

bail (bāl) *v*. to remove water with a pail or similar container.

ban · dit (ban′ dit) *n*. a robber or outlaw.

ban · ish (ban′ ish) *v*. to punish someone by making him or her leave the country.

barb (bärb) *n*. **1.** one of the narrow bristles growing from the shaft of a bird's feather. **2.** a point or hook that extends backward from the tip.

bar · na · cle (bär′ nə kəl) *n*. any of a number of small shellfish that attach themselves to underwater objects, such as ship bottoms and rocks.

barnacle

barn · storm (bärn′ stôrm′) *v*. to tour rural or outlying areas as a stunt flyer or pilot.

bar · ri · er (bār′ ē ər) *n*. something that blocks the way.

bass (bās) *n*., *pl*. **bass · es. 1.** a musical instrument that is able to make a very low sound. **2.** lowest male singing voice.— *adj*. **1.** having the lowest range in a class of instruments. **2.** deep or low in sound.

bat · ten (bat′ ən) *v*. to fasten or strengthen something with a batten, or long, narrow strip of wood or metal, used on a ship to fasten canvas over a hatch, or opening. **to batten down the hatches.** to cover the openings of a ship's deck with canvas and fasten them with battens.

bean ball (bēn′ bôl′) *n.* a baseball that is pitched at or near a batter's head.

Bee · tho · ven, Lud · wig van (bā′ tō′ vən, lüd′ wig vän) 1770–1827, German composer.

Bel · ler · o · phon (bə lãr′ ə fon′) in Greek legend, the hero who tamed the winged horse Pegasus.

ben · e · fit (ben′ ə fit) *n.* advantage; something that helps or makes better.

be · tray (bi trā′) *v.* **1.** to give away a secret. **2.** to help the enemy of.

board · ing house (bôr′ ding hous′) *n.* a place at which people are housed and fed for pay.

bold · ly (bōld′ lē) *adv.* with courage; fearlessly.

bound (bound) *v.* to move in a series of leaps; jump; spring.

box (boks) *v.* to place or pack in a box. **to box the compass.** to name the thirty-two points of the compass in the proper order.

brass · es (bras′ əs) *n., pl.* the section of an orchestra consisting of musical wind instruments made of brass or other metal, such as the trombone, trumpet, or tuba.

breed (brēd) *v.* **bred, breed · ing.** to raise plants or animals, especially in order to develop new or improved kinds.

bri · dle (brīd′ əl) *n.* the part of a horse's harness that fits over the animal's head, used to guide or control the horse.

bridle

broad · cast (brôd′ kast′) *v.* **broad · cast · ed, broad · cast · ing.** to send out information or entertainment by radio or television.

buf · fet (buf′ it) *v.* to knock or toss about.

C

cal · cu · la · tions (kal′ kyə lā′ shənz) *n., pl.* the answers or results of figuring out with mathematics; estimates.

ca · mel · lia (kə mēl′ yə) *n.* a sweet-smelling flower that grows on shrubs and trees. Camellias are grown in warm, damp regions and have white, red, or pink petals.

can · di · date (kan′ də dāt′) *n.* a person who is being thought about for a job.

car · go (kär′ gō) *n., pl.* **car · goes, car · gos.** goods carried by a ship.

Car · ne · gie, An · drew (kär nā′ gē, kär′ nə gē; an′ drü) 1835–1919, U.S. steel manufacturer and philanthropist.

cease (sēs) *v.* **ceased, ceas · ing.** to stop; come to an end.

cel · lo (chel′ ō) *n.* a musical instrument of the violin family that is larger than a violin and lower in tone. A cello is held between the knees when it is played.

cello

cer · tif · i · cate (sər tif′ ə kit) *n.* a written statement declaring the truth of certain facts.

---

a b**a**t, ā c**a**ke, ä f**a**ther, är c**a**r, âr d**a**re; e h**e**n, ē m**e**, ėr t**e**rm; i b**i**b, ī k**i**te, ir cl**ea**r; o t**o**p, ō r**o**pe, ô s**a**w, oi c**oi**n, ôr f**o**rk, ou **o**ut; u s**u**n, u̇ b**oo**k, ü m**oo**n, ū c**u**te; ə **a**bout, tak**e**n

---

Cho·pin, Fre·de·ric (shō′ pan, fred′ ər ik) 1810–1849, Polish pianist and composer.

cir·cuit court (sėr′ kit kôrt′) *n.* a court that sits at different times in a number of places in the area it serves.

ci·vil·ian (si vil′ yən) *n.* a person who is not a member of the armed forces.

civ·i·li·za·tion (siv′ ə li zā′ shən) *n.* **1.** a condition of human society in which there is a highly developed knowledge of agriculture, trade, government, the arts, and science. **2.** way of life of a particular people, place, or time.

clam·ber (klam′ bər, klam′ ər) *v.* to climb by using both hands and feet; climb with difficulty or in a clumsy manner.

clar·i·net (klār′ ə net′) *n.* a musical instrument of the woodwind family, having a single reed mouthpiece and played by means of finger holes and keys.

clarinet

clas·si·cal mu·sic (klas′ i kəl mū′ zik) *n.* a type of music that is widely accepted as showing the highest standards of form and style. An important quality of classical music is that its value or worth is not changed by the passage of time.

cli·ent (klī′ ənt) *n.* a person or group that uses the professional services of another.

clutch (kluch) *v.* to grasp or hold tightly.

Coast Guard (kōst′ gärd′) *n.* a military service that patrols and defends the coasts and inland waterways of the United States.

cock·pit (kok′ pit′) *n.* open or enclosed compartment in an airplane where the pilot and copilot sit.

col·lapse (kə laps′) *v.* **col·lapsed, col·laps·ing.** to break down suddenly.

col·league (kol′ ēg) *n.* a fellow worker or member.

com·mend (kə mend′) *v.* to praise.

com·mis·sion (kə mish′ ən) *n.* a group of persons who are chosen to do certain work.

com·mit·tee (kə mit′ ē) *n.* a group of people who work together for a purpose.

com·mon (kom′ ən) *adj.* usual; appearing often.

com·pass (kum′ pəs, kom′ pəs) *n.* instrument for determining and showing directions, made of a magnetized needle which is freely suspended on a pivot and points to the North Magnetic Pole.

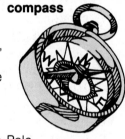
compass

com·pe·tent (kom′ pət ənt) *adj.* capable; having or showing enough ability or knowledge.

com·pe·ti·tion (kom′ pə tish′ ən) *n.* a person, group, or thing against which one competes, or proves oneself; competitor; rival; opponent.

com·pli·cat·ed (kom′ plə kā′ tid) *adj.* having many parts in a complex arrangement.

com·pli·ment (kom′ plə ment′) *v.* to praise; congratulate.

com·pos·er (kəm pō′ zər) *n.* a person who composes, or creates, music.

con·fi·dence (kon′ fə dəns) *n.* **1.** a secret. **2.** firm faith or trust.

con·fi·dent (kon′ fə dənt) *adj.* sure; certain; filled with confidence.

con · spir · a · cy (kən spir′ ə sē) *n., pl.*
con · spir · a · cies. 1. a secret plan; plot.
2. the act of secretly planning together to
carry out some evil or illegal act.

con · stel · la · tion
(kon′ stə lā′ shən)
n. a group of stars
forming a pattern
that looks like a
picture.

constellation

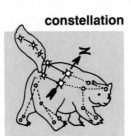

con · sult (kən sult′)
v. to look to for
information or
advice.

con · tend (kən tend′) *v.* to argue.

con · tour (kon′ tür) *adj.* made to fit or
closely following the shape of something.

con · tract (kon′ trakt) *n.* a written
agreement between two or more parties
to do or not to do something.

cool · ant (kü′ lənt) *n.* a substance used to
cool machines.

co · op · er · a · tion (kō op′ ə rā′ shən) *n.*
act of working together for a common
purpose.

cop · per · head (kop′ ər hed′) *n.* a
poisonous snake of the eastern United
States, having a copper-colored head
and a light brown body with dark brown
markings.

Cor · inth (kôr′ inth) a port city in southern
Greece. Corinth was an important trading
city and a center of the arts in ancient
times.

coun · sel (koun′ səl) *n.* a lawyer or
group of lawyers giving legal advice.

coun · se · lor (koun′ sə lər) *n.* a person
who gives advice; adviser.

coun · ter · bal · ance
(koun′ tər bal′ əns)
n. a weight used to
balance another
weight.

counterbalance

cour · age (kėr′ ij) *n.* a strength that a
person has that helps him or her to face
danger by overcoming fear; bravery.

course (kôrs) *n.* a route or direction taken.

cours · er (kôr′ sər) *n.* a swift or lively horse.

craft (kraft) *n.* a trade or job that requires
special skills.—*v.* to make by hand.

crane (krān) *n.* a large bird that has very
long thin legs and a long neck and bill.
Cranes live near water, and wade along
the shore looking for food in the water.

cres · cent (kres′ ənt) *n.* anything shaped
like the moon when only a thin, curved
part of it is visible.

crev · ice (krev′ is) *n.* a narrow crack into or
through something.

cri · tic (krit′ ik) *n.* **1.** one who judges works
of the fine arts or the performing arts,
reviewing them for their merits and faults.
2. one who judges severely or
unfavorably; faultfinder.

cross-ex · am · ine (krôs′ ig zam′ in) *v.*
cross-ex · am · ined, cross-
ex · am · in · ing. to question a witness
who has already testified for the
opposing side to determine the reliability
of the person's testimony or character.

crys · tal (krist′ əl) *n.* a solid body with a
number of flat surfaces.

---

a b**a**t, ā c**a**k**e**, ä f**a**th**e**r, är c**a**r, âr d**a**r**e**; e h**e**n, ē m**e**, ėr t**e**rm; i b**i**b, ī k**i**t**e**,
ir cl**e**ar; o t**o**p, ō r**o**p**e**, ô s**a**w, oi c**oi**n, ôr f**o**rk, ou **ou**t; u s**u**n, u̇ b**oo**k, ü m**oo**n,
ū c**u**t**e**; ə **a**b**ou**t, t**a**k**e**n

cur · rent (kur′ ənt) *n.* a part of a body of water or of air moving along in a path.

cy · cle (sī′ kəl) *n.* a series of events that happen one after another in the same order, over and over again.

D

dai · myo (dī′ myō) *n., pl.* **dai · myo, dai · myos.** before modern times, a noble in Japan who ruled over a large area.

dazed (dāzd) *adj.* stunned; confused; bewildered.

debt (det) *n.* something that is owed to another.

ded · i · ca · tion (ded′ ə kā′ shən) *n.* commitment.

deed (dēd) *n.* something done; act; action.

de · fend · ant (di fen′ dənt) *n.* a person against whom a case is brought in a court of law.

de · lib · er · ate · ly (di lib′ ər it lē) *adv.* on purpose; knowingly; intentionally.

de · mand (di mand′) *n.* something that is demanded; requirement.

dem · o · crat · ic (dem′ ə krat′ ik) *adj.* based on the idea of equal rights for all.

dem · on · strate (dem′ ən strāt′) *v.* **dem · on · strat · ed, dem · on · strat · ing.** to prove or make clear; show.

de · pos · it (di poz′ it) *v.* **1.** to put or lay down. **2.** to put money in a bank or other place for safekeeping.

de · scen · dant (di sen′ dənt) *n.* a person or animal whose ancestors can be traced.

de · scent (di sent′) *n.* movement from a higher place to a lower one.

de · sire (di zīr′) *n.* a longing for something.

des · ti · na · tion (des′ tə nā′ shən) *n.* a place to which a person is going.

de · vo · tion (di vō′ shən) *n.* a strong feeling of attachment or affection; loyalty.

di · ges · tion (di jes′ chən, dī jes′ chen) *n.* the breaking down of food in the mouth, stomach, and intestines so that it can be absorbed by the body.

dig · ni · ty (dig′ nə tē) *n., pl.* **dig · ni · ties.** the state of being noble, worthy, or honorable.

dis · as · ter (di zas′ tər) *n.* any event that causes suffering, distress, or loss.

dis · ci · pline (dis′ ə plin) *v.* **dis · ci · plined, dis · ci · plin · ing.** to keep under control.

dis · tance (dis′ təns) *n.* the amount of space between two things.

dis · tract (dis trakt′) *v.* to draw one's attention away from something.

douse (dous) *v.* **doused, dous · ing.** to throw water or other liquid over; drench.

down · beat (doun′ bēt′) *n.* a downward hand movement made by a conductor to indicate the first accented beat in a measure.

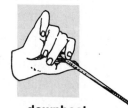

downbeat

down pay · ment (doun′ pā′ mənt) *n.* an amount of money that is paid on a purchase before the rest is paid.

drag (drag) *n.* resistance to the movement of something, such as the air slowing down an airplane moving through it.

drain (drān) *v.* to draw off a liquid gradually.

dram · a · tize (dram′ ə tīz′) *v.* **dram · a · tized, dram · a · tiz · ing. 1.** to act out in a dramatic way. **2.** to put into the form of a play or other dramatic performance.

dril · ling bit (dril′ ing bit′) *n.* a boring or drilling part that is used in a drill.

dwell · ing (dwel′ ing) *n.* the place where a person lives.

E

ef · fect (i fekt′) *n.* **1.** influence or impact. **2.** something brought about by a cause or agent; result; outcome.

el · e · va · tor (el′ ə vā′ tər) *n.* one of the two moveable flaps attached to the tail of an airplane. When the elevators are lowered, the tail of the plane rises and the nose drops.

elevator

e · merge (i merj′) *v.* **e · merged, e · merg · ing. 1.** to rise or come out; come forth. **2.** to come into view.

em · pha · sis (em′ fə sis) *n., pl.* **em · pha · ses** (em′ fə sēz′). a special importance given to something.

en · chant · ed (en chant′ id) *adj.* created by a magic spell; magical.

en · dur · ing (en dür′ ing, en dūr′ ing) *adj.* lasting.

en · gi · neer (en′ ji nir′) *n.* **1.** a person whose job involves studying, planning, and designing machines, buildings, and other structures. **2.** a person who drives or maintains an engine.

en · sure (en shur′) *v.* **en · sured, en · sur · ing.** to make sure or certain of; guarantee.

en · vi · ron · ment (en vī′ rən mənt, en vī′ ərn mənt) *n.* **1.** surroundings. **2.** all of the things that surround and affect living things.

en · vy (en′ vē) *n., pl.* **en · vies.** A feeling of jealousy or unhappiness over not having what someone else has.

e · ro · sion (i rō′ zhən) *n.* a gradual wearing away, especially by wind, water, and weather.

er · rand (ār′ ənd) *n.* a short trip to do something, usually for someone else.

es · tab · lish · ment (es tab′ lish mənt) *n.* the act of setting up; creation.

es · tate (es tāt′) *n.* **1.** all the property or things that a person owns, especially at his or her death. **2.** a piece of land with a large house.

ev · i · dence (ev′ ə dəns) *n.* **1.** that which makes something clear; indication; sign. **2.** that which is legally presented to a court, for the purpose of proving or disproving an issue in question.

e · volve (i volv′) *v.* **e · volved, e · volv · ing.** to grow or develop gradually.

ex · cel (ek sel′) *v.* **ex · celled, ex · cel · ling. 1.** to be better or greater than; outdo. **2.** to be superior to others.

ex · hale (eks hāl′) *v.* **ex · haled, ex · hal · ing.** to breathe out air from the lungs.

ex · haust · ed (eg zôs′ tid) *adj.* worn out.

ex · pe · di · tion (eks′ pə dish′ ən) *n.* a journey made for a special purpose.

ex · pel (eks pel′) *v.* **ex · pelled, ex · pel · ling.** to force to leave; kick out.

---

a b**a**t, ā c**a**ke, ä f**a**ther, är c**a**r, ãr d**a**re; e h**e**n, ē m**e**, ėr t**e**rm; i b**i**b, ī k**i**te, ir cl**ea**r; o t**o**p, ō r**o**pe, ô s**a**w, oi c**oi**n, ôr f**o**rk, ou **ou**t; u s**u**n, u̇ b**oo**k, ü m**oo**n, ū c**u**te; ə **a**bout, tak**e**n

ex · pe · ri · ence (eks pir′ ē əns) *n.* knowledge gained through seeing or doing something.

ex · treme (eks trēm′) *n.* **1.** something marking one end or the other of a range, such as hot and cold. **2.** greatest or highest degree.

F

fa · mil · iar (fə mil′ yər) *adj.* used to; not unusual.

feat (fēt) *n.* act or deed, especially one showing great skill, or courage, or strength.

fid · dle (fid′ əl) *n.* a violin or other instrument of the violin family.—*v.* **fid · dled, fid · dling.** to play on a fiddle.

fiddle

flail (flāl) *v.* to wave or swing violently or quickly.

flash point (flash′ point′) *n.* the lowest point at which the vapor of certain substances will catch fire.

flinch (flinch) *v.* to draw back or away, as from something painful or unpleasant.

flint (flint) *n.* a very hard type of quartz, usually dull gray in color, that produces sparks when struck against steel. The American Indians made arrowheads out of flint and used it to start fires.

flute (flüt) *n.* a musical instrument of the woodwind family, consisting of a hollow tube with keys along its length and played by blowing through a mouth hole near one end. It produces a high-pitched tone.

for · mer (for′ mər) *adj.* belonging to or happening in the past, earlier.

foul (foul) *v.* **1.** to tangle or become tangled. **2.** to make dirty.

found (found) *v.* to bring into being; start or set up.

foun · da · tion (foun dā′ shən) *n.* something serving as a base or support.

frag · ile (fraj′ əl) *adj.* easily broken; breakable; delicate.

frank (frangk) *adj.* honest and open in expressing one's thoughts and feelings.

freeze-dried (frēz′ drīd′) *adj.* dried while frozen. Freeze-dried food stays fresh without refrigeration.

frig · ate (frig′ it) *n.* in former times, a sailing warship with three masts and square rigging.

fru · gal (frü′ gəl) *adj.* not wasteful; saving.

fum · ble (fum′ bəl) *v.* **fum · bled, fum · bling.** to look for in a clumsy way; grope

fuse (fūz) *v.* **fused, fus · ing. 1.** to become united or blended together. **2.** to melt something, especially by heating.

fu · se · lage (fū′ sə läzh′, fū′ sə lij) *n.* the main body of an airplane carrying the passengers, cargo, and crew.

G

gal · ax · y (gal′ ək sē) *n., pl.* **gal · ax · ies. 1.** the Milky Way galaxy, in which earth is located, one of the vast groupings of stars, dust, and gases scattered throughout the universe. **2.** any such grouping.

gal · le · on (gal′ ē ən) *n.* a large sailing ship, usually having four masts with square sails, a square stern, and three or four decks.

galleon

gem (jem) *n.* cut and polished precious or, sometimes, semiprecious stone; jewel.

gen·er·a·tion (jen′ ə rā′ shən) *n.* **1.** the period of time between the birth of one generation and the next. **2.** a group of persons born at about the same time.

gen·er·ous (jen′ ər əs) *adj.* unselfish; willing to give and share.

ge·ode (jē′ ōd) *n.* a round stone with a hollow center that is lined with crystals.

ge·ol·o·gist (jē ol′ ə jist) *n.* a scientist who studies the earth, including its history, structure, and what it is made of.

gnash (nash) *v.* to strike or grind the teeth together, as in anger or pain.

goad (gōd) *v.* to try to force someone to do something that he or she does not want to do; prod; stir up.

gold·smith (gōld′ smith′) *n.* a person who makes or deals in objects of gold, such as jewelry.

gos·pel mu·sic (gos′ pəl mū′ zik) *n.* a type of music whose words deal with gospel, or New Testament themes, with elements of modern blues and jazz.

gourd (gôrd) *n.* a rounded, hard-shelled fruit related to the pumpkin or squash. Gourds grow on vines and come in many different colors and shapes.

gourd

grad·u·ate (graj′ ü it′) *n., pl.* **grad·u·ates.** a student who has successfully completed his or her studies.

gran·ite (gran′ it) *n.* rock made up of mica, feldspar, quartz, and hornblende. It is often used for buildings and monuments.

grav·i·ty (grav′ ə tē) *n., pl.* **grav·i·ties.** the force that pulls things toward the center of the earth. Gravity causes objects to fall when they are dropped and pulls them back to earth when they are thrown upward.

Gua·da·la·ja·ra (gwäd′ əl ə här′ ə) a city in southwestern Mexico.

H

half-mast (haf′ mast′) *n.* the position of a flag about halfway down a mast or pole, used as a sign of mourning for someone who has died or as a sign that someone or something is in trouble.

halt (hôlt) *n.* a temporary stop in movement.

hammock

ham·mock (ham′ ək) *n.* a swinging bed that is hung between two trees or poles.

ham·per (ham′ pər) *v.* to get in the way of; slow down the action or progress of.

han·gar (hang′ ər, hang′ gar) *n.* building for sheltering and servicing aircraft.

har·mo·ny (här′ mə nē) *n., pl.* **har·mo·nies.** a combination of musical notes sounded together so as to form chords.

hasp (hasp) *n.* a hinged clasp, usually of metal, that fits over a staple and is fastened to a pin or padlock. A hasp is used to keep a door, window, or box closed.

---

a **b**at, ā **c**ake, ä **f**ather, är **c**ar, ãr d**are**; e h**e**n, ē **m**e, ėr t**er**m; i **b**ib, ī **k**ite, ir cl**ear**; o t**o**p, ō r**o**pe, ô s**aw**, oi c**oi**n, ôr f**or**k, ou **ou**t; u s**u**n, u̇ b**oo**k, ü m**oo**n, ū **c**ute; ə **a**bout, tak**e**n

hast·i·ly (hās′ tə lē) *adv.* in a hurry; quickly.

heir (ār) *n.* **1.** a person who has the right to a hereditary title, rank, or office. **2.** a person who has the right to the money or property of a person after that person is dead.

her·o·ine (hār′ ō in) *n.* a woman who is admired and looked up to for her bravery.

hor·i·zon·tal (hor′ ə zont′ əl) *adj.* flat and straight across; level; parallel to the horizon.

hor·i·zon·tal sta·bi·liz·er (hor′ ə zont′ əl stā′ bə lī′ zər) *n.* a fixed, flat surface on each side of the fuselage at an aircraft's tail to keep it from unwanted up-and-down motion.

horn·blende (hôrn′ blend′) *n.* a mineral, usually dark green or black, found in granite and other rocks.

hull (hul) *n.* **1.** the frame or body of a ship. **2.** the outer covering of a seed.

hull

hur·ri·cane (her′ ə kān′) *n.* a storm with winds of more than seventy-five miles per hour that spin around a calm center. Hurricanes bring heavy rain, high tides, and flooding in coastal areas.

hys·ter·i·cal (his tār′ i kəl) *adj.* feeling or showing great terror; terrified.

I

i·de·al (ī dē′ əl) *adj.* the best possible.

i·den·ti·fy (ī den′ tə fī′) *v.* **i·den·ti·fied, i·den·ti·fy·ing.** to find out what something really is.

id·ly (ī′ dlē) *adv.* without purpose; uselessly.

im·pa·tient (im pā′ shənt) *adj.* **1.** having little or no patience; easily annoyed. **2.** restlessly eager.

im·prac·ti·cal (im prak′ ti kəl) *adj.* unwise; foolish; not practical.

im·press (im pres′) *v.* to have a strong effect on the mind or feelings.

im·pro·vise (im′ prə vīz′) *v.* **im·pro·vised, im·pro·vis·ing.** to make up and perform on the spur of the moment.

in·ci·dent (in′ sə dənt) *n.* an event or act; happening.

in·come (in′ kum′) *n.* money received for work or from property or other things that are owned.

in·flu·ence (in′ flü əns) *v.* **in·flu·enced, in·flu·enc·ing.** to change or have an effect on the thought or actions of; persuade.

in·ju·ry (in′ jər ē) *n., pl.* **in·ju·ries.** damage or harm done to a person or thing.

in·jus·tice (in jus′ tis) *n.* unfairness.

in·scribe (in skrīb′) *v.* **in·scribed, in·scrib·ing.** to write, carve, engrave, or mark words or characters on something.

in·spi·ra·tion (in spə rā′ shən) *n.* an idea or force that leads to action.

in·stru·men·tal·ist (in′ strə ment′ əl ist) *n.* a person who plays a musical instrument.

in·tense (in tens′) *adj.* very great or strong.

in·tent·ly (in tent′ lē) *adv.* in an intent way; with the mind firmly fixed on something.

in·ter·mis·sion (in′ tər mish′ ən) *n.* a pause, or recess between events, such as the parts of a play or other performance.

in·ter·view (in′ tər vū′) *v.* to take part in a discussion or question-and-answer session.

in·ti·mate (in′ tə mit) *adj.* close and familiar; well-acquainted.

in·ves·ti·gate (in ves′ tə gāt) *v.* **in·ves·ti·gat·ed, in·ves·ti·gat·ing.** to look into or examine carefully in a search for information.

is·sue (ish′ ü) *n.* a subject or topic that is being discussed.

i·tem (ī′ təm) *n.* object.

J

jer·ky (jèr′ kē) *n.* meat, especially beef, that has been cured or dried.

ju·ry (jùr′ ē) *n., pl.* **ju·ries.** a group of people chosen to hear the facts in a matter that has been brought before a court of law. The jury makes a decision on this matter based on the facts they hear and on the law.

K

ki·mo·no (ki mō′ nə, ki mō′ nō) *n., pl.* **ki·mo·nos.** loose robe or gown tied by a sash, traditionally worn as an outer garment by Japanese men and women.

kin·ship (kin′ ship′) *n.* **1.** any relationship or close connection. **2.** a family relationship.

L

lab·o·ra·to·ry (lab′ rə tôr′ ē) *n., pl.* **lab·o·ra·to·ries.** a room, building, or workshop for teaching science or for making scientific experiments or tests.

la·goon (lə gün′) *n.* a shallow body of water partly cut off from a larger body of water. A lagoon sometimes has a narrow strip of land or a coral reef going part way around it.

lagoon

Lat·in A·mer·i·ca (lat′ in ə mār′ i kə) the countries in the Western Hemisphere south of the United States, in which the languages, such as Spanish and Portuguese, are of Latin origin.

lead (lēd) *n.* a piece of information that serves as a guide; clue.

league (lēg) *n.* **1.** a group of athletic teams that compete regularly with each other. **2.** a number of people, groups, or countries joined together for a common purpose.

lev·er (lev′ ər, lē′ vər) *n.* **1.** a bar or handle that is used to operate or control a machine. **2.** a rod or bar used to lift things or pry things open, such as a crowbar.

lift (lift) *n.* resistance to falling; tendency to move upward.

light-year (līt′ yir′) *n.* the distance that light travels in one year, or about six trillion miles.

lime·stone (līm′ stōn′) *n.* a rock used for building and for making lime.

---

a b**a**t, ā c**a**k**e**, ä f**a**th**e**r, är c**ar**, âr d**are**; e h**e**n, ē m**e**, ėr t**er**m; i b**i**b, ī k**i**t**e**, ir cl**ear**; o t**o**p, ō r**o**p**e**, ô s**aw**, oi c**oi**n, ôr f**or**k, ou **ou**t; u s**u**n, ù b**oo**k, ü m**oo**n, ū c**u**t**e**; ə **a**bout, tak**e**n

lin · ger · ing · ly (ling′ gər ing lē′) *adv.* with an unwillingness to leave; with a desire to keep on doing something.

log · i · cal (loj′ i kəl) *adj.* reasonable; sensible.

long · boat (lông′ bōt′) *n.* the largest boat carried by a sailing ship.

lyr · ic (lir′ ik) *adj.* having to do with a kind of poetry that expresses strong feeling or emotion.

lyr · ics (lir′ iks) *n., pl.* the words written for a song.

M

maes · tro (mīs′ trō) *n.* **1.** any outstanding or well-known conductor, composer, or teacher of music. **2.** distinguished master of any art.

main · mast (mān′ mast′, mān′ məst) *n.* the largest and most important mast of a ship.

ma · jor · i · ty (mə jôr′ ə tē) *n., pl.* **ma · jor · i · ties.** the greater number or part of something.

man · ag · er (man′ i jər) *n.* a person who directs, guides, or controls.

man · u · al (man′ ū əl) *n.* a book that gives instructions or information on a particular subject; handbook.

man · u · al con · trol (man′ ū əl kən trol′) *n.* **1.** the act of operating controls by hand. **2.** controls operated by hand.

ma · rine ar · chae · ol · o · gist (mə rēn′ är′ kē ol′ ə jist) *n.* a scientist who studies objects such as ships and treasure that have been under water for a long time.

mas · sive (mas′ iv) *adj.* having great size and weight.

mas · ter (mas′ tər) *v.* to gain control over; become expert.

mate (māt) *n.* **1.** officer on a merchant ship, ranking next below the captain. **2.** one of a pair.

mat · ting (mat′ ing) *n.* a floor covering made of woven grass, straw, hemp, or other fiber.

ma · zur · ka (mə zur′ kə, mə zùr′ kə) *n.* a lively Polish dance resembling the polka.

me · di · o · cre (mē′ dē ō′ kər) *adj.* not outstanding; ordinary; average.

mem · brane (mem′ brān) *n.* a thin layer of skin or tissue. Membranes line parts of the body.

mem · o · ra · ble (mem′ ər ə bəl) *adj.* not to be forgotten; notable.

Men · dels · sohn, Fe · lix (mend′ əl sən, fē′ liks) 1808–1847, German composer.

met · al de · tec · tor (met′ əl di tek′ tər) *n.* a device used to find metal objects that are buried or hidden.

me · te · or (mē′ tē ər) *n.* a piece of rock or metal that comes into the earth's atmosphere from space. Friction with the atmosphere causes the meteor to become very hot and burn with a bright light as it falls to earth.

meteor

me · te · or · ite (mē′ tē ə rīt′) *n.* a meteor that has fallen to earth.

mi · ca (mī′ kə) *n.* any of a group of minerals that look like transparent or cloudy glass and can be separated into thin sheets.

might · i · est (mī′ tē əst) *adj.* showing the greatest skill or power.

min · er · al (min′ ər əl) *n.* a natural substance that is neither a plant nor an animal.

min·is·ter (min' is tər) *n*. **1.** a person who is the head of an important part of government. **2.** a person who is authorized to conduct religious services; clergyman; pastor.

mint (mint) *n*. a place where money is coined by the government.

mis·sion (mish' ən) *n*. a special job or task.

mod·ern (mod' ərn) *adj*. relating to the present or recent time.

mod·es·ty (mod' is tē) *n*. the quality of being modest; humbleness.

molt (mōlt) *v*. to shed the hair, feathers, skin, or shell and replace with a new growth.

mo·men·tum (mō men' təm) *n*. the force or speed that an object has when it is moving.

mon·o·plane (mon' ə plān') *n*. airplane with only one main supporting surface or only one pair of wings.

monoplane

mon·u·ment (mon' yə mənt) *n*. a building, statue, or other structure set up in memory of a person or event.

mo·tion (mō' shən) *n*. movement.

Mount Hel·i·con (mount' hel' ə kon) a mountain in southern Greece regarded by the ancient Greeks as the home of the Muses, the nine goddesses of the arts and sciences. Artists and poets believed they received their inspiration from Mount Helicon.

Mous·sorg·sky, Mo·dest (mü sôrg' skē', məd yest') 1839–1881, Russian composer.

mute (mūt) *adj*. **1.** not speaking; silent. **2.** unable to speak because of an illness, birth defect, or injury.

mu·ti·ny (mū' tə nē) *v*. **mu·ti·nied, mu·ti·ny·ing.** to revolt or rise up against one's leaders.

my·thol·o·gy (mi thol' ə jē) *n*. myths, or traditional stories that have gods or heroes as characters. Myths often try to explain natural events.

N

nar·y (när' ē) *adj. Informal*. not a; not one.

NASA (na' sə) National Aeronautics and Space Administration, an agency of the United States government established to direct and aid civilian research and development in aeronautics and aerospace technology.

nav·i·ga·tion (nav' i gā' shən) *n*. the act of sailing or steering a ship.

niece (nēs) *n*. the daughter of one's brother or sister.

no·ble (nō' bəl) *adj*. **1.** showing greatness of character; worthy. **2.** having high rank or title.—*n*. person of noble birth; member of the nobility.

no·to·ri·ous·ly (nō tôr' ē əs lē) *adj*. widely and unfavorably known to be.

No·va Sco·tia (nō' və skō' shə) a province of Canada, in the southeastern part of the country.

a b**a**t, ā c**a**ke, ä f**a**ther, är c**a**r, âr d**a**re; e h**e**n, ē m**e**, ėr t**e**rm; i b**i**b, ī k**i**te, ir cl**e**ar; o t**o**p, ō r**o**pe, ô s**a**w, oi c**oi**n, ôr f**o**rk, ou **ou**t; u s**u**n, u̇ b**oo**k, ü m**oo**n, ū c**u**te; ə **a**bout, tak**e**n

O

ob · sta · cle (ob' stə kəl) *n.* a person or thing that stands in the way, or blocks progress.

off · spring (ôf' spring) *n., pl.* **off · spring, off · springs.** the young of a person, animal, or plant.

old-tim · er (ōld' tī' mər) *n. Informal.* **1.** a person who is old or elderly. **2.** a person who has been a member of a group or organization for a long time.

O · lym · pus (ō lim' pəs) a mountain in northeastern Greece that, in Greek mythology, was the home of the twelve major gods.

op · er · ate (op' ə rāt) *v.* **op · er · at · ed, op · er · at · ing.** to work; perform.

o · pin · ion (ə pin' yən) *n.* **1.** a formal decision made by a judge in a court of law; a formal decision made by any expert. **2.** a belief or conclusion based on what a person thinks is true rather than on what is proven or known to be true.

op · por · tu · ni · ty (op' ər tü' nə tē, op' ər tü' nə tē) *n., pl.* **op · por · tu · ni · ties.** a good chance.

op · press (ə pres') *n.* something that causes difficulty, pain, or suffering; hardship.

or · bit (ôr' bit) *n.* **1.** one complete trip of a spacecraft or satellite around the earth or other heavenly body. **2.** the path that a planet or other heavenly body follows as it moves in a circle around another heavenly body.

orbit

or · ches · tra (ôr' kis trə) *n.* a group of musicians playing together on different instruments, usually including strings, woodwinds, brasses, and percussion instruments.

O · ri · ent (ôr' ē ənt) the countries of Asia, especially the Far East.

or · na · men · tal (ôr' nə ment' əl) *adj.* brightly-colored; shiny; decorative.

out · raged (out' rājd') *adj.* greatly offended or insulted.

out · wit (out' wit') *v.* **out · wit · ted, out · wit · ting.** to get the better of; be more clever than; outsmart.

o · ver · pow · er (o' vər pou' ər) *v.* to overcome by greater strength or power.

P

pace (pās) *n.* a single step.

palomino

pal · o · mi · no (pal' ə mē' nō) *n.* a light tan horse having a cream-colored or white mane and tail.

pan · ick · ing (pan' i king) *adj.* overcome by fear or panic.

parch · ment (pärch' mənt) *n.* the skin of sheep, goats, or other animals prepared so that it can be written on.

par · lor (pär' lər) *n.* **1.** a place of business that is decorated to resemble the living room of a home, for example, a funeral parlor. **2.** a room in a home in which visitors are received and entertained; living room.

par · tic · i · pate (pär tis' ə pāt') *v.* **par · tic · i · pat · ed, par · tic · i · pat · ing.** to take part or join in; become involved in.

par · ti · cle (pär' ti kəl) *n.* a very small bit; speck.

pa · tient (pā′ shənt) *adj.* able to put up with delays or trouble without complaining or becoming angry.

pat · tern (pat′ ərn) *n.* an arrangement or design of colors, shapes, or lines.

paw · paw (pô′ pô) *n.* a fruit having yellow flesh and a taste like that of a banana. Pawpaw trees grow mainly in the central United States.

pe · cul · iar (pi kūl′ yər) *adj.* odd; strange .

ped · es · tri · an (pə des′ trē ən) *n.* a person who travels on foot; walker.

Peg · a · sus (peg′ ə səs) a winged horse in the legends and tales of ancient Greece.

Pegasus

pen · e · trat · ing (pen′ ə trā′ ting) *v.* seeping or spreading through or into something.

per · cus · sion (pər kush′ ən) *n.* musical percussion intruments as a group. A percussion instrument is one in which tones are produced by striking one thing against another. The drum, cymbal, xylophone, and piano are percussion instruments.

per · se · ver · ance (pėr′ sə vir′ əns) *n.* the ability to hold to a plan of action, purpose, or belief even if there are difficulties.

pe · ti · tion (pə tish′ ən) *v.* to make a request to a superior or one in authority for some favor, privilege, or correction of a problem.

pierce (pirs) *v.* **pierced, pierc · ing.** to stab; make a hole in.

pin · na · cle (pin′ ə kəl) *n.* **1.** a high, pointed formation, such as a mountain peak. **2.** the highest point.

pit (pit) *n.* a hole in the ground.

plain · tiff (plān′ tif) *n.* the person who brings a case before a court of law for decision.

plot (plot) *n.* **1.** a secret plan. **2.** the events or series of action in a story.

pluck (pluk) *v.* to pull with sudden force; snatch.

po · di · um (pō′ dē əm) *n., pl.* **po · di · a, po · di · ums.** a raised platform from which a conductor leads an orchestra.

podium

pop · u · lar · i · ty (pop′ yə lär′ ə tē) *n.* the quality of being liked by many people.

port (pôrt) *n.* the left side of a boat or ship as one faces forward.

post · pone (pōst pōn′) *v.*, **post · poned, post · pon · ing.** to put off to a later time.

pow · er fail · ure (pou′ ər fāl′ yər) *n.* a temporary cutoff or breakdown in the delivery of electrical power.

pre · cious (presh′ əs) *adj.* valuable.

preen (prēn) *v.* to clean and smooth feathers with a beak.

pre · scribe (pri skrīb′) *v.* **pre · scribed, pre · scrib · ing.** to order or recommend the use of something.

---

a b**a**t, ā c**a**ke, ä f**a**ther, är c**a**r, ār d**a**re; e h**e**n, ē m**e**, ėr t**e**rm; i b**i**b, ī k**i**te, ir cl**ea**r; o t**o**p, ō r**o**pe, ô s**a**w, oi c**o**in, ôr f**o**rk, ou **ou**t; u s**u**n, u̇ b**oo**k, ü m**oo**n, ū c**u**te; ə **a**bout, tak**e**n

pres·en·ta·tion (prez′ ən tā′ shən, prē′ zən tā′ shən) *n.* exhibition or showing, as of a play.

prey (prā) *n.* **1.** a person or thing that is a victim. **2.** an animal that is hunted or killed by another animal for food.—*v.* **1.** to take advantage of. **2.** to hunt or kill for food.

pri·ma·ry (prī′ mãr′ ē) *n., pl.* **pri·ma·ries. 1.** one of the long feathers of a bird. They are used for flying and are located at the outer edge of a wing. **2.** an election in which contenders from the same party oppose each other for the nomination, or the right to run for office with the party's support.

priv·i·lege (priv′ ə lij) *n.* a special right or advantage given to a person or group.

proc·la·ma·tion (prok′ lə mā′ shən) *n.* an official public announcement.

pro·pel (prə pel′) *v.* **pro·pelled, pro·pel·ling.** to cause to move forward; put or keep in motion.

pros·per (pros′ pər) *v.* to have success, wealth, or good fortune; thrive.

pro·tec·tive (prə tek′ tiv) *adj.* protecting; keeping from harm.

pub·lic·i·ty (pub lis′ ə tē) *n.* public notice or attention.

pur·su·er (pər sü′ ər) *n.* a person who follows or chases in order to catch up with or capture.

put·ty (put′ ē) *n., pl.* **put·ties.** a soft, claylike material used to fill cracks in wood, or to fasten panes of glass to window frames.

Q

quartz (kwôrtz) *n.* a clear, hard mineral found in many rocks and in crystalline form.

quote (kwōt) *n.* the act of repeating or reproducing the exact words of.

R

raid (rād) *n.* **1.** a sudden attack by a small number of soldiers, pirates, bandits, or any other armed group. **2.** a sudden, surprise entering of a place by police to seize stolen goods and to make arrests.

rain for·est (rān′ fôr′ ist, for′ ist) *n.* a dense, tropical forest in a region having a high yearly rainfall.

rain forest

ran·som (ran′ səm) *n.* the price paid for the release of a person or property.

rare (rãr) *adj.* seldom happening, seen, or found.

re·al-es·tate a·gent (rē′ əl or rēl′ es tāt′ ā′ jənt) *n.* a person who sells land and buildings for another person or a company.

re·al·i·za·tion (rē′ ə li zā′ shən) *n.* **1.** the act of making real; achievement; accomplishment. **2.** the act of understanding completely.

re·bel·lion (ri bel′ yən) *n.* resistance to any control or authority.

re·ceipt (ri sēt′) *n.* a written statement that something, such as money, goods, or mail, has been received.

re·cit·al (ri sīt′ əl) *n.* a performance of music or dance, especially by single performers.

rec·om·men·da·tion (rek′ ə men dā′ shən) *n.* a favorable statement about someone's qualifications.

re·cov·er·y (ri kuv′ ər ē) *n., pl.* **re·cov·er·ies.** to get back something that is lost or stolen; regain.

re · duce (ri düs') *v.* **re · duced, re · duc · ing.** to make less or smaller.

ref · uge (ref' ūj) *n.* a place that gives shelter or protection from danger or trouble.

refuge

re · fund (ri fund') *v.* to give or pay back.

reg · is · ter (rej' is tər) *v.* **1.** *Informal.* to make an impression on; cause to become aware of. **2.** to put in a register; record.

re · hearse (ri hėrs') *v.* **re · hearsed, re · hears · ing.** to practice a dance, song, or role, in preparation for a performance.

re · luc · tant · ly (ri luk' tənt lē') *adv.* unwillingly.

re · place (ri plās') *v.* **re · placed, re · plac · ing.** to take and fill the place of.

re · port (ri pôrt') *v.* to give information or tell about things that have happened.

rep · u · ta · tion (rep' yə tā' shən) *n.* public recognition; what people think of someone.

re · quire · ment (ri kwīr' mənt) *n.* something that is necessary, needed, or required.

res · cue (res' kū) *v.* **res · cued, res · cu · ing.** to save or free from danger.

res · i · dence (rez' ə dəns) *n.* a place where a person lives.

re · sist (ri zist') *v.* **1.** to fight off; oppose. **2.** to keep from giving in to.

re · veal (ri vēl') *v.* to show; make known.

re · verse (ri vėrs') *v.* **re · versed, re · vers · ing.** to change to the opposite.

re · vive (ri vīv') *v.* **re · vived, re · viv · ing.** to come back to consciousness; become stronger.

ri · a · ta (rē ä' tə) *n.* a long rope with a loop at one end; lasso.

rig · ging (rig' ing) *n.* all the lines of a boat or ship used for supporting the masts or working the sails.

rig · id (rij' id) *adj.* stiff; not changing.

risk (risk) *v.* to take a chance.

rou · tine (rü tēn') *n.* a regular part of an act.

rum · mage (rum' ij) *v.* **rum · maged, rum · mag · ing.** to search through something thoroughly by moving things around.

S

sac · ri · fice (sak' rə fīs') *n., pl.* **sac · ri · fic · es.** the act of giving up, foregoing, or destroying something, especially something valued or desired, usually for the sake of something else.

Saint Ber · nard (sānt' bər närd') a large dog having a large head, a long bushy tail, and a very thick coat. The St. Bernard is famous for rescuing people lost in the snow in the mountainous areas of Europe.

Saint Bernard

a b**a**t, ā c**a**ke, ä f**a**ther, är c**a**r, ãr d**a**re; e h**e**n, ē m**e**, ėr t**e**rm; i b**i**b, ī k**i**te, ir cl**e**ar; o t**o**p, ō r**o**pe, ô s**a**w, oi c**oi**n, ôr f**o**rk, ou **ou**t; u s**u**n, u̇ b**oo**k, ü m**oo**n, ū c**u**te; ə **a**bout, tak**e**n

sal · vage (sal′ vij) v. **sal · vaged, sal · vag · ing.** to rescue or save from being destroyed.

sam · i · sen (sam′ ı sen′) n. a Japanese musical instrument similar to a banjo but having only three strings.

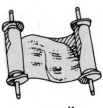
samisen

sam · u · rai (sam′ ủ rī′) n., pl. **sam · u · rai.** a member of the warrior class in Japan before modern times.

schol · ar (skol′ ər) n. a person having much knowledge and an interest in learning and study.

scout (skout) n. a person or thing sent out to gather and bring back information.

scrag · gly (skrag′ lē) adj. having a rough or rugged look.

scribe (skrīb) n. before printing was invented, a person who wrote down or copied letters, books, contracts, or other documents.

scroll (skrōl) n. a roll of paper, silk, or other material that is often wound around a rod or rods. Scrolls can be written on and are often used for keeping records.

scroll

sec · ond · ar · y (sek′ ən dãr′ ē) n., pl. **sec · ond · ar · ies.** one of the feathers of a bird, used for flying. They are attached to a bird's forearm.

sen · sa · tion (sen sā′ shən) n. feeling; impression.

shaft (shaft) n. **1.** a long, narrow passage. **2.** the stiff, central part of a feather from which the web or vane extends on either side.

sheath (shēth) n. **1.** a covering for some part of the body; membrane. **2.** a case of a blade or some cutting weapon, such as a sword or knife.

Si · be · li · us, Jean (sə bā′ lē us, jēn) 1865–1957, Finnish composer.

sim · i · lar (sim′ ə lər) adj. alike.

sim · u · late (sim′ yə lāt′) v. **sim · u · lat · ed, sim · u · lat · ing.** to give the appearance of; imitate; act out.

sin · cer · i · ty (sin sãr′ ə tē) n. honesty; lack of falseness.

site (sīt) n. **1.** the place where something happened. **2.** the position or location of a town, city, building, or the like.

slight (slīt) adj. small; unimportant.

slum · ber (slum′ bər) n. a light sleep.

sneer (snir) v. to make a facial expression showing hatred or scorn.

soar (sôr) v. **1.** to fly upward; rise high into the air. **2.** to glide along without losing altitude.

sol · emn (sol′ əm) adj. **1.** dignified; majestic; noble. **2.** serious and earnest; grave.

so · lo · ist (sō′ lō ist) n. one who performs a musical composition or passage for a single voice or instrument.

so · na · ta (sə nä′ tə) n. a musical work, often written for the piano. A sonata usually has three or four movements in different rhythms.

son · a · ti · na (son′ ə tē′ nə) n. a short sonata.

sooth · ing (sü′ thing) adj. calming; quieting.

sort (sôrt) v. to arrange or separate into groups according to kind or type.

speck · led (spek′ əld) adj. covered with small spots or marks.

spec · ta · tor (spek′ tā′ tər) *n.* a person who watches but does not take part; observer.

stalk (stôk) *v.* to hunt or track down.

stal · lion (stal′ yən) *n.* a male horse.

stallion

star · board (stär′ bərd) *n.* the right side of a boat or ship when a person on deck faces forward.

St. Ber · nard, see **Saint Ber · nard**

steed (stēd) *n.* a horse, especially a high-spirited riding horse.

stern (stėrn) *n.* the rear part of a boat or ship.

stream · lined (strēm′ līnd′) *adj.* smooth; designed or built so no part interferes with movement.

stress (stres) *n.* strain or pressure.

strike (strīk) *v.* **struck** or **strick · en, strik · ing .** to attack.

strings (stringz) *n., pl.* the section of an orchestra made up of string instruments. A string instrument uses thin strands of wire, gut, or nylon to produce musical tones. The violin, viola, cello, and bass are string instruments.

struc · ture (struk′ chər) *n.* the way something is arranged or built.

strut (strut) *v.* **strut · ted, strut · ting.** to walk in a very proud, show-off way.

stunned (stund) *adj.* **1.** shocked; bewildered; dazed. **2.** made unconscious, as by a blow.

sub · merge (səb mėrj′) *v.* **sub · merged, sub · merg · ing.** to cover with water or other liquid.

sub · stance (sub′ stəns) *n.* **1.** matter; material. **2.** solid quality; density; body.

suit · a · ble (sü′ tə bəl) *adj.* right or proper for a particular purpose or thing.

sum · mit (sum′ it) *n.* the highest part or point.

sum · mon (sum′ ən) *v.* **1.** to bring to action; rouse. **2.** to send for, especially with authority.

surge (sėrj) *n.* a sudden increase; burst.

sur · vey (sər vā′) *v.* to look at or view as a whole.

sur · vive (sər vīv′) *v.* **sur · vived, sur · viv · ing.** to stay alive; endure.

swift (swift) *adj.* moving with great speed; fast.

sym · pho · ny (sim′ fə nē) *n., pl.* **sym · pho · nies.** a musical work for an orchestra, usually having three or four movements, or main divisions.

syn · the · siz · er (sin′ thə sī′ zər) *n.* an electronic device having a keyboard that can imitate the sounds made by a wide variety of musical instruments.

T

tame (tām) *v.* **tamed, tam · ing.** to bring under control.

taunt (tônt) *v.* to make fun of; mock; jeer.

tem · po (tem′ pō) *n.* pace; rate; speed.

---

a b**a**t, ā c**a**ke, ä f**a**ther, är c**a**r, âr d**a**re; e h**e**n, ē m**e**, ėr t**e**rm; i b**i**b, ī k**i**te, ir cl**ea**r; o t**o**p, ō r**o**pe, ô s**a**w, oi c**oi**n, ôr f**o**rk, ou **ou**t; u s**u**n, ů b**oo**k, ü m**oo**n, û c**u**te; ə **a**bout, tak**e**n

ten · sion (ten′ shən) *n.* **1.** strain; pressure; stress. **2.** the act of stretching or the state of being stretched.

ter · ti · ar · y (tėr′ shē ār′ ē) *n., pl.* **ter · ti · ar · ies.** one of the feathers of a bird, used for flying. They are attached to the upper arm bone of a bird.

theme (thēm) *n.* the main subject or idea of something.

thrust (thrust) *n.* a driving force; push, such as the forward movement of an airplane.

tide (tīd) *n.* the regular rise and fall of the oceans and other large bodies of water, caused by the pull of the sun and moon on the earth.

trace (trās) *n.* something left behind showing that some person, thing, or event has existed or taken place.

tra · di · tion (trə dish′ ən) *n.* **1.** long-established and generally accepted custom or practice. **2.** the knowledge, beliefs, customs, or the like handed down from one generation to another.

trag · e · dy (traj′ ə dē) *n., pl.* **trag · e · dies.** a sad happening.

trav · erse (trav′ ərs, trə vėrs′) *n.* the act of passing across, over, or through; crossing.

tread (tred) *v.* **trod, trod · den** or **trod, tread · ing.** to walk on or over; step upon. **to tread water.** to keep the head above water while staying in an upright position, usually by moving the feet up and down in a walking motion.

tre · ble keys (treb′ əl kēz′) *n., pl.* the keys on the piano that are above middle C.

tribe (trīb) *n.* a group of people who are joined because they have the same ancestors, social customs, and other characteristics.

trust (trust) *n.* faith; confidence.

tune (tün, tūn) *v.* **tuned, tun · ing.** to adjust a musical instrument so that it can make the correct sounds.

tu · tor (tü′ tər, tū′ tər) *n.* a teacher who gives private lessons to a student.

u

un · a · ware (un′ ə wār′) *adj.* not knowing or realizing; not conscious of.

un · con · scious · ness (un kon′ shəs nis) *n.* the state of being unconscious, or not knowing.

un · der · tak · er (un′ dər tā′ kər) *n.* a person whose job or business is arranging funerals and preparing dead people for burial.

un · per · turbed (un pər tėrbd′) *adv.* without fear or anxiety; calmly.

ut · ter · ly (ut′ ər lē) *adv.* completely; totally.

v

var · y (vār′ ē) *v.* **var · ied, var · y · ing.** to change or make different.

ven · ture (ven′ chər) *n.* an undertaking that involves some risk.

vi · brate (vī′ brāt) *v.* **vi · brat · ed, vi · brat · ing.** to move back and forth or up and down rapidly.

vic · tor (vik′ tər) *n.* a person who wins or conquers.

vil · lain (vil′ ən) *n.* a wicked or dishonorable person; scoundrel.

vi · o · la (vē ō′ lə) *n.* a stringed musical instrument of the violin family, slightly larger and lower in pitch than the violin.

viola

vise·like (vīs′ līk′) *adj.* having a hold or grip like a vise. A vise is a tool with two jaws that is used to hold an object in place while it is being worked on.

vo·cal·ist (vō′ kə list) *n.* a singer.

vol·ume (vol′ yüm, vol′ yəm) *n.* collection of written or printed pages bound together; book.

vow (vou) *v.* to make a solemn promise or pledge.

vul·ture (vul′ chər) *n.* a large bird that has dark, dull feathers and a bald head and neck. Vultures feed on the meat of dead animals.

vulture

W

war·lord (wôr′ lôrd′) *n.* a strong military leader who controls a large area.

war·ri·or (wôr′ ē ər, wor′ ē ər) *n.* a person who fights in battles.

web (web) *n.* **1.** the flat weblike part of a feather, made up of many individual barbs. **2.** a network of fine threads that are spun by a spider; cobweb.

won·der (wun′ dər) *n.* something that seems unusual, astonishing, or marvelous.—*v.* **1.** to want to know or learn; be curious or doubtful. **2.** to feel or express admiration and astonishment.

wood·winds (wùd′ windz′) *n.*, *pl.* the section of an orchestra made up of woodwind instruments. A woodwind instrument consists of a tube with holes in it that can be opened and closed to vary the sound produced when air passes through the instrument. Flutes, clarinets, and saxophones are some of the woodwind instruments.

wrath (rath) *n.* great anger; rage.

wrench (rench) *v.* to twist or pull with a sharp, forceful motion.

Z

Zeus (züs) in Greek mythology, the highest and most powerful god and ruler of heaven and earth.

zone (zōn) *v.* **zoned, zon·ing.** to divide a town or city into zones, or sections where only certain types of buildings or ways of living are allowed.

---

a b**a**t, ā c**a**ke, ä f**a**ther, är c**a**r, âr d**a**re; e h**e**n, ē m**e**, ėr t**e**rm; i b**i**b, ī k**i**te, ir cl**e**ar; o t**o**p, ō r**o**pe, ô s**a**w, oi c**oi**n, ôr f**o**rk, ou **ou**t; u s**u**n, ù b**oo**k, ü m**oo**n, ū c**u**te; ə **a**bout, tak**e**n

This section of *Great Endeavors* includes a review of letters and the sounds they stand for. Good readers know that letters in a word are clues. Looking carefully at these letters is one way to figure out how to say a word. Some words may look new, but once you *say* them you may discover that you already know them.

Lessons

Word Work

Beginning Sounds

Letters stand for sounds at the beginning of words.

__oes __ebbie's __evoted __og __are to __isobey?

Without the letter that makes the beginning sound in the words above, the sentence makes no sense. What letter could you use to finish the sentence?

Number your paper from 1 to 10. Copy the sentences below. Fill in the missing letters. Choose the letters from those in the box. Be sure the words make sense in the sentence.

b   d   g   l   m   p   qu   t   v   w   y   z

1. __onna __went __o the __ibrary __esterday after school.
2. She __anted to __ick out a __ood __ook to read.
3. __efore she started __o __ook on the shelves, she joined some __irls who were __alking in the corner.
4. "__iet, please!" the __ibrarian said. "This is a no __alking __one."
5. __onna __eft the girls.
6. She __alked __ast the __agazines and found the fiction section.
7. She __ickly scanned the __itles on the __ook spines.
8. "What a __onderful __ariety of __ooks there are here," she thought.
9. After she found a fiction __ook, she asked the __ibrarian for a __olume of __oems.
10. Then she brought __oth books to the check-out __esk.

Same Sound—Different Spellings

Some beginning sounds can be spelled more than one way.

Read the words below. Look at the underlined letters.

<u>f</u>estival	however	<u>k</u>ernel	<u>s</u>erpent
<u>ph</u>ase	<u>wh</u>oever	<u>c</u>atalog	<u>c</u>entury

What ways can you spell the sound you hear at the beginning of *festival*?

What sound can the letters *wh* stand for?

Does the beginning sound in *century* sound like the beginning sound in *catalog* or *serpent*?

Number your paper from 1 to 12. Read each group of words below. Write the two words from each group that begin with the same sound.

1. whole
   wharf
   horizon

2. whom
   huff
   wince

3. cycle
   kindle
   captive

4. fence
   pesky
   phone

5. celery
   carrot
   soybean

6. feeble
   physical
   pulse

7. civil
   campaign
   suspense

8. cereal
   kennel
   conversation

9. salary
   common
   ceramic

10. window
    whole
    haze

11. pose
    focus
    photo

12. keen
    cease
    collar

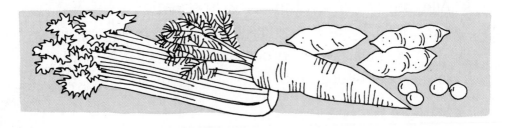

One Sound—Two Spellings

Some beginning sounds can be spelled more than one way.

Read the words below. Look at the underlined letters.

nickel   research   justice
knead   wrinkle   genuine

What two letters together can spell the sound you hear at the beginning of *research*?

What letters can stand for the sound you hear at the beginning of *justice*?

What two letters together can spell the sound you hear at the beginning of *nickel*?

On your paper make a chart like the one below.

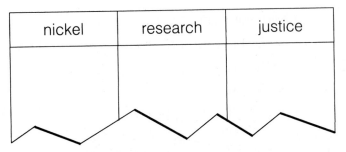

nickel	research	justice

Add these words to your chart. Write each word in the column under the word that has the same beginning sound. HINT: You will *not* use *all* of the words.

kindle	wreck	refuge	jazz	wrapper
wreath	notice	wrench	knowledge	geology
gesture	garage	wonder	recognize	keen
knack	jewel	general	weigh	knuckle

Ending Sounds

Letters stand for sounds at the end of words.

Read each word below. Look at the underlined letters.

crib	cud	haul	grim	hilltop
vain	ox	nudge	foreleg	pat

The letters *dge* stand for the sound you hear at the beginning of *jury*.

The letter *x* stands for the sound you hear at the end of *packs*.

Number your paper from 1 to 10. Each sentence below is missing one word. Notice the sound at the end of the under-lined word in each sentence. Then find the word in the box above that ends with that same sound. Write both words on your paper.

1. I once watched someone try to <u>coax</u> an ____.
2. I've <u>seldom</u> seen anyone look so ____.
3. It wouldn't <u>budge</u>, so he gave it a ____.
4. Pulling on the <u>rein</u> was in ____.
5. A <u>tug</u> on the ____ did no good.
6. The ox just <u>stood</u> there and chewed its ____.
7. At last the man grabbed a <u>cob</u> from the corn ____ and held it in front of the animal's nose.
8. By tempting it with a tasty <u>morsel</u>, he finally got that ox to ____!
9. It didn't <u>stop</u> until it reached the ____.
10. Then the farmer <u>sat</u> down and gave the ox a ____ on the back.

Spelling Ending Sounds

> Some ending sounds can be spelled more than one way.

Read the words below. Look at the underlined letters.

brief	bleak	alas
staff	democratic	distress
telegraph	track	

What are three ways to spell the sound you hear at the end of *bluff*?

What letters can be used to spell the sound you hear at the end of *historic*?

Two *f*'s can make the same sound as one. What other letter can you say this about?

Number your paper from 1 to 6. Copy the sentences below. Fill in the missing letters. Choose the letters from those in the box. Be sure the word makes sense in the sentence.

f	ff	ph	k	c	ck	s	ss

1. This is a histori__ day.
2. We are voting for new members of Congre__.
3. Voting is an important part of the democrati__ proce__.
4. After everyone vote__, the election sta__ will che__ the result__.
5. The newspapers will send someone to take a photogra__ of the winners.
6. The losers will have to loo__ for new opportunities.

Short Vowel Sounds

> There are five short vowel sounds.

Read each word in the box below. Look at the underlined letter that spells each short vowel sound.

a	e	i	o	u
j<u>a</u>b	p<u>e</u>lt	h<u>i</u>tch	pr<u>o</u>d	n<u>u</u>dge

A. Number your paper from 1 to 5. For each sentence below, decide which vowel will fit *all* of the blanks. Use the same vowel to complete each word. Then write the sentence on your paper.

1. My cl__ss h__d a cooking and cr__fts fair.
2. K__m had st__tched a qu__lt.
3. B__b and I sold a l__t of the p__ttery we had made.
4. M__l sp__nt the afternoon under an __lm tree reading.
5. I had f__n j__mping in p__ddles in my waterproof r__bber boots.

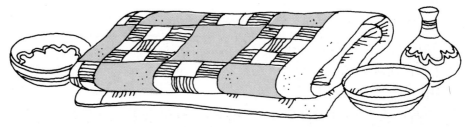

B. Number your paper from 1 to 5. Write the words below. Next to each word, write three words that rhyme.

1. am 2. fell 3. ill 4. lot 5. plug

C. Now try to write a sentence using one group of rhyming words that you have written. For example:

> I am Sam, ma'am.

Consonant Clusters with *l*

> The sounds of some letters blend together. These letters are called consonant clusters.

Read this riddle.

> What is the same about <u>block</u> and <u>blossom</u>,
> About <u>cloudless</u> and <u>flutter</u> and <u>glorious</u>?
> It is also true of <u>plump</u> and <u>sliver</u>.
> Do you have a <u>clue</u>?

Notice that the two letters at the beginning of each underlined word blend together. *Bl, fl, gl, pl, sl,* and *cl* are consonant clusters.

Number your paper from 1 to 10. Read each word clue below. Write your answer. Use one of the consonant clusters in the box below to finish each word.

bl	cl	fl	gl	pl	sl

1. I am the color of hair that is yellow. __ond
2. You can write on me with chalk. __ate
3. I am one of the large heavenly bodies that revolve around the sun. __anet
4. I can help you see in the dark. __ashlight
5. I make shoes for horses. __acksmith
6. You can use me to find the meaning of a word. __ossary
7. I am another word for a large number or group. __ock
8. If I have four leaves you may think I'm lucky. __over
9. I am a musical instrument. __arinet
10. You put your arm in me when it is broken. __ing

Consonant Clusters with *r*

> Consonant clusters are made up of two or more letters whose sounds blend together.

Read the paragraph below. The underlined words begin with a consonant cluster.

> Brontosaurus and triceratops were dinosaurs. Such great creatures might look dreadful and frightening to us, but they were probably not fierce.

What letter is part of each consonant cluster in the paragraph?

Number your paper from 1 to 7. Complete each sentence below by adding a consonant cluster to each unfinished word. Choose the consonant cluster from those in the box. Write the completed words on your paper.

br	cr	dr	fr	gr	pr	tr

1. We can only guess what __ehistoric animals really looked like.
2. __awings of dinosaurs are just the __eations of scientists and artists.
3. Often they have only a few __umbling __agments of bone to use as evidence.
4. We do know __om these fossil bones that some dinosaurs were of __emendous size.
5. Wouldn't you like to see a __oup of them __azing?
6. Or would you __efer the __ama of __ave dinosaurs in battle?
7. Maybe you could __avel back in time and __ing some back as pets!

Consonant Clusters with *s*

> Consonant clusters can be two or three letters whose sounds blend together.

Many consonant blends begin with *s*. Look for consonant clusters as you read the story below.

The captain was skillfully steering our space-craft straight toward the landing site. Suddenly we swerved to the right. Something had scraped against one side of our spaceship! As we began to scan with our radar, something smashed squarely into the other side. The crew was left sprawling in the cockpit. I snatched my helmet and raced for the hatch. This would not be such an easy landing after all!

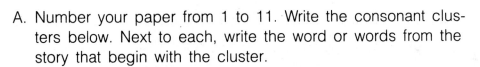

A. Number your paper from 1 to 11. Write the consonant clusters below. Next to each, write the word or words from the story that begin with the cluster.

1. sc   2. sn   3. sw   4. squ   5. sk   6. sp   7. scr
8. str   9. sm   10. st   11. spr

B. Number your paper from 1 to 4. Read each group of words below. Write the two words in each group that begin with the same sound.

1. smudge	2. strap	3. spruce	4. skyscraper
snoop	slack	stress	scarce
snorkle	stallion	spin	skinny
spur	steeple	sprint	script

Ending Consonant Clusters

Consonant clusters can come at the beginning or at the end of words.

A Riddle

In this lesson you will <u>find</u>,
That <u>last</u> is like <u>first</u>,
And <u>best</u> is like <u>worst</u>,
But <u>nice</u> is NOT like <u>kind</u>.
Can you guess why?

Look at the underlined words in the riddle again. Each ends with a consonant cluster.

Some important ending consonant clusters are listed below.

ld	nd	nk	sk	mp	ft	lt	nt	st

Number your paper from 1 to 9. Copy the sentences below. Fill in the blanks of each incomplete word with the same consonant cluster. Use the consonant clusters in the box.

1. John sat by the la__ to work on his sta__ collection.
2. The knight he__ his shie__ as he charged into battle.
3. You must adju__ this knob if you want moi__ air.
4. Marie fou__ a way to me__ the broken recorder.
5. We keep the old coins we found in the tru__ in the ba__.
6. The stu__ woman had an age__ who arranged for her appearances.
7. The ta__ was to find out who was behind the ma__.
8. The cra__ shop was on the le__ side of the street.
9. The flowers began to wi__, and the ice began to me__.

Short Vowel Sounds

Some short vowel sounds can be spelled more than one way.

a	e	i	o	u
tr<u>a</u>ck	bl<u>e</u>nd	r<u>i</u>sk	st<u>o</u>p	pl<u>u</u>ck
	tr<u>ea</u>d			w<u>o</u>n
				t<u>ou</u>ch

What two vowel sounds can the letter *o* stand for?
What are two ways to spell the short *e* vowel sound?
What are three ways to spell the short *u* vowel sound?

Number your paper from 1 to 6. Complete each sentence below with a word that has the same vowel sound as the underlined word. Write the word on your paper. Underline the letter or letters that spell the short vowel sound.

1. Last <u>month</u>, my brother and I made ____ fruit salad.

   great   special   some

2. I <u>got</u> out some walnuts and began to ____ them.

   crack   chop   grind

3. My brother went outside to <u>pick</u> some ____.

   cherries   parsley   mint

4. We had <u>enough</u> ____.

   plums   prunes   pears

5. But we <u>had</u> no ____.

   grapes   apples   peaches

6. <u>Instead</u> we used ____.

   melon   bananas   berries

Long Vowel Sounds

> Many words that end in e have a long vowel sound.

Read the poem below. Notice the vowel sound in each underlined word.

> Without final e, we could <u>not</u> write a <u>note</u>,
> Those who <u>hid</u> could not <u>hide</u>,
> Those who <u>slid</u> could not <u>slide</u>.
> Without final e, we could <u>quit</u>, but not <u>quite</u>.
> I'm glad final e makes these words come out <u>right</u>!

The magic e changes the short vowel sound to a long vowel sound.

The missing word in each sentence below can be discovered by adding the magic e to one of the other words in the sentence. Number your paper from 1 to 10. Write the complete sentences.

1. That polar bear cub is playing with an ice ____.
2. This ____ needle is as sharp as a pin.
3. I would ____ to lose my favorite hat.
4. Chris ____ here in Terry's hot rod.
5. Can Grandma walk without her ____?
6. In the dim light, I couldn't find the ____ I had dropped.
7. That man has hair like a ____.
8. I ____ that rabbit won't hop out of the box.
9. Mom doesn't want us to ____ her typewriter.
10. Let's sit down when we reach the house ____.

Long *a* Vowel Sound

> The long *a* vowel sound can be spelled more than one way.
> d<u>a</u><u>ze</u>   dr<u>ai</u>n   d<u>ay</u>

Read the story below. As you read, listen for the long *a* vowel sound.

It was a special <u>day</u>. My grandmother was coming to visit. My sister had <u>made</u> her a fancy <u>cake</u>. I wanted to do something special for her, too. Should I <u>paint</u> a picture on a <u>tray</u>? Maybe I could <u>take</u> a <u>plain</u> handkerchief and sew on some <u>lace</u>. Finally I decided to <u>put</u> some flowers in a <u>vase</u>.

A. The underlined words in the story show three ways to spell the long *a* vowel sound. Write *a-e*, *ai*, and *ay* at the top of your paper. Write each underlined word from the story under the heading that spells the long *a* vowel sound the same way.

B. Number your paper from 1 to 8. Read each group of words. Write the two words in each group that have the long *a* vowel sound.

1. lane	2. coax	3. stay	4. raid
retreat	claim	wait	achieve
wait	scratch	ready	fate
deny	take	hope	foal

5. hail	6. braid	7. trail	8. fast
brag	brought	happy	strait
boat	boast	smile	rate
crate	baked	haste	steady

479

Long e Vowel Sound

> The long *e* vowel sound can be spelled more than one way.
>
> br<u>ee</u>d   c<u>ea</u>se   boldl<u>y</u>   w<u>e</u>   n<u>ie</u>ce

Read each word below. Look at the underlined letters.

> d<u>ee</u>d   f<u>ea</u>t   dut<u>y</u>   s<u>e</u>cret   gr<u>ie</u>f
>
> gl<u>ee</u>   t<u>ea</u>   lil<u>y</u>   sh<u>e</u>   f<u>ie</u>ld

There is a long *e* vowel sound in each word.

Number your paper from 1 to 6. Find the word or words with the long *e* vowel sound in each sentence below. Write the long *e* words on your paper. Underline the letter or letters that stand for this sound.

1. I can't understand why my friends don't seem to want me on their baseball team.
2. I would never steal a base or anything mean like that.
3. When I'm in the field, I usually strike up a little friendly conversation with the shortstop.
4. Okay. Maybe I'm not too fleet on my feet.
5. But do you really think folks should give a guy grief over a little thing like lack of speed?
6. They could at least let him be the relief pitcher.

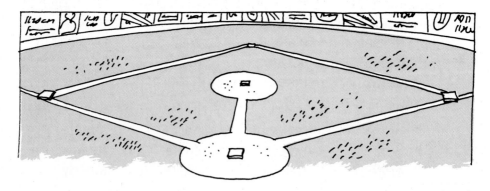

Long *i* Vowel Sound

> The long *i* vowel sound can be spelled more than one way.
> chime   slight   try   tie

Night Kites

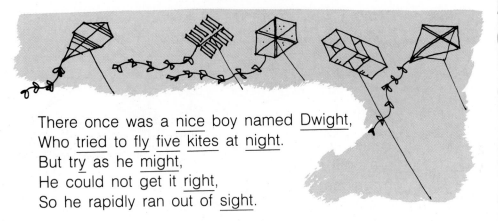

There once was a <u>nice</u> boy named <u>Dwight</u>,
Who <u>tried</u> to <u>fly</u> <u>five</u> <u>kites</u> at <u>night</u>.
But <u>try</u> as he <u>might</u>,
He could not get it <u>right</u>,
So he rapidly ran out of <u>sight</u>.

Read each underlined word in the poem again. The words show different letters that stand for the long *i* vowel sound: *igh*, *ie*, *y*, and *i-e*.

Number your paper from 1 to 15. Read the story below. Then write each word that has the long *i* vowel sound. Underline the letter or letters that stand for the long *i* vowel sound.

> When Tim visited his aunt, she wanted to show him something very special. Just before nightfall, they drove to the harbor and got on board a boat. By the time they got settled, it was getting dark. The crew tied up the anchor and pushed off.
>
> "Why are we going on a boat trip at night?" Tim asked.
> "You'll soon see," was her reply.
>
> She was right! As they began to glide out to sea, white lights went on all over the city. What a magnificent sight! That nighttime view of the skyline was quite a thrill!

Long *o* Vowel Sound

> The long *o* vowel sound can be spelled more than one way.
> sl<u>o</u>p<u>e</u>   m<u>oa</u>t   carg<u>o</u>   gl<u>ow</u>

Read the poem below. Listen for the long *o* vowel sound.

I can't sit around here and <u>mope</u>.
I'll <u>go</u> out in a <u>boat</u>,
Or ski down a <u>slope</u>,
Or climb up a <u>rope</u>,
Or take in a <u>show</u>.
I'll find something to do, I just <u>know</u>.

A. Read each underlined word in the poem again. Number your paper from 1 to 7. Write the words from the poem that have the long *o* vowel sound. Underline the letter or letters that stand for the long *o* vowel sound.

B. Number your paper from 1 to 8. Look at each group of words. Write the two words from each group that *rhyme*.

1. jolt	**2.** loss	**3.** trout	**4.** son
port	doze	shoot	solo
start	toes	float	tempo
bolt	moose	vote	down
5. cloak	**6.** soon	**7.** grope	**8.** moan
sock	known	slope	mane
yoke	ton	hoop	stone
monk	zone	chop	taste

Long *u* Vowel Sound

The long *u* vowel sound can be spelled more than one way.
refuge   few   menu

Read each word above. The underlined letters stand for the long *u* vowel sound. The words show three ways to spell the long *u* vowel sound.

A. Number your paper from 1 to 5. Write each word below. Underline the letter or letters that stand for the long *u* vowel sound.

   1. perfume   **2.** pewter   **3.** humor   **4.** universe   **5.** annual

B. Number your paper from 1 to 8. Choose the word or words from the box that make sense in the sentence. Then write the complete sentence.

musicians	amused	barbecue	argue
transfusion	unit	uniform	fuel

1. A mile is a _____ of measurement we use to talk about distances.
2. We planned to build the fire in the _____ pit an hour before the guests arrived.
3. The joke _____ everybody who heard it.
4. Using solar energy may help us to conserve _____.
5. The lawyer had to _____ his case in a crowded courtroom.
6. The emergency room had a special area for those people who needed a blood _____.
7. Only very skilled _____ could enter the contest.
8. It was an honor for him to wear the _____ of his favorite baseball team.

Review: Short and Long Vowel Sounds

A. Read the underlined words in each sentence below. Notice that they look almost the same but sound different.

Write the headings *Short Vowel* and *Long Vowel* on your paper. List each underlined word under the correct heading.

Plane Plans

1. My brother and I <u>plan</u> to make a model <u>plane</u>.
2. We'll <u>need</u> the help of Uncle <u>Ned</u>.
3. He's worked <u>on</u> his <u>own</u> model planes for years.
4. He lets <u>us</u> <u>use</u> his tools for the tricky parts.
5. When we feel ready to <u>quit</u>, he's <u>quite</u> good at keeping us going!

B. Number your paper from 1 to 8. Read each sentence and the two words that follow it. Write the sentence with the word that makes sense.

1. My friends and I ____ to the zoo. (ran, rain)
2. We saw a very strange ____. (best, beast)
3. It had long legs and a ____ body. (hug, huge)
4. On top of its long neck was a tiny ____. (head, heed)
5. It did ____ have fur, but feathers. (not, note)
6. On its tail were large ____. (plums, plumes)
7. Can you imagine such a bird in ____? (flit, flight)
8. Actually, if you ____ the sign on the fence, you'll learn that ostriches cannot fly. (red, read)

Beginning Consonant Digraphs

> Two or three consonants that stand for one sound are called consonant digraphs.

Read the words in the box below. Look at the underlined letters. They are consonant digraphs.

| chart | shaft | whir | thrive | theme | there |

Notice that the letters *th* can stand for two different sounds.

A. Copy the words in the box on your paper. Then next to each word write the two words from the list below that begin with the same sound.

thrill	challenge	shack	shield
chat	threat	wharf	therefore
theme	wheat	thus	thaw

B. Number your paper from 1 to 6. Add a consonant digraph to complete each word below. Write the complete word on your paper. Be sure it makes sense in the sentence.

1. Wisconsin is the state ____ere my parents grew up.

2. We took a trip ____ere last summer.

3. The ____ing I liked best was touring a factory.

4. We found out how ____eese was made.

5. We were ____own each step in the process.

6. When we were ____ough, the guide gave each of us a generous sample to taste.

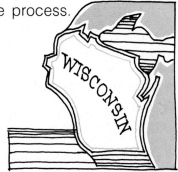

485

Ending Consonant Digraphs

Consonant digraphs can come at the end of words.

Read the words in the box below. Look at the letters that spell the ending consonant digraphs.

clench   blush   sprung   health
sketch

Read the story below. Look at the consonant digraph at the *end* of each underlined word.

Long ago there lived a very selfish giant. He would perch at the top of his mountain and watch people coming up the path. Then he would snatch whatever they had and rush back to his cave with it.

The king heard about this nasty behavior. He decided to teach the giant a lesson. He had a new road built so that no one would have to pass the giant to reach the other side. Foolish giant! Now he was bored to death. He found out that a greedy life can be a very lonely one.

Number your paper from 1 to 5. Write each word below. Next to each word, write the words from the story that *end* with the *same sound*.

1. truth   2. publish   3. sting   4. research   5. stitch

Syllables

> Some words can be divided into parts called syllables. You can hear a vowel sound in every syllable.

Sometimes two or more vowel letters stand for one vowel sound. For example, in the word *globe*, you see two vowels, but you hear only one vowel sound. The word *globe* has one syllable.

A. Number your paper from 1 to 20. Read each word below. The number of vowel sounds you hear is the same as the number of syllables. How many syllables does each word have? Write your answers.

1. blob	2. modern	3. ability	4. dazed
5. extremes	6. tame	7. dedicate	8. independent
9. lead	10. message	11. rescue	12. expedition
13. solo	14. positive	15. treatment	16. genuine
17. banker	18. vary	19. awe	20. importance

When you say a word that has more than one syllable, you stress, or emphasize, one syllable more than another.

In a dictionary or glossary, the stressed syllable is followed by an accent mark (').

mon' ster   a gree' ment

B. Number your paper from 1 to 9. Read each word below. Which syllable is stressed: the first, second, or third? Write your answers.

1. allow	2. cartoonist	3. engine
4. cashier	5. pleasant	6. direction
7. description	8. amusement	9. expect

Schwa

The schwa is a special vowel sound. It can be spelled with *a*, *e*, *i*, *o*, or *u*. The schwa vowel sound is often heard in the unstressed syllable of a word.

Read the words below. The underlined letters stand for the schwa vowel sound.

atl<u>a</u>s	ang<u>e</u>l	dign<u>i</u>ty	seld<u>o</u>m	watchf<u>u</u>l

The schwa vowel sound can also be at the beginning of a word, as in <u>a</u>go, or in the middle of a word, as in neg<u>a</u>tive.

Number your paper from 1 to 7. Write each underlined word below. Underline the vowel that stands for the schwa vowel sound.

1. My grandfather gave me an old photo <u>album</u>.
2. It's great fun to see how he and my other <u>relatives</u> looked as <u>children</u>.
3. Some of the pictures are out of <u>focus</u>.
4. I have to give him <u>credit</u>, though.
5. It certainly is a <u>careful</u> record of family events through the years.
6. He also gave me a <u>journal</u> he kept when he was my age.
7. Reading it is almost like going back to <u>olden</u> times.

Vowel Combinations

Some vowel combinations make the same sound but are spelled with different letters.

j<u>oy</u>	t<u>ow</u>n
n<u>oi</u>se	f<u>ou</u>nd

A. Write the words *joy* and *town* at the top of your paper. Under each word, write the six words from the list below that have the same vowel sound.

enjoyment   fowl
outstanding   rouse
sundown   rejoice
soybean   moisture
royalty   ounce
coward   poisonous

B. *Ou* and *ow* do not always stand for the vowel sound you hear in *cow*. Read the words below. Only eight of them have the vowel sound you hear in *cow*. Which eight are they? Write them on your paper.

sorrow	downward	outlet	vow	compound
rebound	growth	could	tough	follow
trouble	prowl	trout	tow	shower

C. Number your paper from 1 to 5. Read the word clues below. Each answer will have the vowel sound you hear in *tower*.

1. I am a sound a dog makes. ____
2. I am a word that names a person, place, or thing. ____
3. I am the opposite of a smile. ____
4. I am higher than a hill. ____
5. I am *a, e, i, o, u,* and sometimes *y.* ____

489

Vowels + *r*

> The letter *r* changes the sound of the vowel it follows.

Look at each word pair below. Are the vowel sounds the same in—

Tap and tar?
Fame and fare?
Aim and air?
Stem and stern?
Squint and squirt?
Wonder and worker?
Blunt and blurt?

A. Number your paper from 1 to 5. From each list write the two words that rhyme.

1	2	3	4	5
squish	lurk	wish	injure	worse
squirt	lump	whirr	hunch	nurse
hush	stomp	bush	ginger	arose
hurt	work	burr	bench	amuse

B. Number your paper from 1 to 5. From each list, write the two words in which *r* changes the vowel sound.

1	2	3	4	5
trundle	rival	target	stride	rainfall
stirrup	worthless	crank	romp	dairy
ransom	despair	wrist	surf	script
arctic	pretzel	cavern	blare	beware

r-Controlled Vowels

Some *r*-controlled vowel sounds can be spelled in different ways.

Read the two groups of words below. Listen for the rhyming sounds in each group.

1. aff<u>or</u>d
   ad<u>or</u>ed
   ab<u>oar</u>d

2. y<u>ear</u>
   pion<u>eer</u>
   sinc<u>ere</u>

The first list shows three ways of spelling the vowel sound you hear in *for*. The second list shows three ways of spelling the vowel sound you hear in *fear*.

A. Write the words *for* and *fear* at the top of your paper. Under each word, write the eight words from the list below that have the same vowel sound.

restore	fearsome	jeer	information
sneer	important	boar	interfere
severe	forecast	glory	ignore
coarse	atmosphere	weary	career

B. Sometimes two words sound exactly alike even though they are spelled differently. In each sentence below, the underlined word does NOT make sense. Number your paper from 1 to 4. Write a word that sounds the same and DOES make sense.

1. This <u>cored</u> is attached to the kite.
2. The termite <u>board</u> a hole in the wood.
3. Did you <u>here</u> the news about the contest?
4. Would you please <u>poor</u> the tea?

Schwa + *r*

The letter *r* can follow and change the schwa vowel sound.

Read the words below. Look at the underlined letters.

calend<u>ar</u>   goph<u>er</u>   tract<u>or</u>

A. Number your paper from 1 to 6. Complete each sentence by choosing the word that ends with the sound you hear at the end of *polar*. Write it on your paper.

1. Have you ever seen a ____? (termite, beaver)
2. This animal's ____ is truly fascinating. (behavior, personality)
3. It is just about the best ____ in all of nature. (builder, artist)
4. Its home is ____! (wonderful, spectacular)
5. It lives in a ____ lodge made from mud and sticks. (circular, square)
6. Given the same materials, most people could probably not build a house ____ to it. (equal, superior)

B. Find the words below that can be used to identify a person. Underline the letters that make the ending sound of each word you write.

senator   supervisor   fiddler
banker   workshop   harp
kernel   bachelor   scholar
beggar   miner   govern
lecture   percent   professor

Review: Short and Long Vowel Sounds

> The letters *a, e, i, o, u,* and sometimes *y* can be used alone or together to spell short or long vowel sounds.

A. Number your paper from 1 to 8. Copy the sentences below. Complete the sentence by finding a word at the right with the same vowel sound as the underlined word.

Let's get ready for a picnic! The jobs people do will help you review long and short vowel sounds.

1. <u>Mike</u> will ____ the hamburgers.	husk
2. <u>Pete</u> will ____ the bread.	spread
3. <u>Jane</u> will ____ it.	toss
4. <u>Ken</u> will ____ the butter.	fry
5. <u>Tom</u> will ____ the salad.	fold
6. <u>Mother</u> will ____ the corn.	fill
7. <u>Joe</u> will ____ the napkins.	bake
8. <u>Tim</u> will ____ the cups.	knead

B. Read these words: *hungry, satisfy, stay.*
All three words end with the letter *y*, but each ends with a different vowel sound. On your paper, make a chart like the one below.

long *e*	long *i*	long *a*
hungry	satisfy	stay

Add these words to your chart. Write each word in the column that tells its ending sound.

decay	lullaby	dainty	magnify	slay	rely
spray	country	butterfly	delay	factory	ruby

Syllables and Short Vowel Sounds

Learning to divide words into syllables can help you read new words. When you come to a difficult word in your reading, you can work on one small part at a time.

Read these one-syllable words.

yam   get   fig   bun

Now read these words.

cabbage   filter   dismiss

How many vowel sounds are in each word?
How many syllables does each word have?

Below are the same words divided into syllables.

cab bage   fil ter   dis miss

Notice that a vowel comes between two consonants in the first syllable of each word. Do you hear a short or a long vowel sound?

> When two consonants stand between two vowels,
> the word is usually divided between the consonants.
> The vowel in the first syllable is often short.

Number your paper from 1 to 12. Write each word, leaving a space between the syllables.

1. classic
2. contact
3. summon
4. network
5. kitten
6. atlas
7. index
8. dismiss
9. ballot
10. tender
11. baggage
12. member

Syllables and Long Vowels

This <u>robot</u> is really <u>super</u>!
It can dust and sweep and mop.
I only have one <u>major</u> question;
How do I get it to stop?

Read the underlined words above. How many vowel sounds does each have? How many syllables?

This is how the words are divided into syllables.

ro bot   su per   ma jor

Notice that a vowel is at the end of the first syllable of each word. Do you hear a short or a long vowel sound?

> When one consonant stands between two vowels, the consonant usually goes with the second syllable.
> The vowel in the first syllable is often long.

A. Number your paper from 1 to 8. Write each word, leaving a space between the syllables.

1. bison   **2.** labor   **3.** rumor   **4.** legal
5. meter   **6.** polar   **7.** local   **8.** lacy

B. Number your paper from 1 to 6. Find six words below that have a long vowel sound in the first syllable. Write them, leaving a space between the syllables.

pinpoint   cubic   total   burden   pupil
basis   carton   hammock   rival   region

Syllables, Consonant Digraphs, and Consonant Clusters

Read the following conversation. Look for consonant digraphs and consonant clusters.

Hank: We just went to a great concert. Two bands were playing.

Chuck: Which was better?

Phyllis: The "Three Catfish" was more fun to watch. You really should see them!

Stacey: Well, if you ask me, they screamed too much. I liked the "Spring Chicks" better.

A. Look at the underlined letters in each speaker's name. Then look at the underlined letters in the words spoken by each.

1. Remember that consonant digraphs are two or three letters that stand for one sound. List the consonant digraphs.

2. In a consonant cluster, the separate sounds of the consonants blend together. List the consonant clusters.

B. Number your paper from 1 to 12. Write the words below on your paper. Underline the consonant digraph or consonant cluster in each. Then draw a line between the syllables.

1. achieve	7. driftwood
2. cypress	8. wretched
3. fishhook	9. banker
4. earthen	10. camper
5. reflect	11. mouthful
6. reckless	12. between